The Teachers of
Fulfillment

Some Other Titles From New Falcon Publications

Aha! The Sevenfold Mystery of the Ineffable Love   **By Aleister Crowley**
Undoing Yourself with Energized Meditation and other Devices
Secrets of Western Tantra: The Sexuality of the Middle Path
Dogma Daze   **By Christopher S. Hyatt, Ph.D.**
Rebels & Devils; The Psychology of Liberation
     Edited by Christopher S. Hyatt, Ph.D.
Aleister Crowley's Illustrated Goetia
Taboo: Sex, Religion & Magick
Sex Magic, Tantra & Tarot: The Way of the Secret Lover
     By Christopher S. Hyatt, Ph.D., and Lon Milo DuQuette
Pacts With The Devil
Urban Voodoo: A Beginner's Guide to Afro-Caribbean Magic
     By Jason Black and Christopher S. Hyatt, Ph.D.
The Psychopath's Bible   **By Christopher S. Hyatt, Ph.D., and Dr. Jack Willis**
Ask Baba Lon   **By Lon Milo DuQuette**
Lucifer's Rebellion: A Tribute to Christopher S. Hyatt, Ph.D.
     Edited with a Foreword By Shelley Marmor
Aleister Crowley and the Treasure House of Images
     By J.F.C. Fuller, Aleister Crowley, Lon Milo DuQuette and Nancy Wasserman
Enochian World of Aleister Crowley **By Lon Milo DuQuette and Aleister Crowley**
Info-Psychology   *Neuropolitique*   *The Game of Life*
What Does WoMan Want?   **By Timothy Leary, Ph.D.**
Healing Energy, Prayer and Relaxation
The Complete Golden Dawn System of Magic
The Portable Complete Golden Dawn System of Magic
The Golden Dawn Audio CDs
What You Should Know About The Golden Dawn
The Eye in the Triangle: An Interpretation of Aleister Crowley
The Legend of Aleister Crowley   **By Dr. Israel Regardie**
Rebellion, Revolution and Religiouness   **By Osho**
Beyond Duality: The Art of Transcendence   **By Laurence Galian**
Reichian Therapy: A Practical Guide for Home Use   **By Dr. Jack Willis**
Woman's Orgasm: A Guide to Sexual Satisfaction
     By Benjamin Graber M.D. and Georgia Kline-Graber R.N.
The Dream Illuminati   *The Illuminati of Immortality*   **By Wayne Saalman**
An Insider's Guide to Robert Anton Wilson   **By Eric Wagner**
Shaping Formless Fire   *Seizing Power*   *Taking Power*   **By Stephen Mace**
Lovecraft Lexicon   **By Anthony Pearsall**
The Everyday Atheist   **By Ronald F. Murphy**
The Illuminati Conspiracy: The Sapiens System   **By Donald Holmes, M.D.**
Many of our titles are now available on Kindle!!!

Please visit our website at http://www.newfalcon.com

The Teachers of Fulfillment

Dr. Israel Regardie

Introduction by
Colin Wilson

Preface by
Bhagavan Jivananda

NEW FALCON PUBLICATIONS
LAS VEGAS, NEVADA, U.S.A.

Copyright © 2017 U.S.E.S.S.

All rights reserved. No part of this book,
in part or in whole, may be reproduced, transmitted,
or utilized, in any form or by any means, electronic or mechanical,
including photocopying, recording, or by any information storage
and retrieval system, without permission in writing
from the publisher, except for brief quotations
in critical articles, books and reviews.

ISBN 13: 978-156184-536-1
ISBN 10: 1-56184-536-1

First Edition 1946
Formerly The Romance of Metaphysics

Second Edition 1983
Third Revised Edition 2017

The paper used in this publication meets the minimum requirements
of the American National Standard for Permanence of
Paper for Printed Library Materials Z39.48-1984

Printed in USA

NEW FALCON PUBLICATIONS
9550 South Eastern Avenue • Suite 253
Las Vegas, NV 89123
www.newfalcon.com
email: info@newfalcon.com

Contents

Preface by Bhagavan Jivananda   IX
Foreword by Israel Regardie   XI
Introduction by Colin Wilson   XVII

PART I Christian Science

CHAPTER 1	Introductory	1
CHAPTER 2	Mesmerism	15
CHAPTER 3	Philosophy	45
CHAPTER 4	Mary Baker Eddy	75
CHAPTER 5	Metaphysic	105

PART II New Thought

| CHAPTER 6 | I.N.T.A. | 125 |
| CHAPTER 7 | Neville | 171 |

PART III Unity School of Christianity

| CHAPTER 8 | History | 205 |
| CHAPTER 9 | Teaching | 233 |

CLARE
dear friend, this book is
dedicated to you, with
fond and grateful memories
of the early thirties.

"Prove me now herewith, said the Lord of Hosts,
if I will not open you the windows of heaven and
pour you out a blessing, that there shall not
be room enough to receive it.

Malachi
3, v. 10.

PREFACE

By Bhagavan Jivananda

One remarkable correspondence emerges when reading this book. And that is the extraordinary similarity between Eastern Vedanta, Buddhism and the ideas expressed by the teachers described in this book.

Perhaps the major difference lies in the goals sought after by these various systems. In the East the goals yearned for are almost entirely spiritual and unworldly. The Western teachers mentioned here appear to be far more practical. They continually stress that if you are harassed most of your everyday life by poverty, sickness and loneliness, the life of the spirit may be difficult to achieve.

This may ultimately be due to the difference between the East and the West, both in climate and in point of view. So long as one swelters under a broiling sun, with the temperature almost constantly above 100° F., without the air conditioning which is such a blessing in the West, the conquest of Nature which is so characteristic of the West is almost impossible. The Western temperate climate conduces to a life of vigorous activity, both physically and mentally.

This quite evidently has influenced the teachings of the Western metaphysicians. One can not conceive a Patanjali or a Sankaracharya recommending the aims and goals for example of Mary Baker Eddy or an Ernest Holmes. They are poles apart. And yet despite the different practical ends of their respective systems they come very close together where their philosophies and their metaphysics are concerned. In fact, it is quite a miracle that an almost untutored woman in New England could have evolved a philosophy that is so akin to Vedanta and Buddhism. But there it is. These are facts.

There is some discussion about how similarities and differences often become one. But this is not the essential point. For as I see it as a spiritual teacher, this is the essence of all mystical experience which is the same whether Eastern or Western. However the method or the technique in the West has mostly been left to science, while in the East it still remains part of religion. An integration between these two is a religious science, so appropriately named for Mrs. Eddy's work and that of many of the other teachers mentioned here. And this too is entirely my position–to improve life both inwardly and outwardly, facing each day with the hope and fortitude and anticipation of seeking and finding the ineffable Bliss.

This is It!
Bhagavan Jivananda

FOREWORD

By Israel Regardie

This book is a presentation in brief of the major metaphysical systems now operative here and throughout the world. Amongst its other aims was to demonstrate how these various systems have evolved from the stem and root of Mary Baker Eddy's Christian Science. This is why so much space has been given to a consideration of her personality, her life and work.

One of my friends of many years ago, the late Dr. Hereward Carrington complained that I was leaning over backwards in my attempt to be fair to Mrs. Eddy. If this is in fact the case, then I must confess to a profound respect for this really extraordinary woman. Insofar as she was constantly ill and a self-confessed failure through to her sixtieth year, it seems a remarkable achievement to have completely turned around the direction of her spiritual energies for creative ends during the remaining years of her life. There are not many people of whom this can be said. The average person is fairly well played out by sixty. The fires of life are beginning to dim, if not to go out altogether. She is thus worthy of detailed study and attention.

What she also had to say is no less significant. Perhaps she might not agree with an ancient injunction to "enflame thyself with prayer," but nonetheless whatever success Christian Scientists have had with their "demonstrations" must surely depend on an enormous amount of intensity and concentration. This may not be immediately evoked, but given sufficient time and study and prayer. I am certain this inner enthusiasm must arise. And this is the *sine qua non* of success.

It reminds me of some of the stories told by Emily Cady of the Unity School of Christianity. It is said she used to pace up and down her study, concentrating utterly on her affirmations and denials, and the contents of her prayers. In this way, she achieved the fulfillment of her desires through enflaming her mind in prayer. Her intensity was the dynamic factor which bought about the results in various fields of life activities for which she is known.

There are almost exact parallels to these examples in many widely disparate areas. The gulf between them is so wide the individual protagonists within those fields would very likely be horrified to see this parallelism drawn.

For example in the book *Sacred Magic of Abremelin the Mage* translated by the renowned occult scholar of the past century S. Liddell Mathers there is a description of a process of enlightenment which entails total withdrawal from the world for a period of six full months, beginning at Easter in any given year. The whole time cycle is to be spent praying to the Almighty that he vouchsafe illumination to the student and help him obtain the Knowledge and Conversation of his Holy Guardian Angel. Prayers are more or less scattered a the outset of the retreat. There are many tasks to be performed. But as the time proceeds, more or less all the hours of the day and night come to be spent in fervent and ardent prayer. This is the book where is first found the phrase "enflame thyself in prayer."

Now compare this with the experience of one of the founders of the modern Pentecostal movement. It is described at some length in *They Speak With Other Tongues* by J. L. Sherrill (Spire Books, Old Tapper, N.J., 1973) A young Methodist minister Charles F. Parham decided he must do something about his religious life. He had found it wanting when compared with the experiences described in the New Testament. So, in the year 1900, he set out in Topeka, Kansas, to see whether he could discover the secret of living faith which was so conspicuous by it absence in his heart. He was reasonably sure it existed; the scriptures were adamant on that score. "The next morning, everyone in Stone's Folly joined in this prayer. They prayed throughout the morning and into the afternoon. The atmosphere around the mansion was charged with expectancy. But the sun went down and nothing unusual had occurred.

"Then about seven o'clock that night–it was New Year's Eve, 1900–a young student named Agnes N. Ozman remembered something. Wasn't it true that many of the Baptisms described in Acts were accompanied by an action, as well as prayer? Miss Ozman went to find Charles Parham. She told him about her thought.

'Would you pray for me in this way?' she asked.

Parham hesitated just long enough to utter a short prayer about the righteousness of what they were doing. Then, gently he placed his two hands on Miss Ozman's head. Immediately, quietly, there came from her lips a flow of syllables neither one of them could understand.

At Stone's Folly, everyone now prayed with increased fervor for the coming of the Holy Spirit. Over the next three days there were many Baptisms, each one signaled by the mysterious tongues. On January 3, Parham himself and a dozen other ministers from various denominations present with him in this room received the Baptism and spoke in tongues."

It is this fervor which in no way differs from the prayer based on the scriptures and Science and Health which apparently is the indispensable factor leading to success, though I am sure each particular group could cite dozens of different reasons to emphasize the vast differences between them. In the last resort, however, these are of little account.

Another example of this from an entirely different quarter comes from Aleister Crowley. He was no stranger to these phenomena, however incredulous one may be. After all, he was the modern writer who to a great extent has popularized the phrase "Enflame thyself in prayer." In his early thirties, shortly after his return from a visit to the lower borders of China, he wrote a series of what come to be called the Holy Books. Highly inspirational, he considered them in a totally different category from all his other literary work. In one of the *Liber VII vel Lapidis Lazuli*, there is an opening section entitled "Prologue of the Unborn." And it is here that the evidence presents itself that he was once in the company, as it were, of the Pentecostalists and present day charismatic adherents. "To me only the distant flute, the abiding vision of Pan. On all sides Pan to the eye, to the ear: The perfume of Pan pervading, the taste of him utterly filling my mouth, so that the tongue breaks forth into a weird and monstrous speech."

Is this so far from Pentecostalism and the Baptism by the Holy Spirit?

Though this does not deal per se with the technique or methods employed by the various metaphysical movements, enough actually is stated to enable the interested student to formulate his own technique. There is so little difference, ultimately, between any of them, that this should present no real problem. It is only when metaphysics is left behind and the area of the occult and practical magic is approached that there appears a vast gulf. This however in no wise concerns us here and now, though even in this area, the Abramelin injunction still holds good.

The intensity can be of a quiet apparently restrained type so typical for example, of the Episcopal Church or the Christian Scientist, or it could be of the more overt emotion of the Pentecostalist or, let us say, of the Bhakti yogi of the Indian continent. Without this, there is nothing. And nothing can not persuade the window of heaven to open to scatter its largess on the petitioner.

I had intended many year ago to include a chapter on the work of the late Ernest Holmes. For one of several reasons the task eluded me until one Saturday morning some years ago I ran into him in a flower shop on La Brea Boulevard just north of Wilshire Boulevard in Los Angeles. Having heard him speak many times a the Wilshire Ebell Theatre where he held his services on Sunday mornings I recognized him immediately. Having introduced my-

Foreword

self we had a very pleasant chat; he was very friendly and open. This moved me, at least in determination, to write a chapter about him, his life long quest and his very successful work in some subsequent edition of this book. But the exigencies of everyday life and the pressure relative to the maintenance of a psychological practice proved too much to permit me to devote any thought or time to writing this very necessary essay.

Now that I have retired to the quiet mountains of Arizona I am still a little undecided as to how to approach this essay on Holmes. He is a considerably different person from most of the people mentioned in this book. For while he is indebted to some extent to Mrs. Eddy, many other thinkers and philosophers have had a broadening effect on his metaphysical approach which demands a bit more attention to the development of his inner life than was necessary with the others. I felt therefore more time was needed for me to absorb the spirit of his metaphysical contribution. This is taking a great deal more time and effort and contemplation than I originally anticipated, and so to date this essay remains only in rudimentary form in my mind. I would fancy that in the very near future some clarification may develop about this very solid and enthusiastic teacher which will permit finally the completion of my evaluation of both him as a person and Science of Mind as a system. When that day arrives, whenever that will be, I am sure my publishers will include it in this volume or another.

Israel Regardie
Arizona
1983

INTRODUCTION

By Colin Wilson

The author of this fascinating book on metaphysics is the last representative of the great occult and metaphysical tradition of the late 19th century, whose names include Madame Blavatsky and her contemporary Mary Baker Eddy, MacGregor Mathers and W.B. Yeats, and many another famous writer. Even in such distinguished company, Regardie stands out as a figure of central importance.

Frances Israel Regardie was born in London on November 17, 1907, on a dark foggy morning. In 1921 he moved with his family to America, living in Washington D.C. until 1928. In the meantime he attended the Corcoran School of Art in Washington D.C. and then later an art school in Philadelphia where in his own words, he suddenly realized "that I was no artist." Forthwith that was the end of his art studies. Fate had marked him out for a rather more strange and exotic career. The first intimations of this came when he was about 15 years of age, when he saw a reference to a never before heard of Madame Blavatsky, in a nutritional book, of all things, belonging to his sister. Intrigued by the name, he looked it up in the public library to learn of the eventful career of that tempestuous lady. "From then on," he says, "I was hooked." It was a kind of awakening, characterized by the interest in Blavatsky extending to all forms of oriental philosophy and to the practice of yoga. By the time he was 18 Regardie was familiar with most major works on yoga.

So it was with considerable excitement that, at the house of an attorney friend in Washington D.C., he made the discovery of a new text on yoga by a man who unmistakably knew what he was talking about. The work–which was read aloud–was called rather cryptically, *Part I of Book IV*, and was written by one Aleister Crowley. This excited Regardie so much that he wrote to Crowley at the address of a publisher of some 20 years earlier. When some months later he received a reply from Paris he had totally forgotten about the letter in the meantime, and so was thoroughly elated despite the long lapse of time to receive a response from a man who later was to prove one of his mentors and idols.

Crowley suggested that Regardie get in touch with his New York agent, a German named Karl Germer. From Philadelphia Regardie went to New York to meet Germer whom he discovered to be an ex-Wehrmacht officer who regarded Crowley with profound admiration. Some of his enthusiasm was communicated to Regardie so that the latter purchased from him a set of books entitled the Equinox, a periodical of gigantic proportions that Crowley published every six months between 1909 and 1914. For the next few months Regardie neglected his art and plunged deeply into an altogether foreign and strange but familiar world of magic, mysticism and occult philosophy with Nietzschean overtones all tinged with the *fin-de-siecle* flavor of the 1890s, the period of the yellow book and Aubrey Beardsley and others of his ilk. The end result of this was that two years later, on Crowley's birthday October the 12th, 1928 Regardie first sailed and arrived in France, there to meet at Gare St. Lazare Aleister Crowley. The "Great Beast" had invited Regardie to become his secretary. Without knowing anything about what that entailed the invitation had been accepted with alacrity.

The next two or three years must have been traumatic for the young Americanized Londoner. Crowley was just publishing his most important book, *Magick in Theory and Practice*. It failed entirely to attract much attention. A quarrel between Crowley and his public relations man, C. de Vidal Hunt, led to Hunt notifying the Surete Generale that Crowley was amongst many other things a "dope addict." As a consequence of this Crowley was expelled from France. Because of the dogma "guilt by association" Regardie, who had failed to obtain a carte d'identite, was also ordered to leave. Comedy followed tragedy, and because of his association he was not allowed to land in England though he had been born there, and return to France was impossible so he had to go to Brussels. It took him six more months before he was allowed to enter England.

Once there however he moved in with Crowley and his mistress Marie de Miramar at a house in Knockholt in Kent, not too far from London where he began preparing some of Crowley's work for press. Crowley had in the meantime befriended a young enterprising Australian writer P. R. Stephensen who was one of two principals conducting the Mandrake Press. Unfortunately, Crowley's reputation established by *John Bull* as the wickedest man in the world was now so firmly established that his books were thoroughly rejected by most English booksellers, and Mandrake soon went under. In Knockholt Regardie and Stephensen collaborated on a short book defending Crowley, *The Legend of Aleister Crowley* (Falcon Press, 1983). It did nothing to improve Crowley's sinister reputation or to improve the finances of the Mandrake Press. Shortly thereafter Crowley was invited to Berlin to give an exhibit of his so called paintings, so that Regardie went his own way. For awhile, he visited a meditation house in North Devon conducted by a disciple of the silent guru Meher Baba but after a few weeks of this sweetness and light he returned to London, where he became for a short while the secretary to the writer Thomas Burke, author of the once famous, *Limehouse Nights*, which was made into a movie in Hollywood. There Regardie also wrote his own first two books *The Garden of Pomegranates* and *The Tree of Life*.

Both are studies in the Qabalah and the occult, the latter being regarded by many as one of the most important books on Magic ever written. It is dedicated "with poignant memory of what might have been, to Marsyas." The latter name is one used by Crowley years earlier in his epic poem AHA.

Many years later when Regardie sent copies of one or more of his books to Crowley the latter received them with something less than appreciation, making some unkind jokes particularly about Regardie's adoption of the name Francis–a name that had been bestowed upon him by a lady friend who like Regardie at that time was an admirer of St. Francis of Assisi. Regardie gave way to outraged vanity. He wrote Crowley in London a sarcastic letter addressing him as "Dear Alice," a possible reference to the "Beast's" homosexual inclinations as well as to a diminutive of Aleister. The result was a complete break between the two. Crowley produced a scurrilous document about his ex-secretary accusing him of theft and betrayal which he circulated anonymously to all Regardie's friends and acquaintances. Some copies of this document still circulate. It says a great deal for Regardie's forgiving nature–and for his capacity for objective admiration–that he reproduced this document in full in his later study of Crowley, *The Eye in the Triangle* (Falcon Press 1982).

After the publication of the *The Tree of Life*, Regardie found himself at the centre of a violent but unsought after controversy. He had revealed many of the ceremonies and teachings of a society known as the Golden Dawn of which Crowley had been a highly disruptive member in the earliest years of the century, while a young wild bohemian. Some ex-members attacked Regardie. Others, like Dion Fortune, supported him with some reservations. The upshot was that he was invited to join the Stella Matutina, a reincarnation of the original Golden Dawn. This transpired in an immense disappointment. As magicians some of the Chiefs of the Stella Matutina struck him as ignorant and inept. Disgustedly he left the Order and decided to publish the Rituals of the Golden Dawn–an act which has earned him much odium in occult circles though every student of occultism remains in his debt. In fact Francis King a modern historian of this area has determined that the rebirth of magic in recent years is entirely due to Regardie's work.

These details are necessary so that the readers of this book should understand something of Regardie's significance in the history of 20th century occult and metaphysical movements. The remainder may be told more briefly. Regardie remained in England until 1937, continuing to study Magic, Alchemy and writing another important text, *The Philosophers Stone* about the mysteries of Alchemy. This is one of the most interesting and exciting books about Alchemy as a search for a kind of unity of being, and an attempt to unite the conscious and unconscious forces of the psyche. (It is all the more fascinating that in more recent years, Regardie changed his mind to some extent and came to believe that Alchemy is as well an attempt at a chemical transformation of matter. In other words he believes that Alchemy has metaphysical as well as chemical components. I tell the whole story in my book *Mysteries*.)

In 1937 with the recognition that war seemed inevitable Regardie returned to the United States. There he threw himself into the study of Psychology–he had undergone Freudian analysis in England and became a lay analyst. When America entered the war he enlisted in the Army–a step he wryly admits to be a ghastly error. After the war he continued his professional training, moved to California and practiced Reichian therapy. He admits that this "with Magic has changed the whole course of my life." In 1980 he retired to Arizona where he continues to write.

The present book on metaphysics began with his realization, after treating several patients who were heavily involved in metaphysics, that he knew nothing at all of what they were talking about. So he began an extensive study of the subject soon to discover that his patients also knew next to nothing of the origins and nature of the subject they professed to practice. After lengthy discussions with them and with some of the exponents of the different metaphysical systems in New York where he was living at the time, he concluded that most of the adherents of the different schools were wholly unaware of the Christian Science origins of what they believed in. So there appeared to be no alternative, since none of the books he had read dealt with this history, but to start a study of the origins, history, nature and psychological interpretations of the various metaphysical beliefs then current in the late 1930s. This current book is the outcome of those preoccupations and studies of that time.

For many years now I have been an avid reader of Regardie's books. The last one I read *Foundations of Practical Magic* was published in England in 1979. It fascinated me because it reveals that with every advancing age Regardie's mind becomes more clear and vigorous–a tribute to the disciplines to which he has devoted his life. But the chapter that impressed me most was not concerned with Magic but with Meditation. It is a remarkable synthesis of all he knows about magic, meditation and psychotherapy.

Now for those who understandably regard Magic as an absurd superstition it is important to bear in mind Crowley's own definition: "Magick is the Science and Art of causing Change to occur in conformity with the Will." He is echoing a remark of the great 19th century occultist Eliphas Levi, who wrote: "Would you learn to reign over yourself and others? Learn how to will."

Many students of magic and metaphysics are no doubt attracted by its romantic aura and high promise and so indulge in every kind of wishful thinking. But I suspect that the true students have all started from the same intuition; that in some absurd paradoxical way human beings have greater potentials than they realize. Everyone knows that odd feeling we get at times that all is well, that nothing can go wrong. Just as there are days when nothing seems to go right, so there are days when we experience an exhilaration that is like the first smell of Spring: an excitement that

Introduction

seems to be based on some knowledge, some recognition. The romantic poets of the 19th century were always experiencing these moments of vision, then wondering the next day whether it was all an illusion. Magic is first of all an attempt to achieve some kind of control over that inner world of intuition. It escapes us because we are so poor at focusing the attention. Some one of the first steps in magical and metaphysical practice is to attempt to train the mind to visualize, to be capable of conjuring up (and it is interesting that we use this particular phrase about imagining) objects and scenes and endowing them with the smell of reality. And this ability is in fact one of the basic psychological disciplines. That is to say that a person who had become accustomed to doing it at will would have achieved a far higher level of mental health than the rest of us. Students of Metaphysics also believe that when a person achieved this level of intensity it is to some extent possible to make things happen. The metaphysician does not, like the wizard in the "Sorceror's Apprentice" turn brooms into water carriers. But he does believe that it is possible to shape his own destiny. Again everyone knows the feeling of being completely determined to do something, and how, when this happens, events often seem to "come out right." Jung would probably state that this is the operation of the immense unknown forces of the unconscious mind.

Regardie believes, as I do, that this knowledge is very old indeed–that it was probably old when the Egyptians built their first temples. One of the most exciting things in the world is to discover that latest findings in psychology, in structural linguistics, in split-brain physiology, blend smoothly into the pattern of the earliest recorded human knowledge. It is this insight that pervades this remarkable book on metaphysics, and which makes it, to me, the most personal and moving of all Regardie's writings.

Colin Wilson
England

Some of the Teachers...
1. Israel Regardie
2. Mrs. Eddy Baker
3. Neville
4. Emma Curtis Hopkins
5. Myrtle Fillmore
6. Charles Fillmore
7. Dr. Emilie Cady

PART I
Christian Science

CHAPTER ONE

Introductory

It was on June 13th, 1888 that delegates from every state in the union gathered in response to Mrs. Eddy's appeal "to let no consideration bend or outweigh your purpose to be in Chicago." Delegates and students arrived by the trainload. This high-water mark in the development of Christian Science was the nation-wide convention called in Chicago by the National Christian Scientist Association. When, on the second day of the convention, the doors of the Central Music Hall were opened wide, eight hundred delegates and three thousand eager visitors clamoured to see her who had come to known as the "Boston Prophetess."

"When she entered," narrates Stephan Zweig dramatically in the chapter on Mary Baker Eddy in his work *Three Mental Healers*, "the whole assembly rose to greet her. A hush fell upon them as she recited the first verse of the Ninety-first Psalm: 'He that dwelleth in the secret place of the Most High shall abide under the shadow of the Almighty.' Then she began to speak, without notes, and, moved by the enthusiasm of her audience, was so enthralling that (as on the occasion of Abraham Lincoln's famous speech in Bloomington) even the reporters were spellbound and forgot to take notes. No sooner had she finished, then the crowd stormed the platform, not a few of them being invalids who had come in the hope of cure. Some of these stretched forth paralysed hands and begged for help. Men wrestled with one another to get near her and touch her dress. Mothers who could not get through the crowd held their children and shouted for a blessing. Many of the sick declared themselves cured on the spot, as by miracle. There was a real danger in this outburst of enthusiasm, and the faithful had to form a cordon to protect the heroine of the hour from injury."

This experience surely was the peak of the life of a most unusual and amazing woman. Born a nobody, so to say, with out great charm or the beauty which ordinarily we think a woman should possess as one of the adjuncts of success, suffering most of her life from various ailments, penniless and helpless for years, here was Mary Baker Eddy in the rôle, literally, of a saint. She was the centre of a tremendous stream or movement, which since her day has spread entirely around the world. It is calculated to be one of the most powerful religious movements of our day and age. Inestimable is its wealth—its influence incalculable—so completely has it penetrated and infiltrated the thinking of our time. One wit has expressed it that when whoever it is that composes popular jokes takes cognisance of any movement, that movement is important. If this be one of the indices of importance, then since there are many popular jokes about Christian Science, by that token it has achieved great importance and success.

This woman Mary Baker Eddy was consumed by one idea, which some critics assume to have been an extremely questionable idea. But, credit to her, she thought of absolutely nothing else. It consumed her. She had only this one standpoint. To this, however, she clung as though her feet had emerged from solid rock. Motionless and unshakable like the rock from which she had emerged, deaf to every objection, sound or otherwise, with her frail lever of "God is truth, intelligence, life and love, and both mortal mind and matter are error," she attempted to move the world. In twenty years, out of a pre-existing maze of metaphysical confusion, she created a new method of religio-therapeutics. She established a doctrine which was promulgated in text books credited with divine inspiration, counting its adherents by the myriad, with colleges and periodicals of its own. A Church was established and numerous churches were built. She appointed a council of preachers, practitioners and lay-priests, and not least of all won for herself a private fortune amounting to three million dollars. This last acquisition alone would have been an enormous achievement for any woman who, alone and lonely, was penniless for fifty years.

As Stephan Zweig has said referring to *Science and Health*, "anything which exerts an influence throughout the world, modifying the thoughts and lives of millions, is certainly important in a psychological sense; and besides, the circumstances under which the book came into existence indicate the author must have been possessed of extraordinary resolution, must have been endowed with a heroism rare in our days."

Because of this indubitable importance of Mary Baker Eddy, it is incumbent upon those of us living today to trace out the various lines of thought that influenced and produced her. It is often asserted that great characters are the products of their age. They are evoked by the needs of the people around them. Evoked, they voice the need and aspiration of those who, thaumaturgically, evoked them. The age in which she lived was a strange one. Some have thought it a materialistic one—an age devoted solely to the acquisition of the dollar and the neglect of high spiritual principle. The opposite is true, however. People were seeking and investigating vigorously. Their minds and spirits were alive, even if their critical sense was dull. While she was still in her twenties, the towns of her New England background were the playground of a variety of neo-occult cults, each displaying its wares with considerable vitality. Animal magnetism and mesmerism, clairvoyance, mental healing and spiritualism—all these, individually and collectively, served as a symbol of reaction, of protest against the prevailing agnosticism and lack of spiritual security of the times.

Moreover, we must not neglect mention of Emerson. He had just previously published his essay on "Nature," with its clearly defined idealism, its uncompromising opposition to any materialistic concept of life and the world. It was in this milieu that Mary Baker Eddy was born and lived. It was a world in which gross opposing intellectual forces were at war, and it was by these forces that she was torn. The conflict was much too much to be borne easily by her, causing a pendulum swing of her mind out of the realm of such dichotomy.

Science and scientific research had thrust out their feelers, and were firmly establishing themselves on a sound footing. In opposition, there were the churches and organised religion, entrenched in their tradition, and from them all inspiration and spiritual spontaneity had departed. In the middle were spiritualism and some of the mesmeric cults, which in reality stood for a species of transcendental materialism. Mrs. Eddy severed any intellectual contact with all of them by denying substance and reality to matter, and affirming that mind and mind only is the one and supreme reality. God was the One Mind, and all was derived from Him, lived in Him and partook of His divine nature of truth, life and love. Consequently, matter was but a seeming, an illusion which blinded us sensuously to the true state of affairs. Her work, in one sense therefore, was the expression of her age. It was the cry of the outraged soul of the mass of mankind. It was rebellion against autocracy of matter, the insecurity and worthlessness of life, and its dissatisfaction with the so-called normal life of work and money-grabbing. She unconsciously voiced her *zeitgeist*, this rebellion. And in this sense, she was the product of her particular age. But the presence of great minds modifies without question the character of the age they live in. The era is never the same when they have passed on. While she lived however, innumerable influences of environment and time played upon her, moulding her in certain directions. To understand her truly, some historical account has to be presented of at least two distinct trends that operated. The first is hypnotism and mesmerism with which she came to be acquainted through the person of Quimby, for here is the emphasis upon mind and a rudimentary psychotherapy. The second trend is that of transcendental philosophy, of Hegelianism in particular, through the accident perhaps of knowing Hiram Crafts. These two trends will be considered at some length in the following pages.

Within the past several years, many writers by virtue of critical research and scholarship, have come to suspect that Mary Baker Eddy had plagiarised from a wide variety of different sources. Her thefts allegedly were multiform. Yet, though interrupting my narrative, it is worthwhile to interpolate here that while there may seem little doubt but that such plagiarisms do exist, they do not in the least explain Mary Baker Eddy, nor her offspring, Christian Science. Rather, it is evident that she borrowed here and there and everywhere. And this melangé of ideas and theories and facts, stored in her retentive mind, was sifted, co-ordinated, and fertilised into something new, bearing no recognisable relationship whatsoever to the original sources drawn upon. It is this synthesis which assuredly is a creative one, for which there may be the justification for her own belief that she was divinely inspired. Inspiration is a psychological phenomenon. As such, it must be related to other phenomena and events that preceded it, and must be referrable to well-defined laws and principles.

The opening paragraph of her masterpiece *Science and Health*, states that, "in the year 1866 I discovered the Science of Metaphysical Healing, and named it Christian Science. God had been graciously fitting me, during many years, for the reception of a final revelation of the absolute Principle of Scientific Mind-healing." Her statement can be accepted on its face value. In the year 1866, she may well have undergone some psychological stimulus or spiritual experience, the result of which was to completely organise, rearrange and synthesis a multiform brood of ill-fitting and widely diffused materials.

A picture, a friend, a conversation, may be such a stimulating experience, that afterwards, in order to explain what has transpired, we rationalise by stating that we were inspired. A walk in the country with the glory of nature, her trees and skies and earth all around and about one, may set up such a train of psychic events and currents as to revolutionise and vitalise the mind to inspiration just as powerfully as will the hearing of beautiful music or poetry or prose. Likewise, an inspiring experience may result from a book with the ideas and emotions that it may communicate. We shall find that in the year that Mary Baker Eddy states she was inspired by a *final* revelation of her system of metaphysical healing, she has access it is alleged to a manuscript on Hegel's philosophy. This manuscript may have provided her with just that allegorical peg she needed, around which to integrate the disconnected mass of theories she had accumulated for many years. This integration, which may well have been a wholly unconscious psychological process, was an event which she labelled an inspiration and revelation, and which we cannot criticise in any way, but simply try to listen and understand.

As a result of this experience, a new system issued creatively from out of her mind. A painter will procure pigments made by one manufacturer, a dozen brushes and pallet from another, oils and turpentine purified by the refinery, and canvas woven at the loom. Using these, regardless of whether he came by them honestly or not, he can produce a colorful masterpiece which lives forever as a thing of beauty in our minds and imaginations. In fairly much the same way, we may conceive of Mary Baker Eddy's "plagiarisms," if so we must call them, in relation to Christian Science. Hosts of possibilities follow, is a question worth asking ourselves. Artistic and spiritual creativity is its own justification. None other is needed.

Despite this justification, we are told there were literary thefts for which no acknowledgment was ever offered, running slightly counter to her own self-contradictory condemnation of plagiarism.

Carlyse, Swedenborg, and many other literary sources can readily be traced out. In his satirical book, *Christian Science*, Mark Twain has clearly indicated that behind the sometimes faltering and inexpert literary style exhibited in *Science and Health*, another more skilled and erudite hand may be perceived. It would appear as though at least two writers contributed in diverse ways to the formation of this tome of hers.

Quimby and his practise of hypnosis and auto-suggestion without a doubt played a tremendous part in the subsequent shaping of her creed. Of this there can be little question, and it would be sheer futility to attempt to belittle this historical connection. In every family, there probably is some history of crime, if we took the trouble to trace back ancestry far enough. A murderer, a thief, a prostitute may easily be found on some part of our family tree. The discovery of these facts, however, should not endow us with any kind of inferiority feeling. These undesirable ancestors are not elements about whom we should feel ashamed. We are responsible solely to ourselves and our environment, not to the past. Likewise, Christian Science does not need to feel shame or inferiority because of its own terrestrial origins.

For years Mrs. Eddy carried about with her a manuscript of Quimby's empirical philosophy in the form of questions and answers. She must have taken over, maybe involuntarily, the bulk of his ideas. Any didactic material with which one saturates one's thinking for long periods of time, eventually become assimilated, becomes part and parcel of the intellectual equipment, altogether unconsciously. This may have happened to Quimby's system. Possibly, she was not even aware that it had influenced her to the wide extent that it did despite some naïvely enthusiastic journalism of her own creation. So thoroughly, however, did it seep into her mind that eventually she came to believe that the whole fundamental material of metaphysical healing was her own property, she being not in the slightest degree indebted to him.

Some people, forgetting this commonly found mechanism of unconscious assimilation of ideas, have mistakenly accused her of ingratitude. Ingratitude, I believe, plays a far less significant role here than does Freudian forgetfulness. It was more convenient, less painful to her line of life and aspiration, to permit this obligation to undergo complete obfuscation. Her debt to Quimby became repressed. It is unnecessary to labour here the tremendous influence that repression plays in the lives of each one of us.

We know that repression must have played a highly prominent role in her girlhood. From early infancy she was sick and indisposed in such a way as finally to ruin her efficiency. Ideals she had aplenty, though these were nearly always nullified by her indecision, inferiority, and ill-health. In her several biographies, the psychologist finds a wealth of illuminating material to suggest that from a very early age she manifested a wide range of hysterical symptoms. Repression is the mechanism of hysteria. Hysterical manifestations of any kind, from inefficiency to so-called "spinal disease," from which she is said constantly to have suffered, are typical conversion phenomena. Repressed ideas and emotions that have been thrust out of the sphere of consciousness by a process of deliberate forgetfulness, become symbolically represented by a host of dynamic psycho-somatic symptom materialisations. We can readily understand that repression was not too difficult a task for Mary Baker Eddy. It was a weapon forged ready-to-hand. Its use was second nature. For this reason it is, that the theme of ingratitude is far less psychologically valid than that she wilfully forgot the effect Quimby had previously exerted on her.

On the other hand, another group of critics are inclined to discount Quimby's influence altogether. For example, when the book, *The Quimby Manuscripts*, was reviewed in the New York Times in 1922, the reviewer stated: "It is a gigantic task which the editor of *The Quimby Manuscripts* has undertaken when he offers this loosely arranged mass of writings and reflections as not only containing the beginning of spiritual healing, but also the origin of

Christian Science...*Science and Health*, whatever views may be held concerning it by individuals, has served to build up a mighty organisation which could hardly have been reared on the uncertain foundations of *The Quimby Manuscripts*." In effect, while *Science and Health* may certainly betray the influence in some measure of Quimby, yet the distinctive element which is Christian Science, is definitely absent within the pages or thought of *The Quimby Manuscripts*. Some other line of thought must be sought which will effectively explain the intrusion of ideas apart from Quimby.

Most critics and metaphysical investigators have suspected that German transcendentalism is represented in *Science and Health*. By transcendentalism, is meant the philosophies of the great German idealists, Kant, Fichte and Hegel. For example, on the very first page of the text of *Science and Health*, Mary Baker Eddy uses the unusual term "apodictical." It occurs only on the first page, and its usage is never repeated anywhere else in her book. The term was frequently employed philosophically by Immanuel Kant to indicate a judgment enunciating a necessary and absolute truth. It is curious that she used this word once, and only once. But just how Mrs. Eddy came to be influenced by transcendentalism, what the channels were, and how she came to have access to such philosophy, have never really been explained. Suspected, it certainly has been. The clues were there. How they came to be there, however, was not known.

In 1936, Reverend Walter M. Haushalter published a book in Boston entitled, *Mrs. Eddy Purloins from Hegel*. To state it briefly, for I propose referring to it again later, Reverend Haushalter claims that a certain Francis Lieber wrote a manuscript entitled "The Metaphysical Religion of Hegel." Significantly, it is dated April 1866 — the year of supposed revelation. Is it the work that inspired her mind to create that dynamic synthesis?

The manuscript was forwarded to Hiram Crafts to be read before the Kantian Society, of which both Lieber and Crafts were members. We know that Mary baker Eddy, during her lean years penury, the period of her probationship as it were, lived in Crafts' house. He actually became the first Christian Science practitioner. We can only suspect that she must have gained access to this document. Suspect, did I say? Whole paragraphs of Lieber's essay on the religious philosophy of Hegel have been lifted bodily from context and incorporated it is alleged, word by word, line by line, in *Science and Health*. Reverend Haushalter has patiently compared the text of both the essay and the book together, and has given innumerable parallels between them.

The central thesis upon which Christian Science is made to stand, is in reality said to be one of the Hegelian concepts as understood and enunciated by Lieber. "There is no life, truth, intelligence nore substance in matter," is the keynote of the Christian Science catechism. It is a variation of Lieber's formulation that "For Hegel and his true disciples, all is infinite mind. Thus matter has no reality, it is only the manifestation of Spirit...Therefore science is spiritual, for God is Spirit."

As I have stated, this relationship between German transcendentalism on the one hand, and Christian Science metaphysics on the other, has not been entirely unsuspected. The clues were certainly discovered and recognised years ago. But the significance of them never completely transpired. Dr. Woodbridge Riley of Vassar, was one of the few professors of philosophy in America who ever lent serious attention to *Science and Health*. Of the thousand and more analysts of Mrs. Eddy, he alone it is said guessed the truth. In his work, *American Thought from Puritanism to Pragmatism*, Riley declared the intelligible parts of Science and Health to be Hegelianism.

This may well be true. To have proved it was another story. This proof has now been provided to Reverend Haushalter's work which thus gives significance and new meaning to the many clues that previously made themselves known. Since the theoretical parts of Mrs. Eddy's work may have been borrowed from Hegel, so the allegation asserts, through the medium of Lieber, and the practical elements from Mesmer by way of Quimby, it is necessary to examine these claims at some length. Other writers, unknowingly and unconsciously, have likewise contributed certain elements. But to dismiss Christian Science wholly as a collection of plagiarisms is unwarrantable and entirely to have missed what I consider a most significant and important point.

Quimby, Mesmer, Hegel and Swedenborg and others have written, lectured and taught. Undoubtedly their works reached large audiences, and unquestionably their influence can be traced throughout many modern institutions of thought, philosophy and politics. Marxianism and socialism of many shades and hues have emanated from quarters which were Hegelian in origin. It is hardly necessary to indicate in what manner the whole course of world events has undergone modification by them. Modern medicine, wittingly or otherwise, has been more than tinged by the influence of Mesmer. For Freud, the father of modern dynamic psychology, was originally a neurologist who employed hypnosis as one of his therapeutic modalities. The Church of the New Jerusalem was founded by Swedenborg, and now has branches the world over. New Thought, a movement incorporating dozens of small sects and cults, involving, when considered as a whole, hundreds of thousands of people, openly admits its indebtedness to Quimby. But none of these figureheads have become directly, by any means of comparison, that world-wide influence that Christian Science became. Christian Science, though neither Christian in the historical sense and certainly not scientific, nonetheless gained considerable momentum. Within a very few years, it had permeated every level of society and influenced many different types and groups of people.

The miracle as I see it—for miracle it surely is—is not that Mrs. Eddy integrated a system from innumerable alleged plagiarisms and gave no credit for them. None can say that plagiarism is creative or dynamic. The concrete miracle is that she so transformed that material she had drawn upon as to appeal to thousands and millions of people who would otherwise never have known of Mesmer, Quimby or Swedenborg. People not merely in the United States, but in every country in the world. She appealed to them, influenced them, and vitalised them into an entirely new type of social and spiritual activity. However ridiculous the average person may regard her metaphysical formulation—ridiculous because he stupidly takes the world for granted, never for one moment enquiring into the metaphysical basis of existence—nonetheless when modern psycho-therapeutic and analytical schemes appeared on the horizon, a large number of people were already prepared to accept one basic fact. That mind is able to make people sick and poverty-stricken, and, by the same token, to heal them and enable them to take their rightful place in the community.

To my mind, this is so vast a miracle that were it no constantly under our noses, we would stop short in our tracks. We should be staggered by the phenomenon. Illiterate, mean, avaricious though she may have been, as it alleged, at the same time Mary Baker Eddy must be considered, no matter by what logical process of thought, a woman who was nothing less than a genius.

By a genius, I imply a person who, by his life, ideas, and accomplishments, leaves some indelible impression in some one of the phases of world history. When the average person dies, truism that it is, he really is dead. Nobody will remember him, outside of his own particular family, where the memory of his existence will fade after the passage of a pitiably short space of time. He will not have made any lasting contribution to human thought or endeavor in any way. He will have lived, worked, married, reproduced his kind—and died. And there is the end of him. So far as posterity is concerned, he will be truly dead.

Anyone, however, who can leave some definite mark in the world, regardless of whether it be good or evil, is quite another story. That mankind one hundreds years from now will recall that such a person lived, and that the mere fact of his existence has influenced their lives—that phenomenon must bear the living stamp of genius.

That Mrs. Eddy was just such a genius may appear distasteful to some amongst us. We may prefer to dwell on the more unsavory personal aspects of her life and work. There is something a little devastating and petty in human nature that, unconsciously, we prefer to under-rate people, to mock and deride things not altogether understood. Perhaps we feel insecure when confronted by something we cannot fathom, and our insecurity breeds inferiority. And to cover the shame of our inferiority, we believe we must tear down all before us so that our own lives and minds will not suffer.

We may criticise the philosophy that she espoused, and taught. It is irreligious, unscientific, not common sense. Mrs. Eddy may have been selfish, hard-driven by a lust for power, money-mad. All of this may or may not be true. It does not matter in the least. But she acquired a following that in the last fifty or sixty years must number many millions of people in different levels of society and life. Not only acquired such a following, but taught them to live a nobler life. She helped them over many of the hurdles and crises and despondencies to which all are susceptible. Anyone who can lift up the faint human heart in the dark face of the suffering and pain that we are on occasion obliged to confront, is indeed a benefactor of mankind. She showed people how to transmute their lives into worthy and ideal phenomena. Thousands of people have blessed her memory for the aid she has afforded them when confronted by trials and tribulations. Hers indeed, for many, is a revered memory. This surely, is the highest testimonial. This indeed, the work of genius.

If, after criticism and research, we can in all honesty conclude in just such a manner, most people will admit that nothing can be said which can possibly injure her. When it is stated and alleged that she has plagiarised shamefully, that she was ungrateful and petty, that she failed to recognise her historical debt to great predecessors in the sphere of spirit, none of these things can injure her. Her reputation and the work that has lived after her, are beyond human reach, unspoilable. She is a spiritual genius. That is all that matters.

CHAPTER TWO
Mesmerism

In the recognised biographies of Mrs. Eddy, we learn that when the medical autopsy performed on her late husband revealed valvular disease of the heart, she claimed and insisted emphatically that, in spite of the bacterial vegetations on the cardiac valves which was shown, he had died through "malicious animal magnetism." All her long days she lived in mortal terror of the supposedly evil effects of animal magnetism. Often occurring in *Science and Health* in this phrase "animal magnetism." It is much to be doubted whether the average Christian Scientist really understands the implication, especially when the real issue is woefully confused with very inadequate and occasionally misleading explanations. In various places, animal magnetism is defined as "mortal mind," whatever that may be. In others, it is believed to be a synonym for matter, in which there is "no life or truth or intelligence." The phase is too lightly used. There is no clear philosophical definition. Nor any adequate understanding of the historical and scientific implicit of its background.

However unsatisfactory a term, animal magnetism is a descriptive phrase that came into wide vogue through the efforts of Franz Anton Mesmer. He wished to explain certain psychological phenomena which came to his attention long before the formulation of Christian Science. It was Mesmer who developed the process which came to be known as mesmerism, vital magnetism, and later as hypnotism. From this latter science, all mental healing cults have grown, whether they acknowledge and recognise it or not. Modern psychology too has subsequently developed out of it. Hence, in order to clarify the issue with regard to Christian Science and its antecedents, it is imperative to outline briefly the development of the schools of animal magnetism up to the time of Mrs. Eddy and *Science and Health*. Although some may claim that she was in no way obliged to Quimby as the inheritor of the long line of magnetic and mesmeric tradition, nevertheless it was her particular experience with Quimby that at least oriented her in a certain direction. It gave her some degree of awareness of mind-healing, with all its vast and wide implications.

The phenomena of magnetism, the therapeutic sleep, and instances of miraculous healing by other than physical means, date back not merely to Mesmer, but hundreds of years previously. We know full well that some magnetic method of entrancement was widely practised in Greece. Thousands of years ago, the Phrygian Dactyli, the initiated priests, spoken of as the magicians and exorcists of sickness, healed disease by these processes without recourse to medication. These drugless methods were the principal agents in theurgic mysteries, as also in the Aesculapiea—the healing temples of Aesculapius, where the patients were treated before the images of gods during the process of "incubation," as it was termed, magnetically during sleep.

From a study of Greek and Latin literature, it is certain that a species of healing by a laying on of hands was so commonly practised in ancient days, as not to demand a detailed or particularised description. Underlying such a method was the belief that the human organism is permeated wholly by a vital creative power or spirit, which, for lack of more specific or accurate terms, came to be known as vital magnetism. Or, because it circulated in animal bodies, as animal magnetism. Not only was it supposed to circulate in its own arterial system, but aided by a laying on of hands, directed by a keen imagination and strong will, and exalted by religious enthusiasm, it could be communicated to another person for therapeutic purposes. It need hardly be laboured that the Bible contains many references to cures of an apparently magnetic nature. Many of the healings accomplished by the great prophets and by Jesus are of such a nature, in sharp contrast to the Eddy injunction that there shall be no laying on of hands. Such magnetic methods continued from the earliest times through to the Middle Ages. For centuries they were commonplace in Europe.

Avicenna, a physician of the ninth or tenth century said: "The imagination of man can act not only on his own body, but even on others and very distant bodies. It can fascinate and modify them; make them ill, or restore them to health." Marcus Fienus, a physician of Florence said in the same century: "A vapour, or a certain spirit, emitted by the rays of the eyes, or in any other manner, can take effect on a person near you. It is not to be wondered at that diseases of the mind and of the body should be communicated or cured in that manner."

Petrus Pomponatius of Mantua believed that "Some men are specifically endowed with eminently curative faculties; the effects produced by their touch are wonderful; but even touch is not always necessary; their glances, their mere intention of doing good, are efficient to the restoration of health." Here we have an adumbration, at least, of mesmeric practice and the suggestion theory that was to be elaborated after many centuries.

Van Helmont, the sixteenth century discoverer of laudanum, ammonia, volatile salts, etc., also held opinions very similar to those of Mesmer. He held that "Magnetism is a universal agent; there is nothing new in it but the name. Magnetism is that occult influence which bodies exert over each other at a distance by means of attraction and repulsion." He named this influence the "Magnale Magnum," which Eliphas Levi spoke of in the nineteenth century as the Astral Light. Helmont conceived of it, not as a corporeal thing, but as an ethereal, pure vital spirit or essence. It penetrates all bodies, and in man has its seat in the blood, where it exists as a peculiar energy, enabling him by the force of will and imagination to act at a distance. He also asserted the idea of polarity or the duality of magnetism which he claims is composed of a vital principle and a will principle. The former exists "in the flesh and blood of man, the latter belongs to the soul or consciousness." But since soul and body are not separate discrete entities but together comprise a whole, so magnetism is one, manifesting in different principles on different planes. By a slight translation of terminology into those current today, it seems to accord fairly well with the psychological definitions of libido, and it has many parallels with the metaphysical concept of Universal Mind.

The great alchemist Sendivogius wrote: "Let therefore the searcher of this sacred science know that the soul in man, the lesser world of microcosm, substituting the place of its centre, is the king, and is placed in the vital spirit in the purest blood. That governs the mind, and the mind the body." It is upon such a statement and the philosophy underlying such a postulate, that is built up the hypothesis of vital magnetism and its efficacy to heal.

Sebastian Virdig, a learned philosopher-physician of the same century as Van Helmont, averred: "The whole world exists through magnetism; all sublunary vicissitudes occur through magnetism; life is preserved by magnetism; everything functions by magnetism."

Similar passages are to be found in the works of Paracelsus, and a host of leading authors of these and later centuries. All more or less affirm the existence of a universal vital spirit or energy, the medium both of light and thought-activity. That ether they represented interiorly in man by a vital spirit or magnetism which radiated and emanated a vital influence from him, subtly and invisibly. This spiritual force, so the theory went, could be controlled and manipulated for purposes of healing by a willed transmission through the hands, or by a direct glance of the eye, or simply through reflection and concentrated mental activity, to another ailing person.

There is a fascinating and extraordinary account of a magnetic healer recorded as having operated in England during the seventeenth century. Valentine Greatrakes acquired considerable notoriety from curing various diseases, during the reign of Charles II, by stroking sick people, with his hands. These cures were authenticated by the Bishop of Derry and many other people who have recorded them for posterity. In particular, there is an account of a case of leprosy handled by Greatrakes in the presence of Lord Conway. A boy of about fourteen years old had been afflicted with leprosy for about ten years. One Wednesday Greatrakes began treatment by stroking him, or as the magnetists would have said, by making passes over his body. A few days later, on Friday, desquamation had begun, with the dermatological irritation and inflammation subsiding in very large part. Greatrakes again made passes over him, and rubbed his body over with spittle, a curious parallel to miraculous healings recorded in the New Testament. After this, all symptomatological manifestations disappeared, and the boy was accounted cured. Many other similar healings have come down to us fairly well authenticated as having been accomplished by Greatrakes without the administration of medicine.

But it is only when we come to Mesmer and his disciplines that we realise an advance in the theoretical formulation of the concept of magnetism and the advantages of his particular approach. That approach to a psychological system of healing was pregnant with possibilities, only to be explored fully many years later.

Franz Anton Mesmer was born in Austria in the year 1734, and in 1766 he graduated from medical school in Vienna with his doctor's degree. His inaugural address maintained that the sun and moon and stars affect each other reciprocally and cause tides, not only in the ocean and sea, but in the atmosphere, also. It was his theory that everything is affected similarly through the medium of a subtle and mobile "fluid" or energy which he conceived to pervade and permeate the universe, and to associate all things together in mutual harmony and relationships. His theory further included the idea that all things soever in Nature, possess a peculiar power which manifests itself by special action upon other bodies. That is to say, it is a dynamic power acting without any chemical union, or without the necessity of being introduced physically into the interior of the organism. Mesmer also contemplated the idea that all organic bodies—animals, plants, trees, metals, waters—might be magnetised. By this he meant that they could be charged or impregnated with a flow or current of vital spiritual energy. This cosmic vitality or animal magnetism—could be transmitted, he claimed, by direct contact with a body already magnetised, or by means of the hand, the eye, or even through mere intention, as conceived of by the enlightened will and mind.

So far as the practical application of general theory is concerned, Mesmer, like modern psychological exponents, believed that moral causes and erroneous attitudes towards life, may constitute the basic factors in the production of diseased states. That is to say, an attitude towards life which was in conflict or at variance with reality, could interfere with the psychic distribution of vitality throughout the bodily system. For instance, he states that "disease is nothing but a perturbation in the regular progression of movement and life." Not only were there physical factors that tended towards the lowering of physical resistance which facilitated the development of disease, but responsible also were emotional etiologies. Important factors were pride, envy, avarice, ambition, all the vile passions of the human mind. He also believed to be responsible as precipitating factors such traumatic experiences as the loss of income and social security, as brutal and jealous husband or a faithless and nagging wife, an unnatural father and mother, and ungrateful children.

His theory held that this cosmic, spiritual power or vital magnetism, is constantly circulating in the animal or bodily system. Not only so, but that it emanates to an appreciable degree about the body. When the rapport is established between patient and healer—that is when contact is made either by glance or mesmeric passes, or by prayer and meditation—it circulated through the magnetic systems of the two people, just as blood would were their arteries and veins somehow interconnected.

In the early phase of his career, two Jesuit priests named Gassner and Hehl delivered some very suggestive ideas to him. Gassner imparted the secret of strengthening the curative effect of treatment by moving the hands over the diseased parts of the body. Such movements later became known as "passes." He himself used exorcism as a means of curing certain types of disease. He held the view, modified from the prevailing Roman Catholic belief, that there are two principal kinds of disease. The one is curable by the ordinary chemo-therapeutic means employed by physicians, whilst the other can only be cured by priestly means, by prayer and exorcism. To these he added a third category, which he called "mixed," requiring the aid both of prayer and medication, a group which we would today consider as psycho-somatic illness.

From Hehl, Mesmer had obtained at the outset of his public career, a set of magnetised steel plates which, when laid upon different part of the body, were claimed to have a curative effect. Mesmer did not long persist in the use of these plates, passing on to the employment of the so-called *baquet*, a vast tub containing glass bottles, iron filings and metal rods. Seated on chairs around this enormous *baquet*, numbers of people would congregate in a large salon, grasping the iron rods. The light would be dim and coloured, soft music would fill the air and Mesmer, clad in silken gown, wielding a wand, would flit silently from one patient to another around this circle, touching first one lightly with the wand, and uttering a hushed word to another. Very soon someone would pass into convulsions, the magnetic crisis. Then another. And whether by suggestion and contagion, or by reason of the mysterious magnetic virtue of the *baquet*, the whole audience would be plunged into a variety of psychological states. Some would be cataleptic, others would heave terrific convulsions. Yet another group would weep or laugh hysterically, or sit apathetically, silently gazing at the contents of the *baquet*.

Mysterious humbug or suggestive healing notwithstanding, some patients present, who had been previously dismissed by the medical doctors as incurable, regained their physical and spiritual integrity as a result of these *seances*. No doubt it was the supposedly unscientific atmosphere of the salon, and silk gowns, that netted Mesmer so much devastating criticism. Yet we can wonder today whether the latter was wholly justified. Maybe Mesmer *did* know what he was doing. It is quite possible that he was in reality a master of clinical psychology and happened to hit upon just the most effectual array of suggestive paraphernalia which would rouse dynamically the dormant *vis natura medicatrix*, or the latent psychological possibilities of the individual to produce a cure where nothing else would succeed.

Much later, discarding all these needless contrivances of magnets and *baquets* and similar accessories, he came to rely exclusively upon his own personality, his benevolent mind and magnetism. He pictured man as a closed circuit of the magnetic fluid. But it was a circuit that participated or was contained within a larger cosmic circuit. Or in many larger circuits of magnetism and vitality which flowed through him from the universal storehouse about him, thus renewing the personal vitality and health. We find Mesmer constantly speaking both of increasing the rapidity of the flow of magnetism through the body and of equalibriating that vital flow. He does not care to speak, as did the later magnetists, of "charging" the patient with magnetism, rather as one would a storage battery, nor of "saturating" him with the hypnothetical magnetic fluid. His theory consisted solely in the idea of achieving an equilibrium of the disturbed vitality in the body of his patient. He passes, his benevolent intentions, and the fixed gaze, designated to aid concentration—which process thus becomes the equivalent, psychologically, of prayer—were the means of hastening the magnetic crises, after which health established itself.

Not particularly happy was the reception of his theories and then startling cures. The cures and miraculous healings were manifold, a large variety of disease and disease states came before his attention for therapy. Mesmer's fame spread throughout the whole of

Europe. Royal commissions were authorised to examine scientifically the cures announced by Mesmer and his patients, and following unfavorable reports of these investigations and much antagonism, he fell foul of public opinion almost everywhere. The medical fraternity of that age was just as adamant as it is in modern times in maintaining that outside of the profession, all healing modalities that do not accord with its own rigid views must be classified as sheer humbug or mere imagination. In both cases, however, they should be suppressed.

Following Mesmer, we find the Abbé Faria, a French priest who, after experimenting for some time with mesmerism, announced in 1814 a psychological view of the subject comparable to that entertained today. He did not believe in any actual communication or even equilibriation of magnetism from healer to patient as being the least bit involved in the therapy. He thought that the effects were mainly subjective. The mesmeric state was possible due to changes in the mind and body of the subject, produced by faith and expectancy. In other words, it was an anticipation on general lines of the later theory, that the hypnotic state and the remarkable cures so produced, were the result of faith, expectancy and suggestion. Very little receptivity to this rather modern view, was manifested, and it was soon glossed over and forgotten.

Although at the date of Mesmer's death in 1815, his system of magnetically inducing a violent crisis in the patient, was followed in its entirety by a considerable number of practitioners almost everywhere, but more especially in Germany, there were already two other more or less important schools of animal magnetism in existence. One of these was the school of de Barbarin, which taught that the cures were effected directly through the providence of God, being in reality the result of faith alone. The processes of Mesmer served but to disguise that fact, he held. In no way did they assist the cure which was invariably produced by an "act of the soul." The chief method employed by these operators was religious exhortation, and their chief means was prayer. These enabled them to duplicate the phenomena produced by Mesmer and by de Puységur and his disciples. And it is said that they had a notable proportion of successes, especially among those who were particularly inclined to religious emotion. Here was some anticipation of the metaphysical attitude which became so popular before fifty years had sped by. But, having no new processes to describe, and a theory that was not then sufficiently developed to be acceptable, this school has left very little record of its existence.

The development of Magnetism in the so-called Experimental School of the operators who were undoubtedly the legitimate heirs and successors of Mesmer proper, and of de Barbarin. But who were the "great magnetisers" of this experimental school? These included a great many operators, or practitioners, in almost every country in Europe. Many were physicians who, during the last quarter of the eighteenth century and the first quarter of the nineteenth, devoted themselves to magnetic therapy. Some established private institutions where patients were received, while others operated in various hospitals. The best known of that generation of magnetisers are the Marquis de Puységur, Baron du Potet, Deleuze, and La Fontaine, all of whom have left treatises on the subject.

Very soon, de Puységur, as a pioneer, began to move away from his master, both in the theory and practice of Magnetism. Indeed, we may safely say that the later magnetisers followed the pupil rather than the master. Were we to label as Mesmerism the processes of Mesmer and other violent effects in the artificial crisis that he encouraged, then the real discoverer of animal magnetism as it has been known for the past hundred years, as a phenomenon rather than a theory, is the Marquis de Puységur. He is the acknowledged founder of the experimental school. It is to him that are due the processes now generally known as mesmeric— processes which are productive of results differing considerably from those produced and described by Mesmer himself.

There was a fundamental difference between the theories of Mesmer and those of de Puységur. The former emphatically asserted that magnetism was an ubiquitous ocean of life and vitality, infinite and omnipresent, permeating all things, pervading the earth and all things in and on it. His conception of the magnetic cure was simply the adjustment of the disturbed flow of magnetic currents within the system of his patients. De Puységur on the hand, held the view that the operator definitely imparts his own superabundant magnetism or vitality to the patient, and that such a transmission of power is responsible for the restoration of health.

De Puységur's first discovery of any importance in this realm of drugless or mind-healing, was that in the drowsy or somnambulistic state, which quite early is produced by the application of magnetism, it was possible to address the patient and obtain evidence of a very high order of intelligence. Mesmer was previously aware of the induction of somnambulism, but he rarely interfered with it, considering it as a natural state by means of which the system adjusted its inequilibrium. Dr. Williams Gregory many years later, in describing the somnambulistic patient, declares that his whole manner seems to undergo an improvement and refinement, and "it would seem as if the brute or animal propensities were laid to rest, while the intellect and higher sentiments shone forth." What interested de Puységur most about this new discovery, was that not only did the replies he received from the entranced patients show the most marvellous insight into their own symptoms and the means of treating them, but they gave evidence of the extraordinary phenomenon, of telepathy. Here was the beginning of what later came to be known as the "higher phenomena," which included telepathy, clairvoyance, mind-reading, community of sense and perception, and ecstasy.

His second discovery was made in 1811. It consisted in finding out how to induce the somnambulistic state more quickly and more efficiently than before, namely by the use of the long passes. Several years later, du Potet laid much emphasis on the effect of the will and less on benevolent intentions, relying far more even then did de Puységur on the fixation of the eye and the passes.

Du Potet soon left the trail blazoned by Mesmer and de Puységur. He felt it was followed too servilely by the other magnetisers, and that the phenomena were obtained by means which he considered purely physical. A magnetism founded on spiritual power was the field which he chose to apply himself to, a magnetism which resembled that of Parcelsus, Van Helmont, and others. This he thought to be the true magnetism which Mesmer had refrained from revealing. Du Potet's idea was that there is one "living force," a divine dynamic power which is welded by the soul or the mind of man. This force acts upon "dead forces," by which he meant electricity and magnetism. But those he considered to be only two of the large number of unknown forces in the mind's arsenal which the soul may, by its own inherent activity, set into operation. And these forces, when put into motion, produce effects that have to be experimentally studied, since their operation is at present unknown. Over and over again he claims to have rediscovered the existence of that mysterious spiritual force of thought and will with which the magicians and great saints of yore worked. Du Potet adopted Mesmer's idea that when the spiritual forces are set into motion by thought and will, the action is like that of flame which spreads it's own energy so long as it had material to feed on. With a single match one might burn a whole city. Even so, exciting the spiritualised will, the powers of the soul, a man might do great and universal good. Once this natural force is set going in this way spiritually, the soul imparts to it a kind of intelligence that causes it to do the work demanded of it. No further effort is required. It achieves its ends divinely and effortlessly.

La Fontaine, who has been called the last of the great magnetisers, relied almost exclusively on the passes, except that sometimes he established contact magnetically with the hands while looking into the eyes of his subjects. Of course, his will was exerted powerfully all the time. Unlike du Potet, who was a scientific experimentalist, La Fontaine devoted himself wholeheartedly to the treatment of the disease. Totally disgusted with the derision of the medical world, he appealed to the people themselves, making the successful cure of disease his principal object. He relied for success in his propaganda on the results he obtained in that direction, as much as on his exhibitions of strange phenomena. He received pupils and endeavoured to found little societies which would persevere in their studies and healing work after he had gone.

He produced apparent clairvoyant phenomena at his demonstrations as evidence of the reality and importance of magnetism. But constantly he tried to convince the lay-world, the people themselves, that they had in their own hands an extraordinary power of curing each other's disease without the aid of drugs or doctors. A large proportion of his curs was of persons in the so-called higher grades of society who had tried, in vain, every other means of therapy. When they were cured, these people made the virtues and wonders of magnetism known among their own set. In England in 1840 and 1841, he created a sensation, according to the newspapers of that day, by magnetising a lion in the Zoological Gardens, London. He repeated a similar performance in other English cities. IT was on one of those itinerary demonstrations in Manchester, that Dr. Braid saw him mesmerise a man, and from some curious neurological phenomena witnessed then, received the stimulus which culminated in the discovery of hypnotic technique and the sweeping and magical effects of suggestion.

The disciples of Mesmer had maintained that the best proof of the reality of animal magnetism was the cure of disease—even as no claim the Christian Scientists that the results they achieve demonstrated the validity of their hypothesis. But a new kind of proof was now offered by the Experimentalists. They brought forth the production of anaesthesia, analgesia, clairvoyance and trance. These after all, were merely the symptoms showing themselves during the process of cure, not the really important end in itself, the cure. A patient in coma or in convulsions, however, was not an attractive object except to medical experts. But a mile away, had an interest for everyone. Here entered therefore, one of the most potent reasons for the moral disintegration of the entire field. It began to "play up to the galleries," seeking popular support through the production of psychic phenomena rather as occurred in the spiritualistic realm, instead of adhering firmly to its high primary intention of healing the sick and the lame.

The danger in some measure was anticipated. De Puységur foresaw that this new marvel of somnambulistic clairvoyance would only indispose the majority of serious-minded people from examining the subject scientifically, so he rather restrained himself and those about him from speaking pointedly of these psychic phenomena. Later, however, the facts leaked out, becoming widely prominent so that the phenomena alone were sought after. The somnambules developed by the magnetic passes were supposed to be able to see clairvoyantly into the viscera of the patient they examined in trance, diagnose correctly the nature, site and status of the disease entity present, and name the most effectual remedies and prescriptions that would help. For a long time the most implicit reliance was placed on the prescriptions of somnambules. It constituted a most serious lapse from the older ideas. For it became a sad departure from drugless therapy, and allopathic therapeutics sneaked in by the back door. No longer was reliance placed upon mind or magnetism, but upon the clairvoyantly prescribed drugs. But presently it was noticed that they prescribed chiefly remedies with which they happened to be acquainted. These were bleeding, blistering and purging—the unholy trinity that constituted so large a part of the medical practice of the day. And thus, when doubt was cast upon the clairvoyants and their prescriptions, another era began in which the efficacy of suggestion was recorded, even though a full understanding of its significance did not dawn for some many years to come.

Chiefly responsible for introducing Mesmerism into England was Dr. John Elliotson, who employed it surgically at University College Hospital, London. That is to say, he would mesmerise his patients until they sank into a deep coma characterised by analgesia and anaesthesia, when a capital operation could be painlessly performed. We must recall that these were the incredible days before the invention of chemical anaesthetics such as ether and chloroform, when surgical operations were accompanied by the most horrible anguish and torture. No sooner had Elliotson demonstrated its efficiency, and he did that in a most effectual way, than his medical colleagues instigated a programme of vilification and derision of both him and his practice. He did not permit himself to be too perturbed by such attacks, for he had been subject to persecution from them before. It appears that he had long been a progressive physician. But the medical profession has long had a neophobia, and has accepted scientific advances only with the utmost hesitancy, as if forced against its will to do so. It is recorded that Elliotson broke through the old rules and conventions of his profession by being the first doctor to discard knee-breeches, and the first to cultivate a beard—a shocking breach of professional conduct. Moreover, he horrified his fellow physicians at University College Hospital by experimenting with the effects of enormous doses of drugs, and scandalised them by using a stethoscope, against which, as is well known, the whole profession at first revolted.

He was not only the first to exhibit and practice auscultation, but he also gave the first impulse to clinical instruction, until then almost wholly unknown in England. From this it is evident that he was an enterprising physician, widely consulted by patients and frequently reported in the press, having an extensive and lucrative practice. But no sooner had he employed mesmerism in the hospital and found it more than promising as a drugless therapeutic agent for the amelioration of the sick, then he was obliged to tender his resignation. However, he founded his own institution, the Mesmeric Hospital in London, where he kept the flag flying for many years. He was familiar with that phenomenon known today as unconscious psychical activity, for he speaks of "No point in cerebral psychology is more curious than our unconscious reception of sensations, or unconscious prevention of consciousness of them, and the influence of unconscious knowledge and feelings over our actions." Although the word "suggestion," was not so employed by him in relation to his magnetic therapy, nonetheless, he was more than familiar with it, having spoken of it as the "mesmeric promise," which he employed successfully.

Another eminent pioneer was James Esdaille, a Scottish medico stationed in India. He appears to have been the first British mesmerist to receive some measure of official recognition and support. One of the most curious aspects of his application of mesmerism, was that he found he could not mesmerise to induce anaesthesia and surgically operate at the same time. Too much time was consumed in magnetising. Sometimes it would take hours to magnetise successfully a refractory patient. So he trained several of the hospital attendants in the art of inducing mesmeric sleep preparatory to surgery. From 1845 onwards, he employed the magnetic sleep for painless surgery with great success at various Indian hospitals. Not only was there no discomfort occasioned to the patients during capital operations, but they recovered far more quickly than those patients who had not been so magnetised. The record of his operations by these means, makes thrilling reading. Many of his operations were for the removal of monstrous scrotal tumours weighing nearly a hundred-weight, horrible but deadly convincing evidence of the effectiveness of his technique. The discovery and almost universal application of chemical anaesthetics for surgery put an end to the interest in hypnotic experimental work in England.

The term "hypnotism," as a less objectionable and possibly a more scientific term for certain aspects of the mesmeric state, and the partial recognition of suggestion as the effective agent, was first coined in 1843 by a Manchester physician, Dr. James Braid. It was in 1842 that he first began experimental work with mesmerism, the stimulus to it being derived from his observation of a palpebral tremor in a mesmerised patient magnetised by

La Fontaine in a public demonstration. He seems to have been the first modern practitioner deliberately to use the technique of fixation of sight and suggestion, repudiating entirely the whole magnetic implication. Even the bright object that he employed to procure optic fixation and neural fatigue was soon eliminated, since in some patients it aggravated an acute conjunctivitis, the entire stress being now laid upon verbal suggestion. He book, *Neurypnology*, contains vivid descriptions of a large number of cases which he treated hypnotically and cured by means of suggestion.

Since Braid was a physician, a graduate of the Edinburgh Medical College, trained in clinical methods and diagnosis, we need entertain little doubt that his diagnoses of most of the cases he claimed to have treated and cured hypnotically were fairly accurate. It has always been one of the first devastating replies of the medical profession, in the face of successful therapy by unrecognised methods, that the diagnosis was faulty, or that the patients were hysterics or tricksters. However, we know that hysterics and anxiety neurotics generally are not the easiest of people to hypnotise, as any practicing hypnotist readily knows. There is no question but that he diagnosed cases adequately, so far as concerns the diagnostic principles then known to the medical world, and that the patients were cured by the application of suitable hypnotic treatment. The book can be unequivocally recommended as a careful and methodical statement of hypnotic application. It is from this date that we have the first real indication of a successful psycho-therapy, a mind-cure by a physician trained in scientific observation and diagnosis. The full development of this indication played, indirectly and technically, an important role in the system inaugurated years afterwards by Mary Baker Eddy.

From 1842 to more or less the end of the century, there was a lull in the application of hypnotism in England. On the Continent however, there were famous names like Liébault, Bernheim, Charcot, Janet, Moll, and the beginning of groupings of operators coming to hold vastly different theories, such as the Schools of

Nancy, Salpêtriere, and so on. I have not attempted to describe their work, their discoveries, nor their research, which enabled them to place hypnotic treatment for the first time on a purely scientific and experimental basis, employing the mechanism of suggestion. I have neglected this part of the narrative, only because it is clear that they could not have influenced Mrs. Eddy's mind in any way, nor could their theories of suggestion have played any part whatsoever in the shaping of Christian Science theory or practice. There had not been time for any intercommunication to and from the continent of Europe and New England for, let us say, the suggestive technique of Liébault to have been brought to her attention. In one sense that is a good thing. Otherwise, her critics would surely have said of her that she stole suggestion therapy and incorporated it with a pseudo-religious façade, in her book, Science and Health.

So far as this country is concerned, La Fayette had written very enthusiastically to George Washington about magnetism and the magnetists. But it came to be introduced here by a Frenchman, Charles Poyen de St. Sauveur, and was taken up in New England by a Dr. Collyer, who gave a lecture with demonstrations in Belfast, Maine, in 1838. Many other prominent magnetists and hypnotists played a specific part in shaping and modifying the development of the future system of mind-healing. For example, Dr. Theodore Leger must be mentioned. He was a "psychodynamist" belonging to Braid's generation. In lieu of the term animal magnetism, he invented the term "psychodynamy," from *psyche*, soul, and *dunamos*, power. His system was based upon soul or spiritual power inherent within every individual. However, he was an orthodox magnetiser of the experimentalist school, for he had been an intimate friend and one of the pupils of Deleuze. He practiced and lectured in the United States, accompanied by a medical clairvoyant, and together they were said to be preeminently successful. Although he was fundamentally a magnetist of the old school, yet the subsequent march of events was to some extent influenced by some of the doubts he cast upon the magnetic theories through his own metaphysical doctrines.

Another formidable innovator was Dr. J. Rhodes Buchanan who in 1841 put forward his system of "Neurology," later called Anthropology. While denying the magnetic theories of the mesmerists and ridiculing their manipulations, he himself was able to produce many of the formerly produced therapeutic phenomena. In a letter written to Leroy Sunderland in 1844, there occurs a very interesting passage which, viewed in the light of the historical development of mind-cure, is highly significant. He says: "I do not perceive the necessity of new terms...for facts which were previously known under other names, such as Mesmerism, Neurology, etc. Neither do I think it makes any difference whether we suppose that we operate by a fluid, or a solid, by mind or by matter, by an influence, an attraction or a sympathy, or by nothing at all..."

One of the most remarkable and enterprising of the American magnetisers, however, was a physician names Dr. William B. Fahnstock, residing and practicing in Lancaster, Pennsylvania. He too thoroughly discarded all former theories of magnetism or fluids or powers, simply regarding the magnetic state as a psychological frame of mind which could be self-induced by a specific process of concentration. It would seem that this generation of American magnetists were by far and away more ingenious and speculative than were their European colleagues. Many years before a scientific basis for mind-healing was established in England, the Americans had already invented in their own way, a psychological rationale for the system.

Fahnstocked named his formulation of the observed facts as "Statuvolism," derived from *status* and *volo*, signifying a state, or peculiar condition, produced by the will. His book, *Statuvolism or Artificial Somnambulism*, though published in 1869, was the culmination of intense reflection and experimental work described in several pamphlets published long before that time. In that book he claims to present the results of thirty years of experience and research, which fact gives him some years of priority over Braid and his work in England. His system is entirely psychological, inasmuch as it eliminates passes, fixation of the eyes, and every other mechanical contrivance of technique. It was the will of the subject, not the operator, that produces the result, the operator only being requisite in his role as an instructor. The function of the instructor is only to impart to his subject or patient, the knowledge and methods whereby may be entered the statuvolic state, where the therapeutic and other results are accomplished. Statuvolism, he defines as "the state into which any person can throw himself at once, slowly or otherwise, independently of anyone else, or subject to anyone's control." In November 1842, he wrote in the Philadelphia *Spirit of the Times*, "I have had over three hundred different individuals to enter this state under my care, and have found by innumerable experiments that they are entirely independent of me, and can enter this state, and awaken themselves whenever they please, notwithstanding all I can do to the contrary." This constitutes a tremendous step away from the previously held view that the operator was indispensable to the induction of magnetic or psychological states. It was a very far cry from Mesmer. And it was another step towards the possibility of auto-suggestion as an art and a science coming to be developed. Fahnstock attracted a great deal of attention to his theories and results.

In the book which appeared in 1869, he has something highly important to state concerning this interior psychological state and its results. "The mere entering this state will not relieve disease." Braid on the other hand, did believe that the mere induction of the hypnotic sleep did have a therapeutic value of itself. Many other later hypnotists likewise concluded so. "It requires that the mind of the patients, while in this condition, should be directed to the disease, and a desire, or a resolution, formed on their part that it shall be otherwise when they awaken. It is no matter whether this resolution be taken or be made independent of the instructor or not, the effect will be the same. But it is the duty of every person into whose care they entrust themselves, to see that it is properly done before they awake, or no beneficial effect will follow...." Here is clear recognition of suggestion, described in distinct and valid terms, in the very year when Braid was merely experimenting with mechanisms for the induction of hypnotic states.

It is imperative to point out here, that it was held that the mesmeric or statuvolic sleep was not a sleep in the sense of an alternative and opposite state of the waking state. It was conceive to be a condition of quiescence which partook of some of the characteristics of both sleeping and waking. The magnetisers had conceived of it as a subordination of the outer or normal senses , and an awakening subsequently or simultaneously, of the inner senses and powers—the complete awakening of these inner senses being perfect lucidity. It is of the nature of a state of reverie, of brown study, or that type of reflection as would occur when attempting to concentrate upon a philosophical idea, a book, or pleasant music. If one were to contemplate religious truths, such as that God is infinite and is all intelligence and life and love, and the mind passed effortlessly into a realisation of such truths, a similar state of abstraction would be attained as would be directly comparable to the statuvolic psychological state.

Another investigator who was a thorn in the side of orthodox animal magnetists, and who did a great deal of propaganda work, was Leroy Sunderland of Boston. It was in 1860 that he published a work entitled, *The Trance*, which he claimed to contain the result of forty years of experience and experiment. In this event, if he began his work based upon his particular theory, in 1820, he establishes a priority of some years, even over Fahnstock, and thus long antedates Braid. Sunderland was not a physician, but a clergyman of the Methodist Episcopal Church, who for many years travelled the country as a revivalist preacher. It was his extraordinary experiences with mob-psychology, and people's reactions during those years which led him to the formulation of a theory that he called Pathetism. He defines the term "from *Pascho*, to experience, to be affected with anything, good or bad; to suffer, to feel, to be exposed or affected in a particular manner towards another, or by any event. And from the same root, *Pathos*, passion, affection, that which is suffered; love, kindness, a disease, a mental perturbation, a passive state of the mind or the body; condition, a disposition."

He left the ministry to devote himself entirely to the investigation and demonstration of psychological states. He was disliked by organised religion, for he said that all religions are attempts to throw the responsibility of our actions on something else, and we must rely wholly upon ourselves. Moreover, the mesmerists detested him for his reproduction of some of their most singular phenomena, without adhering to their contacts or passes, without believing in the existence of a magnetic fluid, and questioning the validity of the action of the will and benevolent intentions. His experiences with Pathetism were unique, and his theories well worthy of consideration only insofar as they constitute a link in the development of mental healing away from the magnetic theory to a full realisation of the powers of the mind of man.

When lecturing, Sunderland seemed to have employed no special technical means at all. This was a constant puzzle both to the press and to the public. Numbers of people fell asleep in their seats while he proceeded with his lecture, or else they went up to the platform with closed eyes, and sat down there. Contemporaries assure us that this phenomenon did not occur, as we might have been led to suppose, by the impossible dullness and fatuity of his speech. "What does he do to produce his results?" queried the *New Era* of Portsmouth, Virginia, in January 1847. "We answer, absolutely nothing but a quiet, unassuming address to the mind."

Concerning what he called the trance, a word which he employed in a specific manner and which bore no relation to the mediumistic trance of the spiritists, he states that the term is "used to signify a state of the nervous system in which the mind is said to pass beyond the use of the external senses..."

Its principal characteristics as recorded by him are: "insensibility to the external world...the mind is active...Ecstasy may be said to be the highest state of trance, when the mind is exalted to its utmost capacity in its emotions of joy. This state is rare and occurs very seldom, being mostly confined to religious exercises...The immediate cause of the trance, whether spontaneous or artificially produced, is always in the mind..." Sunderland claimed for his system of Pathetism, that it operated and produced all the results of magnetism without the labour of the will and without its peculiar processes. It produced the same or greater results on people who are wide awake, in full possession of their senses, and that it could affect emotionally and therapeutically not merely one individual at a time, but hundreds in any audience. And that it operated not only on persons in the normal or waking state, but it carried them into the higher states of trance and ecstasy, where phenomena of healing, religious conversion, and moral transformation, were achieved without effort or will. The ability is possessed by every individual to acquire these states of consciousness. These states, he claimed, as did Fahnstock, could be self-induced, for this "inheres in the economy of human life." Furthermore, he said, "By this power, the mind withdraws itself from the consciousness of pain; it cures disease; it induces the so-called 'change of heart' in revivals of religion; it brings on trance, and often induces other changes, which have been attributed to God or Devil."

He cites a case of Mrs. Agnes Nichols whose surgeon had diagnosed a malignant tumour of the breast, and had therefore suggested surgical intervention. For some days previous to the proposed operation, Sunderland applied his technique of Pathetism, ostensibly to prepare her for surgery, intending to produce anaesthesia and analgesia. But when the surgeons came to operate, they were apparently surprised and embarrassed upon discovering that the cancer or tumour was no longer present. "I give this as a remarkable case of self-induction," he writes, "and the self-healing energies of the human organism."

The secrets, for so he called them, behind the induction of the pathematic state, were dual. "First of all," he claimed, "you assume the authority; and invest yourself with the consciousness of the power every way adequate for the performance of the work you have in view." And secondly, "that in the sick, who are to be healed, as also in all who are to be entranced, there be found a negative condition, a corresponding faith, a conscious yielding of the mind and the nervous forces, to an idea—the influence believed to be exerted over them." In other words, the patient must have faith and confidence and thrust out all resistance to the pathematic operator. Moreover, this "negative condition...to an idea," simply implies a willingness and an ability to completely relax not merely the body, but the mind itself. And this is not always an easy task for the average student. But I shall have much more to say on this subject anon.

Before leaving Sunderland, it ought to be mentioned that during his ten years' career as a lecturer, hundreds of thousands of people must have witnessed the trance states that he publicly demonstrated, and thousands must have experienced them. Everywhere, the local press gave full accounts of the proceedings. In this way, his influence spread far and wide, and his thinking and experiments must have influenced large numbers of people, directly and indirectly, as well. His fame and reputation undoubtedly travelled the length and breadth of New England, and many of his contemporary mesmerists and magnetisers, including possibly Quimby, must have become aware of his work and his ideas, and have been influenced by them.

In New England there was another operator well worthy of our attention, for he too constituted a bridge between the older and the newer conceptions of psychological healing. This was John Bovie Dods, who, as far back as 1830, became convinced that electricity "is the connecting link between mind and inert matter...and is the grand agent employed by the creator to move and govern the universe." He delivered many lectures, including one before members of both branches of the Massachusetts legislature, and was invited by Daniel Webster and Henry Clay to lecture at the House of Representatives in Washington before members of the United States Senate. He spoke of magnetism as being synonymous with mind, and as that force functioning in the cosmos as the vital factor. He made the attempt to connect theory with practice. Here they were, the magnetists, performing incredible and miraculous psychotherapeutic feats without having an adequate philosophical basis for their production. The whole subject of the interaction of mind and body was fast becoming a question of scientific experiment rather than, as before, of philosophy—even if the science that Dods employed, seems rather dubious to us today. However, it is not the scientific material accumulated or the conclusions reached, that are important in the world that we today term scientific. Rather, it is the peculiar attitude of patient, objective investigation that counts and which is important, the method of observing various phenomena over a long period of time, and accumulating logical and verified statistics and pertinent data.

For him, electricity is the peculiar dynamic factor involved in mind-cure, and is set into motion by "the finest, most sublime and brilliant substance in being—a substance that possesses the attributes of inherent or self-motion and living power, and from which all other motion and power in the immeasurable universe, are derived. This is the Infinite Mind, and possesses embodied form. He is a living being,...Mind or spirit is above all, and absolutely disposes of and controls all...What is seen is not the reality, but is only the manifestation of the unseen."

He believed, if so we might express it, that God and man contain the same ingredients. And that is man, as in all else beside, the natural forces tend to the preservation and the re-establishment of health. He felt that we have both doctor and chemist within ourselves, in the shape of voluntary and involuntary powers of the mind, both of which are reflections of the divine power of God. And "the formative power of the mind," selects what is wanted from an infinite source of supply, materialising it to employ it for repairing and curing the mind and body. There are no doctors among the plants, he writes: "The invisible electro-nervous fluid is the healing principle in the vegetable as well as in the animal world." It moves "and equalises the sap, the blood, and the blood affects the flesh" in man.

Mind is something real. It has great spiritual powers of its own, altogether apart from ratiocination, understanding and will, as is concretely proven by magnetic experiments. Sensation too is thoroughly psychological, for the sensory neural impulses are assembled in the brain, to undergo a psychological interpretation. "The true philosophical reason why a tooth can be extracted, or a surgical operation performed, without pain, is that all feeling or sensation, is in the mind—strictly speaking, the body itself has no feeling." This is not a very great distance from Mrs. Eddy's formulation that there is no life and sensation in matter, and that all is mind. But he believed rather as did Mesmer that, "there is one great cause for all diseases, and this is the disturbing of the vital force of the body." However, he goes further, laying the ground for later metaphysical belief, that those whose minds are positive, and in equilibrium, resist the attacks of disease; while those who are afraid, and picture disease in themselves—as we would say, who are prone to auto-suggestion—are likely to be attacked. Mental impressions can cure diseases even when those diseases appear to arise from physical causes.

Phineas Parkhurst Quimby was born in Lebanon, a small New England town, in the state of New Hampshire, in the year 1802. His father was a blacksmith, and his life and rudimentary education were such as might be expected in a humble home in a country town in the foot of the White Mountains. As a boy, he attended school for a brief period only, but he had an enquiring and inventive type of mind. We cannot say that he was a voracious reader of books in general, nor that he was well-educated, and although the title "doctor," was often applied to him, he was utterly lacking in medical or other therapeutic training. How he came to interest himself in mesmerism is, in itself, an intriguing story. Apparently he had contracted pulmonary tuberculosis and was fast waning in strength even although under constant medical supervision. Curiously enough, we come across a parallel instance as a stimulant to metaphysical enquiry in the history of the founders of the Unity School of Christianity, elsewhere described in this book. To continue in his own words, he writes, "My symptoms were those of any consumptive; and I had been told that my liver was affected and my kidneys diseased, and that my lungs were nearly consumed...In this state, I was compelled to abandon my business; and losing all hope, I gave up to die."

Riding one day in his carriage, for he was far too enfeebled to ride horseback, he found that the horse had a will of its own, and contrarily refused to budge, save that he walked by its side. This he did, walking uphill by the horse's side, for over two miles. Finally exhausted, he got back into the carriage, and "excitement took possession of my sense, and I drove the horse as fast as he could go, up hill and down, till I reached home; and, when I got into the stable, I felt as strong as ever I did." The effect of this experience upon him was simply that he came to doubt the medical diagnosis of pulmonary tuberculosis with extensive metastasis. He was not yet cured, but at least his mind was operating in an unaccustomed positive manner. It was in this mood that he became acquainted with mesmerism, through the demonstration of Dr. Poyen, as an interesting therapeutic phenomenon worthy of investigation. In 1840, he gave his own first public demonstration. Subsequently, he met a young man, Lucius Burkmar, who turned out to be an ideal subject, and these two made some of the most extraordinary exhibitions of mesmerism and clairvoyance that had been witnessed for many a year. When Quimby was called upon to visit a sick patient, he would put Lucius into the mesmeric state first of all. Becoming lucid, Burkmar would apparently examine the patient clairvoyantly, describe the disease, the site of the principal lesion, and prescribe drugs and remedies for the cure.

After a time, Quimby became convinced that there was a relationship with what the patient or those about him thought with regard to the nature of the disease and the clairvoyant report that Lucius always produced. Later, Lucius clairvoyantly examined Quimby's own kidneys that had probably become infiltrated and metastasised by the tubercular infection, and undertook to heal them by a laying on of hands. When a real cure apparently took place, that is to say when Quimby became asymptomatic, the discrepancy between medical diagnosis and the apparently trivial efforts of Lucius struck him forcibly. In fact, he came to believe that Lucius read the diagnostic opinion in the mind of the sick, rather than stated a truth acquired experientially by himself. And that in his own case, he had cured himself by suggestion and faith, rather than through the efforts of Lucius. Becoming convinced of this, he thereupon discarded mesmerism, clairvoyance, and his subject Lucius, and began to develop mental healing as a technique by itself.

And so, as time proceeded, he came to believe that disease itself was, as he himself informs us, "a deranged state of mind." Disease is embraced within our beliefs. Consequently, since our beliefs can be altered, so disease can be thrust out of our minds, for we have the ability to alter our beliefs and mental attitudes. Cures have been engendered through the agency of drugs, and also without drugs, but the "principle on which they are done, is the question to solve; for the disease can be cured, with or without medicine, on *but one principle*." That principle for him was a change in the attitude of the patient who held the belief in disease. If the viewpoint could be altered, neurological and visceral and cellular changes would automatically follow. It is not too difficult to realise that merely a changed viewpoint could accomplish this. He knew, as we all know, of many phenomenal crises in health, for better or for worse, occurring under the stimulus of a mental shock. The paralysed man, who has been without the use of his leg muscles for years, who suddenly gets up from his bed and runs out of a flaming house, is a common story that illustrates the point only too well. And we can realise that under the stimulus of great grief, for example, far-reaching organic and neurological changes occur so that the hair, for example, can change colour overnight.

It was while he was engaged in his magnetic work that Quimby became totally convinced that disease was an error of the mind, and not a real entity that mesmerism eliminated. So that later, after he discarded his practice of mesmerism, Quimby would simply sit beside his patient. After having heard a detailed account of what the troubles were, Quimby would quietly converse, appealing to the patient's understanding, explaining the cause of the trouble. In this way, he would accomplish a radical alteration in the habitual mental attitude of the patient. He disabused it of its psychological error, establishing in its stead the truth that false beliefs only were responsible for the disease and that a realisation of this fact would eliminate it, inducing a cure.

In the year 1859, he went to Portland, Maine, where he remained till the summer of 1865, treating the sick by his particular method of explanation and suggestion. It was during the period of his important practice in Portland, that those patients visited him who, receiving from him their health, new inspiration, and lofty stimulus, later were to spread all over the country and the world at large, the gospel of mental healing. Amongst these was Mrs. Eddy, whose visit to Quimby terminated a long period of sickness and inefficiency. That he was the one individual who healed her, restoring to her self-esteem and respect as a human being, enabling her to resume some sort of adequate function in society, exalted her to high enthusiasm. She, who had left her native city, where she was well-known, as an ailing, crabby female, now returned, bubbling over with boundless enthusiasm. She was exuberant in her admiration for Quimby and his method of treatment, not disdaining in her incomparable zeal to compare him with the greatest healers who have blessed mankind. In one of the local newspapers, she wrote of him in a semi-fanatical vein: "Christ healed the sick, but not by jugglery or with drugs. As the former (Quimby) speaks, as never man before spake and heals as never man healed since Christ, is he not identified with truth? And is not this the Christ which is in him? We know that in wisdom is life, 'and the life was the light of man.' P. P. Quimby rolled away the stone from the sepulchre of error, and health is the resurrection. But we also know that "light shineth in darkness and the darkness comprehendeth it not."

Such worship as this for the man who, if not restoring her entirely to health, gave her at least a new vision, a new attitude, a new viewpoint to adopt towards her own inner and physical disabilities—such worship, it is evident, can be construed in only one way. She was indebted enormously to him. But she was indebted, I firmly believe, to him in a way that most critics have not contemplated. These have hitherto thought, either that she was indebted to him intellectually and technically, or else not at all. Either that she assimilated his views of healing, or that she did not. But I do not believe the problem can be stated in this simple way. I hope to demonstrate that there is very little in Christian Science that can be attributed directly to the influence of Quimby. As one critic pointed out years ago, while some traces of Quimby may be found in Science and Health, on the other hand, not one vestige of the fully developed Christian Science theory may be found in *The Quimby Manuscripts*.

Nevertheless, Mary Baker Eddy was enormously indebted to Quimby in this way. He pointed out the way. A new road was revealed to her by his processes of mental healing. For the first time, she had demonstrated to her a method of healing which proved that the mind supremely was able to affect and control physiological function. And that was all the hint she needed. He gave her an orientation which her own genius was able to employ in its own unique manner. And she took that road—as history has narrated only too well. But there was a link missing. Quimby had proven the adequacy of the mind in overcoming physical incoordinations, certainly. But some hint was required in another direction—to provide a philosophical rationale for it *modus operandi*. This she was lacking. It had to come from some other direction.

CHAPTER THREE

Philosophy

It can be fairly well established that, Frank Podmore and his book *Mesmerism and Christian Science* notwithstanding, mesmerism as the historical antecedent of a mind-healing system had only a minor effect upon Mary Baker Eddy. There was very little direct influence upon her from this source. None of the major ideas or even the technical procedures peculiar to the magnetists find any place in her system in even the remotest way. But what they did accomplish for her through Quimby, was to suggest an entirely new method by means of which the body and it peculiar disease states might be beneficently affected. However, if the matter was permitted merely to rest here, we have been fair to Mrs. Eddy in the most negligible way. Now that the hullaballoo and noise attending the appearance of her book have died down, we can afford in these modern times to be more than generous and give credit where credit is due.

Quimby and most of the magnetists were concerned either with the production of the weird but impressive psychical phenomena of the trance states, or else with accomplishing spectacular healings of cases which could be dealt with in no other way. But this attitude cannot be said for Mrs. Eddy nor for her brainchild, Christian Science. Whatever its inadequacies in any direction, *Science and Health* does not enunciate merely a system for healing sick bodies—or sick minds for that matter. It indicates a method by which every phase of an individual's life may be affected and benefitted. At this moment, we are not concerned with a critical appraisal of the claims made by Christian Scientists that miraculous cures have been effected, that undesirable moral traits were eliminated, and that material riches and wealth have been obtained. These, for the time being, we will accept on their face value. We will subject them later on to some consideration and, if need be, to criticism. What concerns us now is this one fact that the applicability of Christian Science as an auto-hypnotic method far exceeds in extent anything dreamed of either by Quimby or even by Mesmer and his disciples. Quimby in one sense recognised that disease states might be correlated to states of mind—in a word to ignorance, to false beliefs, to error. But never for one moment did he conceive of an extension of that idea in any of the variable host of problems that constitute the difficulties of human existence. This, however, is exactly the task undertaken by Mrs. Eddy. Sickness, poverty, problems of every kind must respond, so she thought, to the application of a single principle. If that principle casually applied works in one direction, it must operate in all. In the realm of mind-healing, she was a unitarian.

Today, with modern psychology having established a scientific basis for the recognition of the validity of much of what she indicated, we can understand her a little better. Psychoanalysis has done much to show that an individual and his environment—by which we may mean his health, his viewpoint, his job, his immediate friends and social status—can readily be analysed and understood in the dynamic terms of his unconscious psychic life. We very largely live in a world of our own creation. "The world is mine and the fullness thereof" is something each and every one of us can say of his own particular world, unique for every one. This is what Mrs. Eddy tried to teach in her own way many years ago. And successfully too. The success of her organisation, the widespread infiltration of her ideas and teachings into so many aspects of modern life, are eloquent proof of how well she fulfilled her vision. What we are concerned with just now, however, is this. What enabled her to use the Quimby re-orientation in so creative a manner? This is the problem. What stimulus did she receive other than from Quimby which enabled her to develop so all-inclusive and unitarian a viewpoint which only today is beginning to receive some degree of collaboration?

If we are told that from infancy onwards she studied the Bible closely, we do not I am afraid get very far. Surely that assisted her. But it was too near at hand and too familiar to provide a creative stimulus. The prompt, as it were, had to come from somewhere else. Now critics of Christian Science tell us that, techniques and method notwithstanding, philosophically her system stands in historical relationship with at least three other religio-philosophical systems. The first is the Vendanta, the religious philosophy of India which is the supreme achievement of the Hindu sages. The second is the intellectual vision of Bishop Berkeley, formulated to give a coherency to the objective world, the understanding of which was apparently being disintegrated by the onslaughts of Locke. And finally, Hegel's philosophy, the very peak and summit of German transcendental philosophy and idealism. Obviously, in a work of this kind, I cannot even begin to do justice in description to any one of these systems, yet alone all three. But in order to trace out any possible relationship between them and Mrs. Eddy's system—a relationship, rather, that may reveal the possibility of plagiarism, to state it bluntly, as has been alleged—we must examine them at least briefly, and indicate their salient features, so that we can learn what their distinguishing elements are.

We must begin with Vedanta philosophy. This is the first in time and bears, on the surface, the greatest resemblance to Mrs. Eddy's own metaphysic. One of the shortest summaries of the ideas of the Vedanta is contained in two lines from the teaching of Sankaracharya, the most prominent commentator and interpreter of the Vedanta:

*"Brahman is true, the world is false,
The soul is Brahman, and nothing else."*

It is a perfect summary, quintessentialising the entire teaching found in innumerable tomes of this grandest achievement of oriental thought. What truly and really exists is Brahman, God, the one absolute spiritual being. It is what Plato meant by the Eternal Idea, Christ by the Father in heaven, the agnostics by the Unknowable, and what others have called the infinite in nature. This is the Being behind all beings, the power that manifests the universe, sustains it, and draws it back again to its own eternal bosom. This is the supreme reality, all else being phenomenal, a mere appearance. It is the highest concept of God, whose characteristics are *Sat-Chit-Ananda*, infinite being and substance, infinite wisdom and truth, and infinite love and bliss.

The world is false, according to the Vedantists. It is *maya*, illusion. But by illusion they do not infer that it has no existence. It exists all right, as witnessed by our strivings, by our pains and sorrows, our constant frustrations when it impinges too vigorously upon our lives. Everything which is presented to us by means of the senses and the mind is phenomenal and relative, and is subject to many interpretations. The world has existence, but it is not wholly what it appears to be. We do not know the world as it *really* is. All we know of the world is a purely psychological process, an interpretation of sensory impressions that are assembled and coordinated in the cerebrum to result in a series of inner experiences. But what is the world? We do not know. All we know is that it is not in the least what it appears to be. Even modern science arrives at a similar conclusion, though possibly it is more cautious in its deductions from these conclusions than were the Vedanta sages. How do we know this outside world, the validity and reality of which we question, to assume that it is false? Only through our senses.

Before me, on a table, stands my typewriter. How do I know what it is, and that it is there? I see it, feel it, and hear its clicking when it is in operation. Three of my special senses, sight and touch and hearing, are stimulated. A series of light-rays, passing through the lens of the eye, strike the retina, the sensitive membrane of the eye, which is shot through and through with minute neural filaments. Chemical changes occur in the retina, by means of which these light vibrations from the typewriter are converted into sensory neurological impulses that are conveyed along the third cranial nerve to the visual centres of the brain. Some strange and miraculous process there occurs which eludes our understanding. But as a result, these impulses and nerve vibrations are converted magically into a mental picture of a typewriter which stands before me on the desk. My fingers strike the typewriter keys. The terminal end plates and sensory buds in the finger tips are stimulated to convey a complex series of impulses along the nerve fibres to the posterior horn of the spinal cord in the upper dorsal and lower cervical areas, and hence to the brain. There, again, these impulses are translated. Some waves, set into motion by my tapping the keys of the machine, impinge upon the perilymph and endolymph of the inner ear, vibrating the fine hair cells and the organ of Corti within the cochlea. Vibrations are then transmitted along the auditory nerve to the cerebral centre of hearing, to associated with the visual and touch picture, and interpreted finally as the image of a typewriter.

But I have no direct or immediate experience of a typewriter whatsoever. All that my experience consists of, is a series of sensory reactions which mysteriously are converted into psychological states and inner experiences. All this is admitted both by psychology and physiology. These differ principally in a major respect. Philosophy, or some branches of it, is inclined to question whether the mental picture is a true image of external reality, whereas science is inclined to accept it on its face value. Vedanta questions the reality of such pictures, arguing that we live exclusively in a world of mind and ideas. What plays on us apparently from the outside stimulating the nerves to convey impulses to the brain for interpretation, is also a part of that world of mind. Both within and without is mind, and that mind is God. There is no cleavage between ego and non-ego, between spirit and nature. We live in God and his infinite mind. It is God and his omnipresence that affect us objectively, and it is God within that provides the subjective interpretation within the brain.

The Vedanta is based upon the supposition that our ordinary knowledge is simply the result of ignorance. We do not know our true nature within, nor do we know how we become aware of God in the objective world. We suffer from a chronic psychic scrotoma, which they call ignorance, the first and major sin. For from ignorance, all the vast host of other sins and errors must follow. Our ordinary knowledge is to them ignorance, deceitful and untrue. In one sense, this is not unlike the scientific attitude which so distrusts the evidence of the unaided senses, that instruments of varying degrees of sensitivity have been invented in order to offset and correct this sensory inaccuracy.

For example, we say in common parlance with the ordinary knowledge that we possess, that the sun rises every morning. But nothing could be further from the truth. Yet our sense knowledge tells us that this is so. Were we to take the trouble to bestir ourselves from our customary inertia and watch the dawn arise, we would gradually see the eastern horizon with the clouds there become faintly tinted and made beautiful as the hidden glory of the sun swings into view. And as we watch, we would see the great orb gradually move upwards, so that after a while its golden disc is visible well above the horizon. Yet science demonstrates that this is purely illusory. The sun does not rise. It is the earth that encircles the sun. It is the movement of our terrestrial globe that creates the illusion that it is the sun that rises.

Imagine yourself sitting in a modern streamlined express, speeding on its way at some sixty or so miles an hour, over a good road-bed. Let it be an air conditioned car, so that all windows and doors being closed tight a minimum of external sound and clatter is heard inside. In such a car, it actually appears as though the surrounding landscape were rushing furiously by. Trees, bushes, buildings, and telephone poles tear madly by, and the comparative quiet of the carriage, with the absence of any pronounced lateral or rocking movement, all confirm us in this illusion. It does really seem as though the train is stationary, while the rest of the world rushes past us. But we know that this seeming is pure illusion. Our senses *do* deceive us. The do not register the entire truth. We have to correct the sensory evidence by an appeal to our knowledge, and by what intellectually we know to be true.

Medically speaking, a patient may appear to be in perfect condition. He may have a complete absence of any inner sensations from the various viscera that might betoken disease. He may remain completely unconscious of them, and believe himself to enjoy absolute health. Yet I know of many cases of malignant neoplastic activity which must have proceeded secretly for many years, all the time the patient was asymptomatic. Autopsies have been performed, revealing that malignant tumours have been located in brain, in lungs, liver and stomach—tumours evidently requiring for their massive growth and metastasis the lapse of a great length of time. They produced no signs or symptoms, until just a short time period before the end. The seeming health was but an illusion. Things are certainly not as they appear to be. And so, in order to overcome this apparent state of affairs, medical science resorts to a wide variety of ingenious instrumentalities to obtain a better insight into the situation. Röentgen rays dispel this idea of the solidity of matter, enabling us to peer darkly into the secret depths of the body. Blood and urine chemistry, serological tests, biological assays are all attempts to overcome this ignorance and this manifest imperfection of the special senses by an appeal to more exact methods of determining function and organic integrity.

Things are not always as they appear to be at first sight. We must not take them for granted. Madness lies that way. Insight is necessary. It is upon this basis that Vedanta takes its stand.

Only God is true, the world is false. But if God or Brahman is perfect and unchangeable, only He exists. Man, as separate from God, cannot exist, otherwise we would have man and an Infinite being which clearly does not brook of a second. Man and God therefore must be identical. A true identity exists. If there is an Infinite, it can only be one Infinite—one Infinite God of boundless love, truth, substance and intelligence. If there were two Infinites, they could not really be Infinite but would exist in a mutually limiting relationship to each other. But that which exists is Infinite, and there cannot be more than one. Therefore God as the Infinite is One. Hence God and Man's spirit are one Infinite. The Vedantist, therefore, confronted by the supreme reality of God, does not deny the validity of the phenomenal world. It is surely there, only it is not what we think it to be, any more than man is what he feels himself to be—petty, finite, impotent and helpless.

Man, in his highest level of being, is Brahman. He is God and there is none else beside. To express this, the Vedantists coined the phrase *Tat twam asi*. That thou art. "That" is the infinite Brahman, the supreme reality. The "thou" is the highest spirit in man, his true self, unknown to him most of the time. He is unconscious of what he really is. It is the higher self, the Self, the being behind every human ego, free from all bodily fetters of pain, sorrow, poverty, limitation, distorted passion. Free and unattached, unborn and undying, this is the Self—and that Self is God or Brahman. And if we realise this truth, liberation from limitation is achieved.

The question how ignorance laid hold of man, and made him imagine that he lives or moves or has his true being elsewhere but in Brahman, is just as unanswerable really in Vedanta, as it is in any other philosophy. The philosophy of the Vedanta, like Christian Science, states that our thinking arises from the conviction that ordinary human knowledge is uncertain, if not altogether fallacious. True knowledge of the Self, true self-knowledge, expresses itself in the words *Tat twam asi,* the identity of God and man. And until that stage of awareness has been reached, the individual is fettered by the body and by the organs of sense, even by the mind and the conflicting problems which in its ignorance it creates.

A yearning for God as the expression of a hope to overcome all human limitations finds expression in all religions. But according to most of them, a return of the soul to the absolute knowledge of God is possible after death only. Not so with the Vedanta. The final beatitude of the soul can be achieved here and now in this life on earth. That spiritual attainment requires knowledge only, the truth of the eternal unity of what is divine in man with God. The truth brings freedom and beatitude. The Vedantists call it *atmavidya*, self-knowledge—the knowledge that the true self can only be that Self which is All in All, and beside which there is nothing else. Sometimes this realisation of the intimacy between man and God comes suddenly, as the result of an unexplainable intuition, or self-recollection. Sometimes, however, it seems as if the force of logic, or even the hard bitter blows of human experience had driven the human mind to the same spiritual result. Moreover, the Hindu sages invented various forms of spiritual exercises, of prayer, of meditation, of techniques of reflection and thinking having as their objective the achievement of such divine knowledge. India's history is rich with accounts of noble achievements of this kind, of great sages who, by their own intellectual efforts, have arrived at an inward realisation of their own identity with God.

This is the supreme goal of the Vedanta as both theory and practice. The theory posits the statement that God is the sole reality, and the world as something wholly apart from and other than God is pure sensory deception. This being so, and since only one Infinite can exist, man in his true spiritual nature is eternally one with God. Nothing really can separate him from participating in the wisdom and divine being and joy that infinitely is God's except his own wilful ignorance of that fact.

Nothing in the above could not have been immediately accepted by Mrs. Eddy. In fact, by eliminating the Sanskrit words, we could well imagine that in effect we were reading from *Science and Health*. Vedanta and Christian Science are both absolute idealisms. Could Mrs. Eddy have had access to any literature during her life that enabled her to be influenced by oriental teachings? It is possible. Anything is possible. But in assuming that such a possibility had existed, we must produce some evidential material to prove that influence. And in the present instance, not the smallest grain of such evidence can be produced. The Rev. Dr. Lyman P. Powell, in his authorised biography of Mrs. Eddy, quotes the names of several classical authors, fragments of whose writings were reproduced in one of the girlhood books she read. But none among them was a Vedantist.

We know there was a French translation from the Upanishads done by Anquetil du Perron many years before she was born. A translation of the Bhagavad Gita was in existence also, having been rendered into English towards the close of the eighteenth century by Charles Wilkins. A tremendous surge of activity with regard to oriental philosophy and religion occurred around the middle of the century, when Mrs. Eddy's ideas were not yet formed into coherency, or set into a system. But there is no trace, no scrap of evidence to indicate that she was in the slightest degree indebted to the Vedanta for the principal form or inspiration of her philosophy.

Mrs. Eddy's Christian Science developed, I am firmly convinced, independently of any familiarity with eastern teachings. But for the sake of argument and discussion, let us assume that in ways unknown as yet to us, oriental philosophy was brought to the attention of Mrs. Eddy. Let us assume, as would the most uncompromising and devastating of her critics, that she did plagiarise from Vedanta, what then? Really, we get nowhere with such an assumption—altogether apart from the fact that it is unproven. I am willing to admit that the theoretical formulation of the two philosophies are similar. Both place the entire emphasis on God as the true source and ground of human existence. They differ in that

Mrs. Eddy does not regard man's spirit as identical with that of God, for he is only a reflection of the divine order and power. Both place gigantic question marks against the validity of the objective world which presents to man that host of problems with which all are familiar—sickness, poverty, mental and moral conflicts, marital and social discords, and so on.

In many respects they are comparable. But they bear certain resemblances only insofar as theory is concerned. The practical implications are so completely different that well might we wonder how such vastly conceived spheres of applicability could have evolved from a common theme. The Vedantist with his magnificent notion of the identity of God and man, thoroughly neglected the physical world and its problems. The poverty and filth and squalor typical of the Indian village was the well-known result. Spiritual experience alone was the goal of the Vedantist, to feel the inner pulse of complete identity with God. He became so enamoured of his idealistic philosophy that the objective world around him deteriorated. Poverty, in the sense of lack of material things and possessions, instead of being considered a disgrace and a violation of spiritual knowledge, was encouraged. It was believed that material things bound the soul more powerfully to illusions instead of aiding it in its free flight to divine realisation. Success in any commercial or professional enterprise was scarcely encouraged. In fact, the opposite tendency was far more common. To withdraw from active life to devote years to meditation on spiritual matters, in solitude and quiet, was recognised as a superior goal. One of the four main divisions of the Hindy way of life was reserved with just this idea in view. The emphasis was placed wholly on an inward realisation of the power and presence of Brahman as being the true self of man, rather than upon any attempt heroically to remedy sickness, or to destroy the horrid bonds of poverty with their foul injury to the soaring spirit of man, and so render his lot easier. No one even stated that Brahman, as the divine power and spirit in dwelling the heart of man, could eliminate disease and want, heal social inequalities and inadequacies, and raise up the entire functioning of civilised man and his environment to a higher and more divine level of social integration. In Vedanta, none of this was conceived. The entire concentration was on the achievement of the beatific vision, of liberation, *Moksha*, from the terrible bonds of the world and the self, by a realisation of God in a frightened retreat from the world of filth and sorrow.

No doubt, had Mrs. Eddy been born in an eastern environment the bias of her mind, with the background peculiar to it, would have given her a similar point of view. Poverty would have been accepted as a matter of course, and material possessions of money and property would have come to be looked at as positive hindrances to the spiritual life from which deliverance must be sought. But Mrs. Eddy was not born in the East. She lived her life in the New England States, where hardy, strong, and virile peoples pitted their wills against life and the world. Only a few years before her time, we must remember that these gaunt New Englanders were pioneers in a virgin country which had to be bent to their will. All the forces of nature and the savage inhabitants of the land, and the very earth itself, new and uncultivated, seemed determined not to yield readily to the white-skinned invaders of the North American States. By sheer courage, indomitable will, and forcefulness of purpose in the face of every obstacle, and hardship, these pioneers kept themselves occupied with their task, determined to succeed in their chosen goal of conquest and colonisation. It was a vital spirit that Mrs. Eddy inherited, in spite of the fact that her early years, the first half of her life, displayed but little of that tenacity in the tedious repetition of ill-health. But it was just this fact, that she dissipated and squandered her heredity vitality in almost constant sickness, that possibly conditioned her to orientate her brain-child towards achieving success in material things and overcoming the gaunt spectre of sickness and disease and poverty.

Being a New Englander who had assimilated typical American concepts and notions into her being, of course nothing could be more natural to her than to regard sickness and poverty and conflict with considerable distaste. Money and property, implying leisure for culture and thought, were highly regarded as legitimate, even superior ends in themselves. The American spirit had come to regard no problem as fundamentally insoluble. Tackled in the right way, fought with the right weapons, and faced with the right spirit, the intrepid individual could overcome all things. The way and the weapon and the spirit came to be summed up, after Mrs. Eddy's revelation, in the idea of God being infinite intelligence, truth, love, and substance. Armed with these qualities, what could stand in the way? Knowing that God resides everywhere within and without man, could any problem persist before that divine onslaught?

Mrs. Eddy unknowingly brought her typical Yankee background into the picture of her divine science. This background gave direction and fiery determination to what otherwise might have been an insipid parlour fluttering of female gossip about religion. There was nothing insipid about this woman who at fifty was penniless, but died at eighty five leaving an enormous estate. Nor was there anything inept about this thoroughly practical person who wrote the Church Manual, with its definite rules and regulations for governing a vast religious movement with its host of churches sprung up all over the country. There was very little fantasy in her vision of a well-organised Christian Science Church which would cater to those physically and spiritually sick, and bring them to a psychological state whereby they could enjoy and master the physical world. An altogether different view prevails here. It is so completely in opposition to the eastern view, in spite of minor similarities of philosophical theory, that we are justified in drawing the conclusion that she could have known nothing intellectually about Vedanta and eastern spiritual knowledge, and therefore borrowed nothing.

Another set of critics have believed that Christian Science bears resemblances to the philosophy of *Bishop Berkeley*. It behooves us, therefore, briefly to examine this system to determine whether or not Mrs. Eddy could have been obligated in any way to the speculations of George Berkeley, an Irishman, born in 1685. His was the enthusiasm, lofty imagination, and charm of personality that commonly we associate with the Irish. He entered Dublin University in 1700, and in his forties, after returning from Rhode Island whither he had come to convert the Americans, he was appointed to the bishopric of Cloyne in Ireland. As a Catholic scholar, obviously his speculations were motivated by an intellectual bias, the defense and propagation of the Catholic faith. Religion and faith had been dealt hard blows in the preceding years, and Berkeley as a student in Dublin felt impelled to defend them. It was in his early days at college that the vision came to him of a philosophic principle by means of which he hoped to revolutionise human thinking, and in his twenty-fifth year published his chief work *A Treatise on the Principles of Human Knowledge*.

The fundamentals of his philosophy are not easy to present, especially the novelty of his conception, the denial of the independent existence of matter. He argued that the objects of human knowledge are either ideas actually imprinted on the mind through the agency of sense perception, or else are perceived by some process of introspection of the mind itself. Moreover, there is an inner activity which knows or perceives these ideas, exercising certain mental operations such as thinking, willing, remembering, imagining, and so on. This perceiving active being is what he calls mind, soul, spirit. It is the Self. That none of our thoughts and ideas can exist without a perceiving mind is self-evident. It is the mind alone that perceives these psychological reactions. Moreover, the various sensations or ideas imprinted on the mind through the senses, cannot exist otherwise than in a mind perceiving them, as was indicated when discussing Vedantism. All our sensations are psychological reactions to some kind of objective stimulus, regardless of what that objective stimulus is. Any sensation, such as smell, sight, sound touch or taste, is an idea that the Self receives and interprets. It is from a consideration of this fact, that he came to utter his now famous dictum esse is percipii. That is to say, it was totally unthinkable to him that things could exist independently of experience. They must exist only for some thinking mind. As unthinking entities perceived by no one, they could have no existence. For what are houses, rivers, mountains, and valleys of our objective world but the things we perceive by sense? And what do we perceive besides our own ideas or sensations?

If, to continue the metaphor previously employed, I become aware of the idea called my typewriter only through my sensations, what becomes of it when I leave the room, or die, or am not otherwise engaged in perceiving it? Does it cease to exist because I no longer perceive it, on the basis of the formula that if I perceive it it must exist, and that if I do not perceive it, it does not exist? Berkeley says this idea of a typewriter exists independently of my perceptions and sensations because it is a part of God, one of the many ideas of universal Mind.

"I take this important truth to be," he states "that all the choir of heaven and the furniture of the earth, in a word all those bodies which compose the mighty frame of the world, have not any subsistence without a mind—that their *being* is *to be perceived or known*; that consequently, so long as they are not actually perceived by me, or do not exist in my mind, or that of any other created spirit, they must either have no existence at all, or else subsist in the mind of some Eternal Spirit."

This therefore is what Berkeley intended to prove—the immaterialism of the external world, the non-existence of an unspiritual thinking matter, and that all things perceived are ideas in the divine universal Mind of God. So far from violating common sense, he claims that all he is doing is to justify the beliefs of common sense by clarifying the issue. He believes we have first raised a dust and then complain that we cannot see. The root of the evil for him lies in the supposition that we have such things as abstract ideas. Every possible idea must be a concrete fact or image of consciousness. We deceive ourselves by taking words for ideas, and assuming that behind the whole phenomenal world there is an abstract substratum of matter, maybe an invisible, intangible, fine matter which impinges upon the senses to evoke from our consciousness the subjective characteristics of colour, shape, size, etc.

The question he asks is this. Can we represent to ourselves what we mean by matter as something independent of mind and consciousness? It is a word which we use, without any understanding behind it? It is on this assumption that Berkeley rests his case. If we can define what we mean by the existence of objects abstracted from the plain fact of their being perceived, very well. But if we cannot, then we are merely fooled by words, and then we must go back to the common sense dictum that material objects are identical with the very things we see, feel and hear. That is, matter is really nothing apart from our own sensations and perceptions and ideas. And these are phenomena of mind only, not phenomena of matter. Things are thoughts, and thoughts are things. The idea of a substratum of matter which neither acts, nor perceives, nor is perceived, is descriptive of what Berkeley calls non-entity. It does not exist. He wishes to know how anything can be present "which is neither perceivable by sense nor reflection, nor capable of producing any idea in our minds, nor is at all extended, nor hath any form, nor exists in any place." An unperceived material substance then is unthinkable.

Again and again he reiterates, an unthinking material substance independent of mind and perception does not and cannot logically exist. We cannot conceive of any substance to exist otherwise than in a mind perceiving it. The question arises, in consequence, can we know anything outside of our own fleeting thoughts? That is to say, is there really some sort of objective world outside of our minds? In his speculations, Berkeley is obliged to differentiate between the ideas that arise in the mind through memory or imagination, and those that are received by means of sensory experience. There is a difference, as we all know. Objective images seem to be more powerful and lasting than the inner images. We are able to control, to banish, to manipulate the ideas native to our minds. But those ideas that we come to know through the special senses appear to have an order, a significance, and a coherence, an enduring quality, that renders them of a different nature from the former. His deduction is dual. First, "my ideas evidently require some cause beyond my own will; and second, this cause cannot be unthinking matter–a word to which no positive notion corresponds. Nor, clearly, can the ideas be the cause of on another." In other words, God is the answer. God is the ground of these objective ideas. God is the objective world.

Ideas imprinted on the senses from without are real things. They actually do exist, and we cannot deny them. There is no false testimony of the senses. They convey real impressions which answer to real things. But whereas we have in our ignorance imaged that these real things are composed of matter, of unthinking corporeal substance, Berkeley would have us know that these real things are ideas created and perceived by the mind of God. The things perceived by sense are external to our own minds. They are not generated or created from within the mind itself. They are seen to come from outside the perceiving spirit of man. God is a spirit, and man is a spirit. Man therefore is able to partake of and perceive the ideas of God, because he is of essentially the same substance and spirit of God.

In this concept, we have everything that is needed to account for the objectivity, order, significance and necessity of our ideas that are derived from sensation and perception. "That food nourishes, sleep refreshes, and fire warms us; to sow in the seedtime is the way to reap in the harvest; and, in general, that to obtain such or such ends, such or such means are conductive—all this we know, not by discovering any necessary connection between our ideas, but only by the observation of the settled laws of nature." These laws are the known characteristics existing between the ideas of God which seems objective to us. "And yet this constant uniform working, which so evidently displays the goodness and wisdom of that Governing Spirit whose Will constitutes the laws of nature, is so far from leading our thoughts to Him, that it rather sends them wandering after second causes."

That concluding sentence in reality displays the motive of his philosophy. His sole object was to bring man's thinking back to God, and no doubt in such a way as to further concretely the causes of the Roman Catholic Church. Possibly, what was said with regard to Vedanta is also partially true of Berkeley's philosophy. It seems completely impossible that Mrs. Eddy should ever have known of the Vedanta. It is difficult to see in what way she could have access to academic philosophy. There is no reason why not, of course. It is possible, but a little bit improbable. To-date I have come across no direct evidence that would lead us to suppose that she was in any way familiar with Berkeley's tenets. Since we found her using one of the pet clichés of Kant's transcendentalism, as I pointed out formerly with regard to the word "*apodictical*," we might imagine that the phrase "*esse*" is "*percipii*" would have equally impressed what critics have called her naïve mind, and so led her to give employment to it. But actually we find no evidence whatsoever that any of Berkeley's clichés or mannerisms enter in the least into *Science and Health*. I do believe however that the Christian Science system could be intellectually improved by recourse to some of his ideas and arguments as to the non-validity of a world of matter.

On the other hand, it is possible that Mrs. Eddy read material in girlhood, the text and context of which were forgotten, although the basic material remained in her memory. She read numbers of books in childhood, various readers and collections of classical material. We know that she read deeply in Lindley Murray's *Introduction to the English Reader* and *The English Reader* itself. These books give samples of the writing of most of the great eighteenth century thinkers and writers—Goldsmith, Addison, Pope, Hume, Thomson, Samuel Johnson, and so forth. Rev. Lyman P. Powell in his biography of Mrs. Eddy, remarks significantly of these two books that most significant is the evidence that she did read and re-read them till they were so deeply embedded in her memory that sometimes they appeared automatically in her own later speech and writing, possibly, as is familiar to all acquainted with modern psychology, unconsciously to point a moral or adorn a tale. In other words, what we might expect is an unconscious indebtedness to many classical authors. Berkeley is not included amongst the several writers represented in the *Reader*.

We cannot prove therefore that she had access to Berkeley or had been influenced by his philosophy. But it remains nevertheless as a possibility. For example, "All that really exists is the divine Mind and its idea, and in this Mind the entire being is found harmonious and eternal" reads as though it could have been from Berkeley's epistemological treatise, yet in reality it is taken from *Science and Health*. And there are many such. I shall not attempt to establish any further parallels between the two, for it is proposed to review Mrs. Eddy's philosophy later on, when the reader will be able to divine for himself if such a relationship exists.

Apart from the fact that there is a dim probability that Mrs. Eddy may have been influenced by Bishop Berkeley's scheme, which however cannot be proven, what further differentiation can be drawn between the two? Primarily one of technique and practice. Never, throughout his life, could we imagine the venerable Bishop to have conceived of the possibility of utilising practically his deific interpretation of the objective world as a means of overcoming poverty, sin, and sickness. As a Catholic, unquestionably he accepted the basic postulates of faith of the Roman Catholic Church. Never once does he pursue the now familiar line of Mrs. Eddy's logic. "God is truth, love and substance. God is good, and God is all. Matter is nothing. Since disease, sin, evil and death are," let us term them "the properties of matter, and since matter is non-existent, then these properties of matter likewise have no real existence. Man, in his spiritual relationship to the divine mind and order of God, partakes of God's eternal and flawless perfection."

The Irish bishop had no conception of any such train of thought. He would never have agreed with Mrs. Eddy. His epistemological work insisted upon the annulment of non-thinking substance, not with a view to denying the validity and relationships of even the most insignificant objective factor in the world of reality. All these factors he fully accepted, only implying that they functioned within the ground that was the divine Mind.

So far from pursuing a similar train of thought to Mrs. Eddy, we know that a series of perfectly puerile notions were propounded by him. His last appearance publicly was in connection not with epistemology but with a fantastic controversy about the merits of tar water. Berkeley was convinced, partly on experimental, partly on philosophical grounds, that he had discovered a universal panacea for all human ills, and his sincerely deep interest in the welfare of humanity urged him to promote it with his usual fire and enthusiasm. In fact, one of his last works, *Siris*, is a compound of the praises of tar water, intermingled with some of the most profound of his philosophical reflections.

But one more system of philosophy now remains to be considered. If it was difficult to delineate the salient points in Vedanta and Berkeleyan philosophy, it is practically impossible to do justice to Hegel briefly. He is one of the most abstruse and complicated philosophers to read, let alone understand, and I must confess that in large part he baffles me. What I will have to say here is the barest outline only. More would require a volume by itself. But in keeping with my thesis here, we need to know just enough Hegel to determine whether or not there was any obligation to this German philosopher on the part of Mrs. Eddy.

Georg Wilhelm Friedrich Hegel was born at Stuttgart in 1770. More, perhaps, than any other of the great philosophers, his personality is so sunk into his work that outside of this there is but little interest to note in his life. His main thought is the philosophical expression of a new historical sense. The objective world of experience is a progressive embodiment of mind. That mind is conceived largely in terms of reason. Precisely at this point I am sure Mrs. Eddy would part company with Hegel, for reason would be a part of the complex mortal mind which, with matter, is a part of the organised system of errors which she denounced and denied so ardently. Reason, by itself, and unaided by the higher faculties and insight of divine mind, gets nowhere and is a self-contradictory faculty. If the resemblances that are alleged to exist between Hegel and Mrs. Eddy rested solely on this philosophical assumption, we could afford to let the whole matter drop, and assert that neither Dr. Woodbridge Riley nor the other critics had the least notion of what Mrs. Eddy was talking about. Moreover Mrs. Eddy would strenuously have denied the very idea of the embodiment of mind. There are many paragraphs in *Science and Mind* devoted to just such refutations as this.

Hegel asserted that no longer are we led to judge everything by the particular subjective standard which happens to appeal to us as rational. Instead, this new historical sense says a thing is to be judged by its surroundings, its environment, and the part within this which it has to play. In other words, it is a part of a whole, and as such must be understood. We must put ourselves actually in the place of the reality which we ourselves wish to estimate. In other words, instead of reason being a subjective criterion outside the phenomenon observed, it exists also as embodied in the phenomenon of experience itself. We must watch experience unfold and then, if we can, detect the laws involved in this growth. Reason is objective in the phenomenal world of experience and the wide sphere of reality, not merely subjective in ourselves. Reality exists, and that reality reveals itself in history, which is our human process of observing the unfoldment of reason or spirit embodied in the world of experience.

We can understand reality, therefore, only by taking it in all its concreteness, not by making abstract statements about it. Hegel maintains that the world of experience is a system of reason with its own laws. His entire philosophy is an endeavour to disclose and explicate them. This is what he means by his assertion that thought and reality are identical. This statement has sometimes been loosely taken to imply either that our individual thoughts are the sole reality, or that reality is a set of mental abstractions opposed to sensory data. The first of these interpretations had already been subjected to considerable philosophical criticism and finally rejected, and Hegel had not the least intention of affirming it. Nor did he mean that reality is a system only of abstract thought concepts. Concrete experience in the objective world, for him, is the starting point and the end. But this experience is rational throughout. Here too he stands in diametrical opposition to Mrs. Eddy. She tends not to accept life as a whole, a whole which includes both spirit and sensory data as valid. Matter she rejected without a further claim, emphasising that reality consisted of God and the infinite array of ideas in his divine Mind. Hegel on the other hand takes experience as it is presented to man, and is inclined to accept both its spiritual and material factors as integral parts of those whole concrete experiences which alone are real. For Hegel, experience, whether of matter or of mind, is rational and integrated throughout.

Every element of experience for Hegel is connected relatively with a rational whole where it has a definite place and function, and where it can be thought understandingly. The reality of a thing is its possession of significance, of meaning, for the great process of experience into which it enters.

Reality is thus co-extensive with significance and experience. There is no invisible substrate of matter behind the phenomenal world. No opaque thing-in-itself which we can never perceive beyond experience. No transcendent truth is to be reached by an abstract reasoning process distinct from the reason which is in things themselves. What does not enter into experience is for us absolutely nothing at all. The system of experience itself in all its implications is reality, is God. And God thus is the most certain thing in the world, implicated in the existence of any and every reality. God, then, and the laws of spirit, are the real essence of the universe, in terms of which everything is to be understood. There is no necessity to go outside of our experience to find the truth of reality. Reality is present in this very partial experience of mine and yours.

The problem of philosophy is to show the meaning of each experience factor that has ever revealed itself to man through its relation to the whole rational world where it belongs. The instrument by which this is accomplished is through a logical process of development. This developmental process he calls the dialectic, in which the oppositions and contradictions of the world are not denied and annulled. Rather they are combined in a richer whole which gives them each a relative validity. Without in any way wishing to pass judgment on the relative philosophical worth of either Mrs. Eddy or Hegel, it is apparent that there can be no reconciliation here. The dialectical process is unalterably opposed to Mrs. Eddy's scheme and I can see no manner or means whereby Mrs. Eddy could take over the dialectic into her system where God and his ideas alone are adjudged to be real and enduring, and all else is illusion and error. If Mrs. Eddy had read Hegel, she would hardly have found the dialectic to her liking, and would have rejected it forthwith.

The dialectic provides Hegel with a schema of three logical stages. In this, thesis is followed by or negated by antithesis, and this again is negated by the synthesis which negates the negation and includes both thesis and antithesis, transcending them in development. For instance a typical thesis would be God, which is logically opposed by the idea of the world of matter, evil, darkness. But this duality is negated as well as reconciled in the synthesis of the dialectic, which is man. Thus every partial truth is preserved, entering a vigorous protest against all one-sidedness and incompleteness, and it is here more definitely than elsewhere that we find no substantial contact whatsoever between Mrs. Eddy and Hegel. Reality is not any partial stage of development, or even the end of development as a finished product, Hegel thought. It is the *process* of development itself, considered in its entirety. That is the Real, that is Spirit and God.

The identification of thought and object, of the finite and the infinite, as dialectical concepts, is raised to a high power in Hegel's concept of religion. For Hegel, there is here no question of proving the reality of God and the truth of religion in the ordinary sense. He is interested rather in the interpretation of the religious experience, which for him is identical with God. The religious experience exists as a concrete fact which philosophy must understand. Philosophy cannot create nor induce it, but attempt to understand, it surely can. And since God has his existence within and not outside of experience, the more supreme and comprehensive this experience is, the more adequately God is revealed in it. Religion exists in the process of religious development and growth. The stages of this development require not judgment but rational interpretation.

Following Hegel's dialectic process, the elements of the religious idea are God, man, and the relation between them. These elements underlie the successive stages of religious development. For example, Hegel says that in the oriental religions, the idea of the infinite prevails and reigns supreme. God is everything, and man and the world he lives in are mere illusions that must pass away, leaving God resplendent in all his glory. The world is *maya* and must be shunned and hated, for it is all that God is not. The religion of the Greeks, on the contrary, was a religion of naturalism, and the finite. It stands in diametrical opposition to the eastern religious philosophy. Here, man was the final object of worship. Its mythology was a human glorification of man. Its gods are essentially human attributes concretely embodied and raised by art and poetry to the position of types.

These two religious types, the Greeks and the Oriental, are negated as well as reconciled by Hegel in Christianity. For him this was the absolute religion. Here the important thing is neither God by himself, nor man by himself, but the concrete unity of the divine and human in Christ, the God-man. Christ represents the dialectical synthesis, the negation of all previous divine personalities, and the summation of them at the same time. Christianity finds God, the infinite, implicated *in* the finite, in human consciousness, and the process of experience itself.

Hegel's philosophy covers the entire gamut of human thinking and experience. No phase of intellectual endeavor is exempted from the all-inclusive scope of his dialectic. He wrote a philosophy of history, as well as a history of philosophy. His system gives attention to epistemology as well as to aesthetics, religion and institutions, to ontology as to psychology and ethics, all in the light of his integrative logic. It is so vast and so extensive a scheme as to elude all but the best minds, and baffle description in aught else but volumes. All that can be done here is to indicate the broadest and, it must be confessed, the vaguest principles enunciated by his dialectic. In the light of these simplified principle, however, some comparison is rendered possible with the broad outlines of Christian Science.

Above all, Hegel was a logician. Mrs. Eddy was anything but that. It is not derogatory in the least to assert that hers was a realistic rather than an abstract mind. Too many problems remain unsolved in *Science and Health* for us to assume that logic was her forte, or that any major philosophical problems have been logically elucidated by her through the methods of academic philosophy. If mortal mind and matter are illusions, solecisms as she pertinently claims, the problem immediately arises as to their origin. No indication is given in her work as to how such a degenerative process arose whereby false beliefs could be entertained. However unsatisfactorily in places, Hegel does attempt to indicate some emergent or evolutionary process based on the dialectic.

But we are not concerned with more theoretical principles of philosophical discussion. It is with practical elements that we are concerned. And once more, out of fairness to both Hegel and to

Mrs. Eddy, I can see but the most remote relationship between the two systems. If Mrs. Eddy did read German transcendentalism, she borrowed little beyond the mere use of the word "apodictical," and maybe a mite else.

Francis Lieber's account of Hegel's philosophy of religion, as presented in the Rev. Walter M. Haushalter's book, must be recognised to be Francis Lieber's *interpretation* of Hegel, which may or may not be authentic Hegelianism. Academically, there is little similarity between Hegel and Mrs. Eddy. Merely in the concept of the dialectic, there would be enough to indicate that there is a gulf which Mrs. Eddy could not have attempted to cross. But Rev. Haushalter, in presenting Lieber's essay on Hegel, ought to have pointed this out. Lieber himself mentions but little the dialectical process of thesis, its negation, and the negation of the negation, even although it is the groundwork of Hegelianism.

On the other hand, if Francis Lieber did write this essay on Hegel's religious philosophy, and if Mrs. Eddy did have access to in the home of Hiram Crafts, there is an immediate connection between the two. Whole lines and innumerable concepts of the one, are represented in the work of the other. Whether or not there was plagiarism, in not for me to say. I am not able to pass judgment of such complex problems. These are matters for the experts to decide among themselves. The fact remains, as Rev. Haushalter shows, similarities do exist, demanding certain inescapable conclusions.

From the practical point of view, what was said above with regard to Vedanta and Berkeley is equally true of Hegel. None of these three philosophies purports to be anything more than academic speculative philosophy—with the sole exception of the Vedanta. It did make the endeavor, centuries ago, to be practical in another manner. It has developed some of the noblest and loftiest concepts in philosophy and techniques of spiritual development that the world has ever known. But so far as this world of living experience is concerned, none of these three made any substantial attempt to alter radically the lot of mankind by a practical application of it theories. There is not a single individual alive today who can claim to have healed himself of any disease, for example, or to have overcome poverty, or remedied his failure in the business or social world, through a systematic application of the theoretical principles of these philosophies.

But this is exactly what Mrs. Eddy did essay. Because of the hardship of her own early life, the disappointments, the frustrations engendered by sickness and poverty, another orientation altogether to philosophy was provide by her. As a result of this, thousands of men and women may claim to have done similar things with their lives, hapless and hopeless that they seemed before. She may not have added to our scientific understanding of the *modus operandi* of the methods she employed. She has not enriched our psychological knowledge by a description of the mechanism by means of which her employment of ideas and images actually materialise themselves in the objective world. This is what science above all demands, rather than an insistence upon results. The scientific attitude is that any method will produce beneficial results. What science demands is an increased understanding and insight into the workings of the methods used. We have no more insight than before into how the environment where we live can be altered by contemplating the abstractions of her metaphysics. Certainly these results have occurred, as we are constantly assured by objective and critical investigators, although we do not know how. In this sense we cannot include Mrs. Eddy in the same category of philosophers such as Sankacharya, Berkeley, Kant or Hegel.

But she was, nonetheless, a pioneer in the world of spirit in a way that neither Berkeley nor Hegel were. She must be considered a spiritual revolutionary who was dissatisfied with the prevailing dichotomy of the world of spirit and the world of matter. There must be some relationship between them, else anarchy exists. And although she denied categorically the existence of matter as existing apart from mind, nonetheless she acted pragmatically as though matter did exist. Implicitly she made such an assumption, even devoting her entire life to proving that the very sphere of her denial could be impinged upon by mind and its ideas, and so altered and changed in accordance with the heart's desire. She established a necessary connection between states of mind and bodily conditions. If diseases can be caused through faulty mental states, then likewise they can be similarly altered. And so on, with regard to every exigency of human existence. There was no one facet of human existence which could not be affected altogether by new ideas, by a revolution in the process of human thinking.

It was Quimby who first indicated to her that mind could affect and improve bodily health. It may have been philosophy that gave her the broad view of life and living which enabled her to apply Quimby's orientation to mind-healing in such a way as to negate and transcend his findings. Whereas he dealt only with disease states of body and mind, Mrs. Eddy attempted to deal with every adverse condition of human existence, in no matter what field of endeavor it was manifested.

She was a revolutionary, in the true sense of the word. The world was never quite the same place after her advent. She changed the world's outlook in a host of ways. Even if her schema has not been scientifically acceptable, or universally adopted, so as to bring about the millennium she envisioned, yet enough of a millennium was accomplished in the private lives of her devotees to prove her point. Results of such a revolutionary character were produced by her disciples as to challenge comparison with any other previous system. Neither mesmerism nor hypnotism, neither orthodox religion nor any of its reform cults, can produce anything which will stand up for comparison, for example, with a Wednesday night testimonial meeting in a Christian Scientist Church.

As a revolutionary, she was not obliged to think things out concretely to their logical conclusion. Her system may be defective in providing a complete logical system of metaphysics in the formal academic sense. But the full working out and summation of revolution demands the patient work of faithful and inspired successors. It is the task, so to say, of the genius to point out the way to a new and higher level of thought and action than which has hitherto been achieved. Were it not for the great artists, thinkers and reformers, the world would stand still. Since a world stationary in respect of its spiritual and mental life would be stagnant and deteriorating, the genius stands in the role of a luminary. One could even use chemical terminology, and regard the genius as a catalytic agent. Just as a catalyst facilitates a desired chemical reaction, so the genius brings about this revolution in human concepts. Whatever, therefore, may be said antagonistically to the person and work of Mrs. Eddy, it must be granted that she was first of all a spiritual catalytic agent, and secondly, a revolutionary in human thinking that cannot be fully estimated even now. She left her mark on the world, in the lives of men and women, going far beyond mere indebtedness to Quimby.

She challenged the accepted modes of thought and rules of action now current in society. The challenge was bitterly resented by man's natural disinclination to have his settled and established world order upset. That would represent psychological insecurity. The new ideas must not be accepted. They must be derided, and their advocate vilified. She was bitterly reviled and persecuted. In spite of this vilification, and in spite of the vagaries of her own personality, her work endures. Her name lives both in the hearts of those who have good reason to be grateful to her, and in the corroboration afforded to the general tenets of her practical system by modern psychotherapy. The work of a revolutionary becomes the accepted creed of the following generation. This has been accomplished. And it is for this reason that I regard her, in spite of all else, as one of the world's great geniuses.

CHAPTER FOUR

Mary Baker Eddy

The Bakers were a simple farmer people. Neither rich nor poor, they were just ordinarily well off, typical natives of the state of New Hampshire. Originally, their ancestors had hailed from England, as had those of so many of these New England people, and they had been settled in the North Atlantic states for approximately two hundred years. Mark Baker was a vigorous hard-working farmer, level-headed, and Calvinistically inclined, but having nonetheless what was said to be a balanced temperament. Mary was his seventh child. From the outset she seemed imaginative and over-sensitive, growing up to be a frail, pallid, and nervous girl. "A loud voice made her shrink," writes Stephen Zweig, describing her character in one of the chapters of *Three Mental Healers*, "A harsh word caused painful excitement; and she could not even go to school regularly, finding the noisy ways of the other children too much for her weak nerves. The delicate child, therefore, was allowed to stay at home and to pick up what she could in the way of learning there—not much, as may well be imagined, in this isolated dwelling, half a mile even from the road."

The Reverend Dr. Powell, in his approved biography of Mrs. Eddy, emphasises the religious tendencies expressed in the menage during her childhood. He narrates the fact that Abigail, Mark's wife, even while bearing the child, would often have prayer sessions with one of the neighbours. Mark frequently led his family in daily devotions and prayers. He was a religious man. The total effect of such a religious background had a definite effect upon her sensibilities. To have been brought up from childhood on the Bible, to have constantly heard the miraculous stories of divine visitation to the biblical characters, must have stirred so young and sensitive a child. The result of this influence was that she herself, imaginative and fay-like, came to hear voices rather as did the young Samuel under the tutelage of Eli, and rather like Joan of Arc. It is clear that she was an altogether different child from the normal run of children, a fact which Dr. Powell obviously recognises by his reference to the psychological work of G. Stanley Hall and Dr. Weir Witchell. In other words, what both Dr. Powell and Stephen Zweig are attempting circuitously to imply, is that Mary was a neurotic, hysterical child. This is the formal psycho-analytical view, and most of the evidence presented leads in the direction of such a conclusion.

But I think we need to qualify this statement a little, and understand it more thoroughly before we let such a conclusion go. It is too easy to say that Mary was neurotic, and then dismiss the subject without further ado. Nothing is explained thereby, except perhaps to cast suspicion upon her integrity and sanity. And this is not good enough. At the start, I should like to ally myself to the side of Dr. Louis E. Bisch, who wrote that excellent handbook on popular psychology called, *Be Glad You're Neurotic*. It is common knowledge that all the people that the world calls great, and who have succeeded in their respective endeavours, have not been "normal," so far as their emotional reactions to life were concerned. Every single one of them was neurotic. Even their contemporaries looked upon them as being peculiar, queer, or eccentric people. We could name specifically Alexander the Great, Caesar and Napoleon. Certainly St. Francis, St. John of the Cross and St. Theresa of Avila, were all neurotic, as evidenced by their behavior. In another sphere, were Michel Angelo, Pascal, William Blake, Pope, Edgar Allan Poe, O. Henry, and Walt Whitman, and innumerable others, far too numerous to mention. They were certainly not normal. Just what is normal, is difficult to grasp, though, for convenience sake, we usually assume that it represents the statistical average, the commonly accepted norm or pattern of behaviour. If the greatest minds of the race have been neurotic, not measuring up to the conventional standard of the average man, perhaps this is ample reason why we should deify neurosis—even seek to cultivate it. Maybe, had Mary lived today, when neuroticism is a little better recognised and understood, she might have been handled more intelligently than she was in her day. In such a case, there need never have been what Zweig dramatically calls her forty wasted years, with all its personal tragedy, before she found herself. Possibly with a little more understanding on the part of parents and family, her tendency to repression and thence to hysteria might have been overcome quite early in life, to permit her abundant energies more direct and faithful expression.

As it was however, quick and active as were her mind and imagination, emotionally all was not well with her. She had undoubted poetic and artistic trends, had a fine and vivid imagination. In spite of Dr. Powell's rationlisations about the educational tendencies of her day to render girls frail of body and liable to fainting spells on the slightest provocation, she gradually developed neurotic tendencies. Dr. Bisch writes, for our edification, that "both the neurotic disposition and the appearance of a neurosis, as such, are a gradual development. Again would I emphasize that one is not born with neurosis, nor does one inherit it. It comes on slowly and insidiously and becomes more and more manifest and marked as the years pass." It is said that Mary's neurotic trends were present early and that they became the cause of years of needless sorrow and unhappiness. We can only guess what were the underlying and precipitating factors in such a development. Undoubtedly, there was a strong emotional over-attachment to her father, and possibly to her brother was well. These things are not too clearly delineated, for no complete anamnesis was ever taken.

Had not these trends been evolved to serve her own ends, it may well be that Christian Science might never have developed beyond Quimby's rudimentary mental science. That would have been an incalculable loss to the world. It was her more or less continual sickness, her poverty, her inability successfully to function in society, that necessitated the construction of adequate psychic compensations. But whereas the ordinary neurotic fabricates a compensation in fantasy that is adequate solely to his personality, and is valueless for the rest of mankind, she was enabled in this instance, due to a variety of factors operating at the time, to formulate a psychic compensation which has since proved widely invaluable. It is for this reason that I suggest it is unnecessary to fight defensively, to take up cudgels on behalf of Mrs. Eddy, when critics too glibly speak of neurosis. There is no need for dispute, because the neurosis, if such we may call it, has fully justified itself. It is not every normal person, so-called, who is able or is called upon to make lasting contributions to mankind's welfare. The average man probably is far too involved in his own futile sterile rut, ever to conceive of anything much beyond his job, his family, and the ever-narrowing circle of his immediate life. It requires a neurotic, fired up by the urgent necessity to achieve recognition, to apply general principles to the world at large.

Neurosis, while implying a corresponding amount of demoralisation, at the same time represents a creative function of personality. Dr. Jung very eloquently speaks of neurosis as being a creative failure to achieve a successful adaptation to the exigencies and difficulties in life. In most cases this is true. Insofar as a man is neurotic, he has lost some degree of confidence in himself. The conflict which engenders neurosis is felt as a humiliating defeat. Also, to the degree that the neurosis represents a flight from painful and difficult situations, it is a substitute for legitimate suffering. The average neurotic is just a little pathetic in his over-zealous attempt to adjust his conflict-wracked mind to the seething flow of life's activities around him. But the mere fact that an adjustment is sought—even though failure and disease be the result—is in itself a creative function that is rarely undertaken by the normal man. The non-neurotic is born into a world where he manages to function more or less adequately, and where he takes everything for granted without thought. Because of his comparative ease of function, never is a question asked of why, how, or when. Questions such as these, are the spurs to discovery and progress. Such an enquiry would never even dawn upon him. He is too normal. In other words, it seems that to be normal is equivalent to being a cabbage. It means being content dully to live like a cow, chewing the cud in the meadow, being milked twice a day, perfect happiness in horrible mediocrity. He is happy so long as no demands beyond the average, are made upon him, so long as nothing untoward occurs.

But the neurotic, as Jung indicates, strives in his own unique way to achieve some sort of definite spiritual relationship with the world. It is a dynamic gesture. That he most often fails, is altogether besides the point. His knowledge is not equal to his effort. Success and achievement are not a final set of values. It is striving and aspiring that elevate man above the beast. And the neurotic strives and aspires as no one can imagine, save those who know their own hearts and minds.

To say that Mrs. Eddy was neurotic, is surely no insult. Immediately, she becomes classified with the supremely great. To speak of her in this way, is in reality a slur cast not against Mrs. Eddy, but is derogatory to the person who casts such a stupid slur. She was a neurotic. But, to use the vernacular, so what? She was a neurotic, but she strove for fifty years, through those so-called wasted fifty years, to convert it to something of good account. What normal person would strive for half a century against the face of the whole world? She succeeded in ways that seem miraculous to the normal mind. The entire story of her success and attainment is something that the average normal person cannot understand, because her mind and its outlook are so far removed, dynamically and creatively, from the sterile humdrum psychology that he lives by. The neurotic can understand her well. He is the creative personality who strives, in his own life, similarly, to accomplish what Mrs. Eddy did for herself and for the world.

We can accept for the moment the conclusion that Mary was neurotic and ultra-sensitive. Zweig, who attempts a provocative biographical outline of her personality describes her as having hysteria, and say, quite accurately, that hysteria can mimic successfully any organic disease. She had convulsions and seizures whenever her own will was twarted. Any minor frustration was interpreted as a threat to her own psychic integrity, and being defensive and without adequate weapons of offense, what better way than to secure her ends than through unconscious hysterical manifestations? Though in one sense this made her inversely the master of the situation, at the same time, it placed her at a considerable disadvantage where other youngsters of he own age were concerned. Since the doctor had given strict orders that she was not to go to school, and so not to mix with others of similar years, ample opportunity presented itself in her isolation for fantasy and indulgent day-dreaming. Her life of fantasy was in diametrical opposition to her active life, and in the measure that the one became enriched, so the other became impoverished. As a result of this, the schizoid tendencies of isolation, hysteria, moodiness, and physical illness of minor kinds grew, slowly becoming ever more formidable at the years proceeded.

A temporary halt to the neurosis was declared when, at the age of twenty-two, she married Washington Glover. He was a young man trained as a mason, and after their marriage, they went down to South Carolina, to start a small contracting business. Love and marriage, for the neurotic, are far better magicians than any doctor or metaphysician. The difficulty usually with the neurotic is an inability to love. The emotions have become too self-involved. For Mary, a period of great happiness and of respite from her neuroticism ensued. Unfortunately, it was all too brief. Within six months of the marriage, Glover contracted yellow fever, dying after a few days of the illness, leaving her destitute. Stricken with grief at the height of her joy, she had to return to her father's roof, carrying her unborn child.

Frustrations of this kind play havoc with the sensitive neurotic soul, strengthening the unconscious trend away from the sorrow-producing world, by an escape to the inner world of gentle fantasy discovered in the early days of her life. Her bereavement precipitated an involuntary flight from reality into the picture world of her mind, where dwelt the biblical characters of her early girlhood, who talked and walked with God. Hysteria thus is the psychosomatic equivalent of repressed infantile habits which, perfectly proper and right for the youngster, become somewhat incongruous in the adult, pathetic especially when the intellectual powers are good and capable. The world being too searing and painful for her sensitive soul, she did violence however to herself by attempting to escape to the fantasy world within. The old nervous symptoms of fatigue, irritability and maladjustment returned, but in far more aggravated form. And apparently relief could only be obtained by reclining in a sort of rocker, a swinging cradle, the movement of which would soothe her nerves, and bring about a kind of analgesic somnolence.

It is clear that some kind of psychic regression occurred here. Possibly Mary was much in love with her husband, and romance, deeply stirred her soul and fulfilling an urgent need, had pointed gently at the possibilities of happiness which could follow in normal human relationships. And no here she was bereft of husband, romance gone, sorrow and responsibilities on her hands, thrust back once more into the old bitter slough of despond. That indeed, was an involuntary kind of regression, forced upon her by the course of events. Not yet being strong enough to withstand the furious onslaught of life, which later by training she could bend to her will, she recoiled disdainfully under these blows. What more could her psyche do—but regress? To slip back uneasily in memory to earlier happier days of her life when love indeed did prevail, when no problems existed, and all was quiet and secure.

An almost idyllic situation does exist in infancy, where the babe is hugged close to the breast of an adoring mother and father, or rocked by them in the cradle. And it was to recapture this former security of love, now dim in memory, that the readily slipped back out of the unhappy present into the neurotic manifestations of old. The swinging in the cradle-swing brought her some modicum of inner peace and serenity because it was an attempt, unconscious and inadequate no doubt, to revive actively the memories of infancy. By magically creating the appropriate symbolic conditions without, it was a neurotic endeavor to provoke security and happiness from within the mind. If to light a lamp we must screw a bulb in the socket, and insert the plug into the outlet, and then flip the switch, we are in a sense performing a magical ritual. In a similar sense, the antics of a neurotic, when understood, are seen to be unconscious mimes of archaic magical formulae. They comprise entirely a series of symbolic gestures. These archaic memories live deep down in all our minds. And we feel that if we can imitate or create externally a faithful image of the spiritual state we seek after, maybe it will really be materialised. Back of Mary's mind, unknown to herself, was a powerful urge to recover this heavenly dream of early life. She was right in believing that the swinging would bring her relief. She had been rocked before as a child, and in the rocking, her parents had given her peace.

Sad to say, however, infantile regressions are ill-adapted to the adult body and mind. And if the totality of the energies which are an individual, slips out of its proper milieu, through the stimulus of present problems, into an earlier level of psychic functioning, the body suffers from a libidinous starvation, as it were. A terrific conflict implies a vast expenditure of energy — an expenditure which is incurred solely on the unconscious level. But it results is to leave little energy adequately to take care of bodily needs and functions. The physical threshold is lowered, and not one organ or gland is able fully to do its work. And so it was with Mary Glover. Her health grew worse and worse. Neurasthenia, constant fatigue, and irritability, were her constant companions, psychic evidences of the internecine warfare being wages. Finally the time came when she was unable to move upstairs without aid from someone in the house. Lack of muscular employment brought about disuse atrophy. Her muscles became soft and flaccid, wasting away, so that her physician feared the induction of spinal paralysis. It seemed evidently that she was doomed to become a hopeless invalid, incurably crippled.

I stress this aspect of her life because surely her own sickness conditioned her mind to emphasise physical healing more than almost any other theme when subsequently she came to develop Christian Science. Her own sickness had been such a problem to her, the years wasted mercilessly so afflicting her conscience, that it was inevitable that her psychic compensation would concern itself with overcoming bodily sickness. The paralysis that overtook her was undoubtedly genuine. But that it had a psychological etiology, is equally unquestionable. Books describing psychological case histories, contain countless instances of neurosis which induced at first merely functional disorders. Later, becoming protracted and chronic, they finally produce organic disease. Mary Glover's infantile background, which clearly was neurotic in nature, eventuated in the hysterical paralysis which her doctor so much feared, and which produced so much anguish and sorrow for her. For nine long years after Washington Glover died of yellow fever infection, she endured it. And the, in 1852, this remarkable woman gave amazing evidence of the energy that, despite or because of her neurosis, she was capable of calling into operation. When she was thirty-two, she married Dr. Daniel Patterson. She who had been so lonely and shut in, made a desperate gesture to end it once and for all. Patterson was big, handsome and healthy, with a big black beard and the personality which, as Zweig delightfully puts it, would have made the fortune of a gynecologist.

To her, he seemed just the right person who would completely understand her invalidism, and help her get well. He too believed that if he could get her away from the environment in which she was morbidly living, he could be instrumental in the conquest of her health and vitality.

He was an itinerant dentist, with some knowledge of homeopathy. His dwindling practice fast became disappointing. They lived in a small house, with a housekeeper-companion for Mary, kept a cow, and a horse, which the doctor used when making his rounds. Here, however, was no respite from herself. There was no restoration of that first rosy flush of romance which years ago had exalted her briefly out of sickness. Instead, she was steadily growing worse—paler, weaker and more inert, a chronic invalid, useless to herself, her husband, and everyone else. Possibly even her peripatetic husband got fed up with this constant invalidism which daily confronted him, and the Civil War came as his welcome release. He sought a commission on the medical staff of the northern army and, with his customary carelessness, was captured by the Confederates on one of the battlefields. Interned for the rest of the war in Libby prison, he wrote her hoping that she would be able to forage for herself somehow. The Civil War served his unique opportunity to escape from his wife's boring hypochondria, and I have little doubt that being captured was part and parcel of his conscious or unconscious pattern of seeking a release from her.

But here was the pathetic picture of Mary, forty years of age, suffering hopelessly from chronic neurasthenia, poor as a churchmouse, seeking once more the assistance of her family. Many a lesser person would have broken completely under this awful shame, and finally ended the misery. In order to achieve some alleviation from physical suffering and mental anguish, she had experimented with almost everything. The drugs and medication of the allopaths, the mystical attenuations of the homeopaths, countless herbal remedies, mesmeric treatments, and finally hydropathic treatment. All to no avail. She has exhausted almost all the possibilities that her age could offer her in treatment. She had prayed, imploring the high heavens for succor. But the celestial gates were closed fast, and she remained impotent, insecure and ill.

The modern psychological idea about hysteria and anxiety neuroses, is that behind them are concealed a host of repressed infantile ideas and feelings. Whatever these feelings are, they appear obnoxious to the conscious personality with its moral sense that is based upon the need for the affection of the parents. If these are retained in mind, and so acte upon, there is the fear either of bodily punishment or else of some far more abstract punishment, such as the loss of parental love, home, and security. It is evident therefore, that the child cannot afford to risk love and security for mere feelings and ideas that it has nurtured, so they must go. A process of repression is instigated, having as its object the elimination from the sphere of consciousness of just these offensive feelings and impulses. Since emotions and feelings are energies, and since we must define an energy as that which will do work, we are forced to realise that some reaction must be produced by these violently repressed feelings. They cannot force their way directly or indirectly, into the child's mind. That would be too upsetting. It is far easier to repress and deny the existence of such facts. But these energies take short-cuts, as it were. The electric wiring, so to say, of the psychosomatic system becomes short-circuited, and these energies become represented symbolically within the body, by a host of mysterious symptoms which do not respond satisfactorily to any kind of treatment. Moreover, they shift all over the place. They do not remain localised solely in one spot, but can manifest anywhere in the body that they choose.

That Mrs. Eddy later on in her life formulated a philosophy which placed so much emphasis on the denial of matter, leads us to speculate on what the psychological and unconscious picture was. If we substitute the word "matter" by the phrase "undesirable emotions" that it would be wiser for a child she was not to think about, we obtain a highly significant clue. We may assume that she was hard-pressed to thrust out of her mind powerful impulses of emotion and feeling which she, with her religious environment and training as a small girl, felt were evil and wicked. Not knowing how to handle them, she began even then to reject and deny them. An inner conflict ensued, which produced not only the bodily symptoms she complained of, but also a complex series of maladjustments to life and living. Later on, however, relying upon religious experience and religious feelings, she was able to reinforce the conscious point of view so as completely to triumph over her unconscious psychic life with its host of repressed infantile wishes. But meanwhile, she suffered. For fifty years, the conflict was waged and it almost seemed as though she would lose, and remain an invalid and a hypochondriac all her life.

Only one asset remained at her disposal. That was her tenacity, her blind faith in a girlhood vision in some higher goal for which she was intended. Simply by advocating or affirming it with the persistency almost of fanaticism, bred by a sincere belief in her own possibilities, she made the improbable true. With such perseverance, and the illogical tenacity that is true only of the neurotic, something was bound to occur which would save her form herself. And so it was that the fame of Quimby, the one-time mesmerist, now the mindhealer, the faith-healer, reached her New Hampshire village. Wonderful things filtered through in those slow days of intercommunication. Because of her slowness, there was ample time for them to become richly embellished with fantasy, amplified by incredible happenings and miraculous accomplishments. Just before joining the army, Patterson had written an urgent letter to Quimby, asking him whether it was at all possible to visit Concord, to attend his ailing wife. "My wife has been crippled," he wrote, "for a number of years by spinal paralysis. She is barely able to sit up, and we shall be so glad, if it is at all possible, to try your wonderful powers in her case."

Tied down in his Portland office by a thriving practice, Quimby naturally could not leave, no matter what the case was.

A year later, with her husband still in military prison, Mary wrote a despairing call for help to Quimby, but once more Quimby was obliged to refuse, suggesting that she come to Portland. Penniless, however, how could she travel to Portland, Maine? It seemed impossible. But because it appeared so thoroughly impossible ever to get there, her own imagination and faith clothed Quimby in a magical atmosphere. Undoubtedly there in Maine was the only man in the whole world who could cure her. Difficulties only stirred up her own faith, which rose step by step to unimaginable heights of anticipation. It was imperative to get to him, regardless of every obstacle placed in her way. Nothing must impede her determination to make this trip. Salvation was at last in sight.

Importuning everyone she knew, with the help of friends, acquaintances and even strangers, it is said, she laboriously added penny to penny, dollar to dollar, until at the end of October, 1862 she found herself possessing sufficient money to make the trip. For several months before she had been at a hydropathic institute, whither her sister had sent her. She was taking the water cure, but all to no avail. She had sunk lower and lower into despair, and therefore furiously clung with every waning once of desperate strength to this one last straw of Quimby, to prevent herself from sinking. She got to Maine, all right. And in Portland, at Quimby's office, she had to be half-carried, half-supported up the long second flight of stairs into the waiting room above. Emaciated and gaunt, with pale and sunken cheeks, eyes flaming deep down from the orbits, she sat there exhausted and weak. It is said she was shabbily dressed. Every reserve had gone not into presenting a worthy feminine appearance, but simply to get to this office. It seemed as though she were a mere broken vestige of a woman.

Within a week, a miracle had occurred. No longer was she weak and wracked in pain. She who had been given up despairingly by the doctors, was climbing the 182 steps to the dome of the City Hall without any assistance. Her own faith, her own expectancy of recovery had brought her through. She had brought to Quimby more, possibly, than he could give her. Yet he simply showed her how to use her own powers. If we can employ the data of newspaper accounts written long before Mrs. Eddy visited him, we may assume that he spoke to her about his denial of disease as an entity, although he admitted it as a deception that had been handed down as a false belief. He probably told her that disease is an invention of men's minds, and that the mind is what it thinks it is. If the mind contends against the thought of disease and creates for itself an ideal form of health, that form impresses itself upon the animal spirit, and through that, upon the body. But, regardless of how he talked to her, she got well.

"She talked, she questioned, she rejoiced, she glowed with ardour; she was rejuvenated and almost beautiful; she was bubbling over with activity," Stephan Zweig remarks, painting a vivid picture of the recovered Mrs. Eddy, "and inspired with renewed energy—an energy unexampled even in America. She was inspired with an energy which ere long, was to make numberless retainers subservient to her will."

In the Portland Courier, she published an enthusiastic account of her cure, delineating in detail all her former efforts to obtain relief. Concluding this article, she said: "But now I can see dimly at first, and only as trees walking, the great principle which underlies Dr. Quimby's faith and works; and just in proportion to my right perception of truth, is my recovery. The truth which he opposes to the error of giving intelligence to matter and placing pain where it never placed itself, if received understandably, changes the currents of the system to their normal action; and the mechanism of the body goes on undisturbed..."

In other articles, so enthusiastic is she about her healer, that she likens him to Jesus. What happened during her visit to Quimby, the results of which so inflamed her to jubilant heights of eloquence? How are we to explain this phenomenon? Previously, she had undergone every kind of medical treatment, orthodox as well as unorthodox. None had succeeded in really helping her. Yet here she was in Portland, after years of chronic invalidism, suddenly restored, if not to perfect health, at least to a condition where she could moderately function. The most evident factor was her grim determination to get well. The trip to Quimby, with its expenditure of all the money she was able to borrow, had previously seemed so impossible that the difficulty made it imperative for her to do it. Since it was admittedly difficult, and since money was such a rarely come by thing, if she did go to Quimby, she *must* get well. It was the last resort. So long as there was one more healer she could try, she might not have recovered her health. But Quimby and his mindhealing was the last resort. She had experimented with all the others—and failed. This trip to Portland *must* succeed. It is clear she approached Quimby with a rare expectancy of results which, naturally, were forthcoming. Her whole psyche was poised, straining and pulling at the leash to overcome the neurotic paralysis which had crippled and handicapped her for years. She was all aflame with faith. And that alone was the criterion for success.

Before any single event can occur to any individual, he must have been otherwise prepared by his own life, by his mental and emotional equipment for that particular experience long before it actually happens. There is a sort of psychic predisposition for any experience. A neurosis does not descend upon one from the heavens. A long period of preparation antedates it. One does not make a million dollars overnight unless there has been a tremendous anticipation of that fact, a preparation for its final acquisition. Days and months, even years before, must have gone into its anticipation before it became an actuality. For Mrs. Eddy, her whole former life was an approach to this one experience of a psychological cure from conversion hysteria, which thus gave her life new significance and added meaning.

Before her trip to Quimby, she was sick and ill because there was no adequate outlet to her pent-up energies. Her mind was locked up, and her powerful emotions were enclosed as within a prison. The sickness was a defense, a means of self-protection.

Suppose she had recovered her health before, what could she have done? The neurosis of years before had sharpened her mind, had developed a fantasy in which visions of imaginative goals had been conjured up. All these, had she been restored to health, would have been dashed to the ground. Her entire life would have been meaningless. Hence she had to remain ill until the right time came, until the right person came who would vitalise her spirit with an ideal, an impetus, into which her latent energies, her fantasies, and her fiery imagination could be unequivocally poured. Quimby, with his emphasis on both faith and intelligent understanding as the golden key giving entry to the palace of perfect health, served as the sign-post to which she gave heed. She followed, all unconsciously maybe, but followed nevertheless, the way he pointed out.

It was around this time that Dr. Patterson and she parted company. No useful purpose would be served in describing fully the reasons why this occurred, for this is not a biography. The various official and unofficial biographies of Mrs. Eddy will narrate these events far more satisfactorily than could anything from my pen. All I attempt to do here is to indicate a few of the major psychological factors which played their part in shaping the destiny of this extraordinary woman. At the age of fifty, Mary Glover Patterson was alone once more in the world. Washington Glover was dead these many years. Patterson had forsaken her, and had followed his own morbid star where it would lead him. He was an non-entity, anyway. The child of her own womb was boarded somewhere far off, without any real desire on her part to see him. And any link that once had existed with her family was thoroughly broken. Not yet had her third husband, Asa G. Eddy, turned up on the scene.

In a very real sense, she was isolated, and now far more completely than ever at any previous time in her life. The very fact that Quimby had assisted her to regain some degree of physical health, made her lot not easier to bear, but very much more difficult.

Had this solitude overtaken her before, during the days of her sickness, she might have accepted it without too much complaint. She had long grown accustomed to being neglected as a result of her sickness. It was a *post hoc propter hoc* kind of argument that unconsciously she employed, "I am sick, therefore I am lonely." The reverse actually was true—"I am lonely and isolated from the whole world because of my repressed sin-laden emotions, therefore I am sick." Now that she had recovered her health, this involved type of argument ceased to have any meaning. A new torment arose for her. It was a cruel torture that can only be appreciated by those who, at various times in their lives, have unwillingly experienced solitude and have found themselves unable to make any contact with people, even though the whole soul ached excruciatingly for companionship and love.

More or less active now, functioning adequately with a body that hitherto had balked proper use, she discovered at this time that the ideals and visions of her early childhood had become activated. Because of the conflict between this catalytic activation of her psychic life, and the actual objective facts of loneliness, further anguish arose. In a word, there was no niche for her to fit herself into, so far as the world was concerned. She was a misfit. This conflict I believe to be important, and played a prominent etiological role in the immediate course of events.

The fact remains that not long after her return to Concord, a cured woman, she slipped on an icy pavement in February, 1866, and injured her spine. The homeopathic medical man, Dr. Cushing, who was consulted, thought the injuries were considerable, concussion and possible spine fracture. She was semi-hysterical, nervous and only partly conscious.

Meanwhile, Quimby had died. She wrote desperately after a few days to Julius Dresser who had been one of Quimby's patients, to take upon himself the mantle of the master and come to Concord and heal her. Dresser, motivated by a variety of feelings, felt himself unable to do this, and refused. Despair once more settled over her. Fear arose frantically again, gripping her mind and heart in its deadly coils, bringing to the foreground of her mind vision-like anticipations of the return of the sickly condition of years ago. Then she was helpless and impotent and sick—condemned it seemed, to chronic invalidism. Was this same spectre returning to haunt her? She was no longer young. Fifty summers had come and gone. It was quite possible that she began to be afraid of what the future would bring. But despair was ever the mother of great deeds and heroic exploits. Many a man when goaded by the demon of despair has performed miracles that never normally could have been conceived. And so with Mrs. Patterson, when despair gripped her. She fought with it, even as Jacob with the angel of the Lord, and she would not let him go save that he blessed her. Apparently he did bless her, for it was during this sickness that she claimed to have made her great discovery.

Now there are at least two ways of looking at this discovery, and rendering explicable to our minds an otherwise unintelligible phenomenon. The first possibility is that she, with one single stroke of genius, discovered a way of using Quimby's ideas without recourse to a second person. If the revelation consisted in nothing more than this, it was a highly significant and momentous event. Quimby's patients were healed through his suggestions. They hearkened to his quiet sincere suggestions to deny the validity of the disease idea, and build up new mental images of health. But they were not restore to health save as they were in attendance upon him. They made no headway, except when they returned to him for repeated discussions, when he would emphasise the illusory nature of disease. The technique of heterosuggestion is evident here. His suggestions, emanating from his self-confident and magnetic personality, had a soothing relaxing effect upon them, and in this passive receptive mood his suggestions would be accepted to produce their neurological and somatic effects.

Mrs. Eddy, however, must have been the first to realise that she could employ this art of conscious auto-suggestion. She learned how to apply the method to herself and her problems without recourse to any other person in the world. By itself, here was a psychological discovery of startling magnitude, a dramatic step forward from the older method. Even if we concede the fact that she stated nothing more than this in *Science and Health* and that Christian Science is simply a technique of autosuggestion, we have, so far from belittled her, marked her down forever as a psychological pioneer of the first order. In fact, many years after her, a Nancy apothecary named Emile Coué, probably influenced by Christian Science, insisted that everyone of us can by autosuggestion cure himself. Advancing not an inch beyond Mrs. Eddy, except insofar as he refrained from a religious nomenclature, he declared too that there was no necessity for any intermediary between the patient and his sickness, for the patient could always do his own suggesting anyway. The need for some outside healer is only an aid towards the acceptance of suggestions, a psychological convenience only, and constitutes one more illusion to be got rid of. Coué, with his doctrine of autosuggestion, only paid homage to the supreme efficacy of the human kind, by means of faith or will or imagination, to control the body and alter and improve its function. He was antedated by Mrs. Eddy by many years, and for this reason alone she deserves credit as the pioneer and revolutionary that I have claimed her to be.

On the other hand, we can claim a second legitimate way of looking at her discovery by resorting to the fact of spiritual experience. The spirit of revelation came upon her, firing its powerful darts of inspiration into the dark recesses of her mind, illuminating her soul. She had been pouring through the pages of the Bible, reading its simple stories with high zeal, praying fervently to God for a repetition of such miracles as those recounted in Matthew's gospel. It was whilst she was steeping herself in Christ's healing of the palsied man, that we are given to understand the high water mark of her life occurred. Throughout the history of mankind we have records of similar ineffable occurrences happening to men.

Some of them were prepared for it by life and logic. Some have prayed and meditated for days and months and years before it came. Others go their way unsuspectingly in the humdrum stream of life when, suddenly, a bolt from the blue descends, thrusts its way through the outer layers of the mind, exploding like a bomb within the heart. In all instances it is irrevocable and unimpeachable—a revelation of supreme knowledge. Ineffable wisdom to be obtained in no other way suddenly is theirs, and with it an indescribable ecstasy and joy, and a realisation of the everlasting presence and immanence of spiritual power and life.

Such experiences we know have occurred in every race, in every clime, in all periods of the world's history. When these religious or mystical experiences occur, the individual is made new. Never afterwards are they quite the same. Previously they knew of God only as an intellectual abstraction, as a theory which it was only convenient or habitual to believe in. Henceforth, God becomes as real, more real to them than any other single phenomenon they could ever know. The entire point of view shifts over, and a transvaluation of all morals and attitudes and values is automatically accomplished. Magical transformations of character are commonplace results of this interior communion with God which the experience brings. All the world's great religions have been founded by men whose daily bread was nothing less than this divine communion with the source of life and being. And however much the experience may be critised on logical or human grounds, the recipient can only smile and remain silent. How can people born blind realise the nature of properties of light? One could argue and describe from now on until doomsday without every hoping to succeed in conveying true ideas. Likewise with God and the mystical experience. We ordinary people of the world, never having been blessed by this dramatic revelation of God abiding within the soul, can only know of it at second-hand. We can but wonder at it, perhaps express desire for it or, feeling jealous and envious, deny its significance and validity. But nothing we can ever do can alter the basic fact that the world's course and destiny has been changed again and again by men to whom God has spoken directly through the so-called religious or mystical experience.

A Canadian psychiatrist, Dr. R. M. Bucke, characterised these psychological phenomena by the term cosmic consciousness, which term served as the title of a book he wrote on the subject. It comprised a record of many people who had undergone such experiences, and received such expansions of consciousness. In one part of the book he says: "The prime characteristic of cosmic consciousness is a consciousness of the cosmos, that is, of the life and order of the universe. Along with the consciousness of the cosmos there occurs an intellectual enlightenment which alone would place the individual on a new plane of existence—which would place him almost a member of a new species. To this is added a state of moral exaltation, an indescribable feeling of elevation, elation and joyousness, and a quickening of the moral sense, which is fully striking, and more important than is the enhanced intellectual power. With these come what may be called a sense of immortality, a consciousness of eternal life, not a conviction that he shall have this, but the consciousness that he has it already."

The psychologist can say very little of such things. Since it is a psychological experience, that is one affecting the mind and behavior of man, he can only try to understand it. Jung who is probably the most outstanding psychologist today, has attempted to apply his psychological knowledge and acumen to this spiritual phenomenon. He writes, in his book *Psychology and Religion*: "Religious experience is absolute. It is indisputable. You can only say that you have never had such an experience, and your opponent will say: 'Sorry, I have.' And there your discussion will come to an end. No matter what the world thinks about religious experience, the one who has it possesses the great treasure of a thing that has provided him with a source of life, meaning and beauty and that have given a new splendour to the world and to mankind. He has *pistis* (faith) and peace."

All that we can do then, psychologically, is to try to understand. We must recognise that we still know little about the hidden debts of the soul, and that for all we know God in all his glory may dwell there. An abiding city within, the city of the New Jerusalem, is an objective that most of us have still to find. That, at any rate, is the attitude adopted by many a psychologist, and a mechanistic concept of psychic life has been discarded in favour of a dynamic spiritual definition of the mind and its unconscious aspects. So that, when some such experience as the vision or inspiration of God bursts through the narrow horizon of the mind, suddenly and without warning, we must realise that here is a startling phenomenon of the unconscious psyche, one of the utmost importance. For months and perhaps for years, it has been evolving the experience as a possibility, awaiting only the right opportunity when conscious barriers would be down, so that it could manifest fully formed and developed, like Athene issuing full-armed from the brain of Zeus.

So, whilst pondering over the spiritual inspiration of the Bible, some such great and holy experience was vouchsafed her. Of it she wrote: "The lost chord of Truth (healing, as of old) I caught consciously from the Divine Harmony...It was to me a revelation of Truth." Years later she came to realise that it was her particular attitude unconsciously developing during this process of reflection over the Bible, that rendered her at this moment passive and receptive to the spiritual forces of the unconscious. These forces welled up in those few moments of passive reflection and acceptance, and she knew that in some unknown way she had attained to that kind of awareness of divine power which heals and makes all things new.

It marked a new era of expansion for her, as similar experiences ever have for all their recipients in former times. Where previously there was doubt and fear and timidity, the whole psyche has become all ablaze with a new light, imparting self-confidence and vigor and an unquestionable surety that was unchallengable. Sometimes the transformation does not come immediately, but develops slowly and surely, changing and transforming the character and personality in subtle ways that are veritably miraculous. In this process of illumination and quiet growth, the fundamental concept of what some years later she called Christian Science came to her. Quimby planted the seeds. Their burgeoning was the result of her own mind. The full implications of their possibilities may not have dawned upon her for years, but the essential idea came through with startling clarity. Only God is real, and he is truth and infinite being and love and substance. His life the only life, and in Him actually do we live and move and have our being. Hence life in matter, or an intelligent response from matter, or any sensation in matter apart from mind, was for her impossible. Upon these ideas she worked during the many years of her wanderings, adding here, developing there, depending upon the particular intellectual or spiritual stimulus that she received.

Of this essential idea of negating matter, Stephan Zweig writes sarcastically: "The most difficult of philosophical problems has been solved, once and for all. Jubilemus! It has been solved with such miraculous simplicity by the castration of reality. A radical cure has been achieved, bodily suffering has been overcome, through the declaration that the body does not exist. It is as much as if we were to 'cure' toothache by cutting off the sufferer's head."

This nice refutation of Mrs. Eddy's leading idea, by the reduction of it to absurdity, is one of those unfortunate literary gestures that an author comes to regret in saner moments. It casts reflection not against Mrs. Eddy at all, but rather against the author and the medical system he attempts here to defend. Of course the medical profession does not recommend the removal of the patient's head to cure toothache. But sometimes it goes almost to similar ridiculous ends because of its own ignorance of adequate therapeutics. There are now many people walking the streets of modern cities who have had appendectomies in order to "cure" appendicitis, nephrectomies in order to "cure" pyonephrosis. Surgery has been resorted to so that by means of historectomy and oopharectomy certain gynaecological diseases may be "cured," and limbs have been amputated to halt necrosis and gangrene. Why be content to extract all the teeth in rheumatic fever or theumatoid arthritis—far better to lop off the head! Even the despised drugless practitioners, such as chiropractors and osteopaths, know better than that. The history of medicine is a stubborn history of mistaken refusals to appreciate new concepts, with the result that outside of medicine there exist many drugless therapies which claim a far higher percentage of satisfactory results than occurs in medical spheres. It is only years after their mulish inability to have anything to do with these discoveries, that some smart medical doctor sneaks it into his profession by the back door, having taken the trouble first to alter the terminology. This is occurring today, even with the Christian Science concepts. Thus Podmore, one of the most venomous critics of Mrs. Eddy, stated that her metaphysic and science "can now almost shake hands, so narrow is the ditch that divides the two camps." I am afraid Mr. Zweig was not very wise in his use of metaphors. It was hardly well-chosen, and Mrs. Eddy is too easily defended against ill-mannered quips of this kind.

She was alone again, and penniless, as I have said, functioning after a fashion however, due to her self-engineered cure which resulted from her revelation whilst sick. But where was she to go? She knew now that she had some work to do. It was not altogether clear. But slowly it was dawning upon her that destiny was straight ahead. She needed to write a book—one which would embody her spiritual experience, and at the same time clarify her own ideas about mental or spiritual healing. Quimby's concepts, and her wide reading, had given her a key, and her spiritual experience had synthesised all this scattered material in her mind. She understood now what she wanted to do. But she was penniless, as well as homeless.

What happened in the succeeding years when she lived for shorter or longer periods with friends we do not really know. Neither Mrs. Eddy's autobiography nor Miss Wilbur's biography has very much to say about her acute sufferings during those years of contumely and degradation. Its blackness is described fairly vividly in Miss Milmine's biography. Dr. Powell says but little more of what occurred to her from 1866, the year of her accident and revelation, to 1875 when *Science and Health* was first published. She had been drifting from one home to another, putting up in the homes of people who had taken pity upon her, attempting meantime to write her book. Dr. Powell believed that her writing, exhausting as it sometimes must have been, was her anchorage to reality when a lesser soul would have drifted to oblivion. Did she, like St. Paul, have to become all things to all men that she might save them? It was the honest toil she gave the book which taught her tact and courage. Was it necessary to pay attention to the spiritualistic rhapsodies of the Websters in order to keep a roof over her head? She could bring herself to do it for the sake of the precious hours it would give her every day to write. Did she have to sit in at a game of cards to keep on good terms with acquaintances, when she begrudged every minute stolen from her writing so that to some she now and then appeared distracted, even cross?

There were times apparently when children rudely mimicked and mocked her, adults insulted her, wounding her sensitive pride, even threatening her with bodily harm. Surely she was deeply hurt by the wanton cruelties that only human beings can inflict upon each other. It is a great pity that we do not have a fully painted picture of this period. One of the things that gives the impression of real greatness is her fortitude and courage during so distressing a time. Yet I wonder whether the more delineation of the external material events and physical sufferings she endured would help us very much. A knowledge of her inner life at that time would be far more revealing. These many years were a period of growth and unfoldment, when her inner resolve was strengthened to achieve and to attain.

For a while she was the guest of Hiram Crafts, who was a heel-finisher in a shoe factory in Lynn, Mass. She managed to around enough enthusiasm within him for the art of mental healing that he gave up his manual work to apply the principles Mrs. Eddy had taught him. He had read Emerson and had been interested in the philosophy of transcendentalism. Rev. Walter M. Haushalter tells us that the was a member of the Kantian Society to which Francis Lieber also belonged. As a guest in the home of Hiram Crafts, we may well assume that they often discussed Quimby as well as her own ideas about healing, and transcendentalism. She may have learned some little from him of German philosophy and, if he possessed them, to have read from his collection of books. Rev. Haushalter's thesis is that she did have access to Francis Lieber's manuscript on Hegel's religious philosophy, and that it provided her with a philosophical background upon which she could build the Quimby idea of healing. He claims that this is the "revelation" she was vouchsafed—from Hegel, and not from God—and from which she developed Christian Science. Haushalter attempts to prove in his small book that many lines, some two hundred or more in *Science and Health* have been lifted from the Lieber manuscript.

The Christian Science Sentinel reviewed this book in April 3, 1937 at some length. It appears that the Christian Science Board of Directors were not particularly convinced for various reasons of their own. However, they put genuine specimens both of Mrs. Eddy's handwriting and Francis Lieber's handwriting in the hands of two handwriting experts of New York City. The experts were asked to compare these specimens with those reproduced in Rev. Haushalter's book. I quote from the review: "The gist of their findings was that neither the purported notation by Mary Baker Eddy, and that neither the purported signature was in the handwriting of Mary Baker Eddy, and that neither the purported letter nor the purported manuscript reproduced in the book nor the purported signature of Francis Lieber was in his handwriting." In other words, the Board of Directors dismissed the whole document as spurious and as a forgery.

The present writer is not in a position to evaluate fully either Rev. Haushalter's contention nor the conclusions of the Christian Science Board of Directors and their handwriting experts. Rev. Haushalter has employed his own committee of experts who support him in his contention. However, the present writer takes a very simple stand, similar to that previously taken in these chapters. For the time being, let us accept Rev. Haushalter's book on its face value. Also let us assume that Mrs. Eddy, whilst enjoying the hospitality of Hiram Crafts the alleged secretary of the Kantian Society, did see this manuscript on Hegel's philosophy of religion. The question arises—though traces of Lieber may be found in *Science and Health*, conversely are there evidences of Christian Science in Lieber's essay? The answer is definitely negative. There is not the least relationship. As I have indicated earlier, between Mrs. Eddy and Hegel there is very little accord, and I cannot believe that this philosophy played an great part in shaping the ultimate form of Mrs. Eddy's highly practical technique and thought. The debt of Quimby is of far greater import and consequence than this alleged plagiarism from Lieber's essay on Hegel.

I am willing to concede that, whilst in the Crafts' home, discussing a wide series of topics with her host, she became familiar with a variety of philosophical concepts that had not previously come her way. Being a highly intelligent woman, naturally some of these discussions, or the conclusions drawn therefrom, were utilised later when the book was taking concrete form. I see no necessity to argue about this unnecessarily. There is no need for shame here, nor is there anything to hide; no need for fearing to admit that such was even possible. She would have been foolish to reject any intellectual stimulus, and even more foolish for failing to utilise it. Many a great mind has confessed to influences from conversations, arguments and discussions that have profoundly influenced his life. Surely Mrs. Eddy drew material from every direction that she could in order to assist her in shaping her ideas to the ultimate end in view. In so doing, she was wise and practical.

Anyway, none of this helps us to understand how she, a mere nobody, could have evolved during those penurious years into a definite somebody of such world-wide fame. Quimby was known to but a few hundreds or thousands of people. Had there not been this furore about the possible antecedents of Christian Science and

Mary Baker Eddy, no one today I am sure would even know of the former existence of Quimby. He has achieved a fame and notoriety only through the success and wide publicity given Mrs. Eddy. Many of the personalities of his day are lost today in utter obsurity. Emerson was not too well known yet; he was only lust beginning to emerge from the darkness himself. And so far as Hegel's transcendentalism is concerned, like all such philosophies they are known and appreciated only by those with academic training in formal logic and philosophy. There is nothing in Hegel that could even begin to be remotely popular. Nothing, certainly that could sweep the world by storm. In the world of scholars and professional philosophers and in the universities, it could make a narrow appeal. But surely not the universal appeal that was made by Christian Science.

In this space of nine years of hardship and incredible misery, something tremendous must have happened to Mary Baker Patterson. Rev. Haushalter has suggested that this tremendous event was the discovery of the Hegel document which gave her a philosophy ready made to which she could attach the practical elements of Quimby's technique. On the other hand, some inner series of spiritual experiences must have occurred enabling her to appropriate an idea or two from Quimby, learn about Hegel through Lieber from Crafts, and assimilate them thoroughly in her own mind. Through this assimilation, vitalised possibly by a mystical experience, she produced a full-fledged Christian metaphysic devoted to the amelioration of sickness and disease, the restoration of health both of body and mind, and the absolute conquest of the material world. But what was it that happened in those nine years of hardship? We learn nothing from the official biographies save the most fragmentary facts.

There is a formula however that does help us in some slight manner to explain, at least partially, this phenomenon. It is a formula that we can apply to all men of spiritual genius. What happened to those people whom we regard as religious geniuses? At one time nobody had ever heard of them. A time elapses. They later take the citadel of the world by storm, and we have never forgotten them since. A nobody all of a sudden becomes somebody. And they did this without propaganda machines, publicity agents, or press advertising. Elaborate lives have been written of all these people, and in each there is a significant parallel. There is an omission. We hear nothing of what Christ did between the age of twelve and thirty. Mohammed, the founder of Islam, was a mere camel driver, unknown and unimportant, but he disappeared into a cave for quite a long while. Buddha left his place where he was born a prince, giving up all his royal privileges and luxuries, and went for a long while into the desert. This omission is true also of Moses, and likewise of St. Paul—and a host of other men. It is also true of Mrs. Eddy in the penurious years prior to the publication and success of *Science and Health*. When each of them came back, no longer were they inarticulate as prior to their disappearance. Each returned to preach immediately a new spiritual law. What happened during this period of silence?

Each states, upon his return, at least one thing significant of the omission. That God spoke to him. In other words, some ineffable mystical experience transformed the whole of their lives, imbuing them with a new sense of self-esteem, poise, self-assurance, and the ability to assert themselves in such a way that the world is forced to take notice. In this retirement from the world— whether an actual literal one in the desert, or a psychological retreat inwardly, locked in the fastnesses of their own soul—each of these many people discovered an interior path to God. By prayer and meditation, or other equally apt psychological methods, they opened their minds to the influx of a noetic spiritual being. As a result they were never quite the same people. They came back armed with knowledge and power, manifesting shining dazzling eyes and bright faces, bearing a heart that pours out boundless love unceasingly.

Psychologically, by concentration and emotional exaltation, they achieved a unification of all the aspects and levels of the mind. The conscious and unconscious psychic levels, instead of being disrupted, and separated by an almost impenetrable barrier, draw together in reciprocal relationships. Dissociated elements that had been repressed and so split off, as it were, from the main stream of the personality are recovered and integrated into the whole psychic structure. There is, consequently, a sense of discovery, of wholeness and holiness, an overwhelming effect of being blessed and sanctified by something not of this earth. A new decisiveness appears, bringing with it a predisposition for social adjustment and mastery that never could have been conceived before. In a word, there is a transformation of the entire personality, a transmutation of the neurotic elements into the white hot fire of genius and creativity.

In those long years of travail that she passed through, between the time of her own recovery and the appearance of her book, her psyche must have been undergoing some such transformation as I have indicated. The fuse was set off, as it were, by the psychological phenomenon of the revelation—regardless of how we try to explain this phenomenon. But a lengthy time was required for the consolidation of its effects upon her character. The magical transformation may not have occurred in one fell swoop. Possibly, during those long, lonely, sad years, there may have been frequent repetitions of that initial mystical experience. Whatever did occur, however, transformed her from the neurotic nonentity that she was before into a notable whose name swept around the world like wildfire. And the transformation was due, not entirely to the enunciation of the principles which she taught much later on, but to a primary experience of so dynamic and exalting a nature as to alter the whole course of her life.

It is people such as these, blessed by the descent of the spirit from above, who become the world's leaders. These are they who begin the powerful new movements which anticipate later developments in world's history, secular, economic, as well as spiritual. And Mrs. Eddy is undoubtedly a spiritual genius, created so not from birth, but one who evolved through personal suffering and striving to bear a hallowed fruit.

CHAPTER FIVE

Metaphysic

Constant suffering tends always in the direction of compensation in some direction or other. Insecurity and inferiority demand some firm foundation upon which to stand, a support upon which safely to lean. Sickness desires an infallible remedy, and poverty ever yearns for a constant and never failing source of supply. Fifty frustrated years of loneliness will surely evoke idealised aspirations of an ever constant friend upon whom unlimited demands of love and affection can be made. No human being can ever measure up to such an ideal which, therefore, has to be sought in a metaphysical realm.

The psychological method of enquiry attempts to show that all systems of human thinking and activity, no matter how abstract or universal, are inevitably based upon, or incorporate within themselves, some personal problem. The man, for example, who becomes a psycho-analyst in adult life does so because of powerful inner tensions impelling him in that direction. And this fact is true equally of the business magnate and street-cleaner, the mechanical engineer or artist's model, and the philosopher as well. Each profession undoubtedly represents symbolically a specific attempt to express some inner urge. Had we an anamnesis of such people, it might be possible to depict with graphs and charts the drives and impulses that were operating against the inertia of the environment to produce the results we know.

Though we have no complete anamnesis in the case of Mrs. Eddy, nevertheless we do have a self-written history and an authorised biography which, together, are partially revealing on this score. Using our present-day psychological knowledge, we can piece together the isolate fragments presented and understand just what the emotional conflict was in her inner life that necessitated her later development. One of the most startling revelations vouchsafed to us by modern scientific psychological research into dreams is insight into man's motives and aspirations. From this unconscious psycho-motor activity we are able through analysis to divine why it is than an individual acts and thinks in certain ways, and why certain events ineluctably occur to him. But more intriguing than mere dream analysis is the logical deduction that the dream interpretation can be extended to man's waking world also.

For example, we can investigate the significance of objective phenomena by regarding them as integral parts of a dream. If unconscious psychic activity is the motivating factor in dream production, it is similarly operative in waking behavior. Once the actual environment can be regarded in the same light as a dream, we can apply all the laws of dream interpretation to it. Thus we can find out why such events, and only such events with no possible alternative, occur to a certain person. They occur because they have meaning. And meaning after all is a psychological and spiritual value. This has been one of the most extensive and fundamentally revealing of the psychological discoveries that have been developed out of the analytical schools of today. To all the events of life, therefore, can be applied by the laws of association, condensation, symbolisation, displacement of emphasis, secondary elaboration in order to obscure issues, and so on. The unconscious purpose can therefore be divined back of every kind of individual activity—a purpose of which the individual may be totally unaware, but which nonetheless expresses itself unconsciously in his every thought and deed.

The events in the life of Mrs. Eddy likewise have a similar significance, partly suggested in the previous section. But I have not attempted to indicate this more fully because, as was there said, this is not a biography. However, I have intimated this idea because, regardless of what other conclusions we draw, we must understand much of her philosophy and methodology in the light of her personal life. On an earlier page, I did suggest that the technique of denial is the way of neurosis. Denial is the infantile corrective to forbidden sensuality in all its broad and intricate details. In order to escape from what the child imagines or feels to be the more anti-social and amoral of its impulses, a process of repression or denial has to be instigated.

This is hardly to suggest that we have to mark off the higher idealistic directions of her philosophy for that reason. But it does enable us to understand etiologically the tremendous force of the attitude revealed in *Science and Health*. Mrs. Eddy was burdened by a consciousness of sin. In other words, she carried with her throughout life a sense of unconscious guilt and fear, which even towards the end of her days erupted violently into the open to be mistakenly attributed by her to malicious animal magnetism. Christian Science is, above all, a personal system depicting the battle by means of which she climbed out of the slough of despond, up the mount of hope, to the full glory of freedom from sin. It is a personal system, having therefore primary and particular reference to her. It could have application to other people only secondarily, insofar as their unconscious psychic problems coincided with her. But since denial plays such a great role in Christian Science—the denial which can be read as the denial of sin and guilt as the result of repressed sensuality—this point requires some emphasis.

In the inner lives of neurotics, there are evidences of the swinging of a psychic pendulum. There is a vigorous forward movement away from the repressions toward a goal that the individual feels it clean, spiritual, bearing no resemblance whatsoever to the neurotic content that has had to be denied. Frequently, in the dreams of such people we find employment of such symbols as flying in the air, going up an elevator, climbing to the top of a tall building, or of going to the attic of a house and finding that the staircase ascended has become very flimsy and shaky. Apart from all other significances, the ascension to the top of the building and the attic are symbols of sublimation, of rising above the sphere of temptation. They are symbolic representations of the height of the mind. They represent ideals, high mental concepts, that peak of intellectual exaltation which is far removed from the basement, the unconscious and its repressions. In Mrs. Eddy's life, her goal *had* to be very lofty effectually to remove her from sin.

The summit of the building becomes represented symbolically in her philosophical system by the postulate of God as the spiritual goal of man, as the all-inclusive principle of the universe in which there is no "otherness." There must be no matter, no "otherness" of God—for this "otherness" was the sin she must eradicate in her own self by denial. This led to the formulation of her famous scientific statement underlying Christian Science. "There is no life, truth, intelligence or substance in matter. All is infinite Mind and its infinite manifestation, for God is All in all. Spirit is immortal truth; matter is mortal error. Spirit is the real and the eternal; matter is the unreal and temporal. Spirit is God, and man is His image and likeness; hence man is spiritual and not material."

It was the material world with its problems and conflicts and sorrows that had hurt her. Consequently this was the motive that caused her intellectually to turn for solace and help away from that painful world to a nobler higher sphere of ideals which she conceived as real in the supreme sense, denying reality and validity to that upon which she had turned her back. If we had no repressions, it is possible we would have no ideals. As I have already tried to show, neurosis breeds great minds, and the neurotic character bears within itself the nucleus of the regeneration of mankind because of its inherent need to progress out of sterility and conflict to evolve creative ideas. Civilisation is based entirely upon repression and sublimation. Ideals are necessary to defend us from the impulses of our animal nature. These intellectual concepts are emotional necessities. The neurotic mind, impelled to escape from and deny the force of its emotional repressions, is able to employ every device of formal logic and academic philosophy as will best serve its own ends.

In this higher sphere of mind, where the trend of her compensatory reactions turned, she saw only one omnipresent Spirit or Mind, and the infinite ideas of that Mind. Only this was real and enduring. All else was fleeting and appearance. All other than this divine Mind had a fictitious reality, since all we could know of matter was through mind. It was an attempt to rob her repressions of any power over her by denying their actual existence. She attempted to devitalise the material world, accordingly, by withdrawing its energy into an inner world of mind. It was a mental world where she lived, a world of mind and its ideas. Since some distinction had to be drawn between the ideas contained within her own mind and these other objective realities perceived through the medium of the special senses, she, like Berkeley, could only conceive that these other ideas were held in the mind of God. Therefore nothing existed save God and His ideas. And insofar as God evolved ideas in His mind, and since too her mind could entertain ideas, there existed an intimate relationship between the Mind of God and the mind of man. The latter was a reflection of the former, but partaking of the same creative nature and spiritual substance of the former.

A logical development then led away from her own personal problems. After all, the latter were simply the prompt, the motivating impulse that gave direction to her mind. And her mind, now on its way, proceeded to propound a system which came to have universal applicability. She propounded four propositions which to her were self-evident and self-consistent, and these she conceived basically to underlie Christian Science.

"1. God is All in all.

"2. God is good. Good is Mind.

"3. God, Spirit, being all, nothing is matter.

"4. Life, God, omnipotent Good, deny death, evil, sin, disease.—Disease, sin, evil, death, deny Good, omnipotent God, Life."

From this it is evident that the bases of Christian Science are very simple. The whole system is based, theoretically as well as practically, upon these four self-evident propositions. Only God is real, and God is the all, the totality of all things. Whatever is, is God. And the divine characteristics, so to say, of God are omnipotent, omnipresence, and omniscience. So that if in theory we argue that God is everywhere and infinite, the can be nothing anywhere that is not of him. Such a conclusion contradicts "forever the belief that matter can be actual," to quote from Science and Health. Our being is not therefore a material but an ideal existence, that we function entirely as minds or spirits, reflections of God, in a mind world which is God. Our whole life depends completely upon God, and there is no life other than His. That is why, in Christian Science, God is considered to be the only Life, Truth, and Love. Whatever life there is, is God. The truth about anything likewise is God. And wherever love is seen, there we know that God is present. As Mind, God is the life and substance and continuity of all things, and Mrs. Eddy says that all life and substance "belong wholly to Mind, are inherent in Mind." "God's thoughts are perfect and eternal, are Substance and Life." Therefore the substance of everything we think and live and handle in our daily lives, that which stands under or behind all phenomena, is not a material substance but the very mind stuff of God himself. Because of this we are, in reality, closer to God than ever we could formerly imagine, even though we are not normally conscious of this divine relationship. That we are not conscious of participating in this divine life is no argument against the concept—especially in these days when the possibilities of unconscious psychological activity are being more and more realised. Christian Science seems to be in accord with one phase of modern psychology which demands that, in order to be healthy in every phase of our personalities, we require to make conscious what before was unconscious to us.

Mrs. Eddy asks us to become more and more aware of the true facts of this relationship of ourselves with God, by intellectually affirming that this is so, and strongly denying anything which would detract from its truth. As a religious movement, therefore, Christian Science must be placed amongst the loftiest attempts of man to realise God not merely as a transcendental principle, but as an immanence involve in even the most minute and trivial details of our lives. It attempts to give credibility and substance to St. Paul's dictum "Whatsoever ye do, whether it be eating or drinking, do it unto the glory of God." Insofar as it does this, it is probably more highly successful than any other popular religious movement the world has ever known. It cuts the gordian knot of theological speculation as to what, where and who God is, by claiming that whatever it is that we are confronted by has it reality in God.

But since God is defined as infinite Good and Love, Mrs. Eddy could not possibly conceive by any mental effort that He could be responsible for any of the evil that had once occurred to her. No decent father would ever wish upon his child the tragedies and awful sorrows that descend upon man. Would God therefore do less than human father? Mrs. Eddy's reply is emphatically in the negative. God does not inflict sorrow upon man, for God is essentially good, and is synonymous with good. His nature is love, and we who partake of Him likewise feel love springing from deep bottomless wells of spiritual emotion. If God is good, and infinite and omnipresent, and if we say that he would not inflict pain and hardship upon his children, whence therefore come these evils that we see? Do these also exist in the omnipresent infinite body of God, since God is All in all? To this Mrs. Eddy also is definite. These evils have no real existence. Only that which God creates as powerful ideas for good in his universal Mind, can exist and have reality. God does not create evil. Evils are the result of our own false ignorant thinking.

As an ideological reflection of God, partaking of His truth and love and intelligence, man creates with his divine mind. Nevertheless he has so forgotten his spiritual nature that he has permitted an erroneous development of mind to occur. It has no real existence, this mortal mind, yet since an illusion is powerful and seems real while it lasts, so also does this mortal or human mind seem real. It is this part of our mental structure which, because of its ignorance of divine truths, is responsible for all human woes, for sin, sickness, and death.

To understand this is not really too difficult, in spite of adverse criticisms. For example, if I hypnotised a man and, giving him a blank card, told him that it was really a picture of his dearly beloved mother, we would see an appearance of love and tenderness creep over his face, and he would even kiss the apparent picture. He is subject to an illusion which, while it lasts, seems very real. His mind, in response to the suggestion of an illusion, really creates that false image of his mother which elicits reactions of love, affection and tenderness. His reactions are real enough, even although deception has been the cause of them. So likewise with our own lives. Having lost the knowledge of the fact that we are actually rooted in divine wisdom and love and truth, our minds actually function as though this were no so, and falsely create illusions by an unconscious process of auto-hallucination. We create our own illusions and hallucinations which, according to Christian Science, is this material world which we regard as being real. Once imbedded in the illusion, we create powerful but destructive images which have the power of leading us still further astray. "Sin, sickness and death" wrote Mrs. Eddy in *Science and Health*, "are comprised in human material belief, and belong not to a divine Mind. They are without a real origin or existence. They have neither principle nor permanence, but belong, with all that is material and temporal, to the nothingness of error, which simulates the creations of Truth."

God's thoughts, she says, are perfect and eternal, are both substance and life. The more we approximate to Him, live always with that thought in mind, act ever with that end in view, the nearer do we draw to Him and become more and more like Him. "The immortal and spiritual man is really substantial, and reflects the divine Substance, or Good, which mortals hope for. He reflects divine Life, Truth and Love, which constitute the only real and eternal entity. This reflection is transcendental, only because the spiritual man's substantiality transcends mortal vision, and is revealed only through divine Science. As God is Substance, and man also is the offspring of Substance, being made in the divine image and likeness, man should wish for, and in reality has, the substance of Good. The belief that man has any other substance, or mind, is not spiritual."

One of the great problems which, unfortunately, remains unanswered in Christian Science is that relating to the origin of mortal mind and its belief in matter. In the case cited, we know the origin of the hypnotic illusion or false belief. The hypnotist imparted it. In the case of mortal mind, what is its origin, and how did it become into being? If God is All, and if the universe "is filled with spiritual ideas which He evolves," and which therefore are "obedient to the Mind which makes them," what room is there for a pure illusion? How possibly could a false belief or opinion originate in a mental world where the only realities are spiritual ideas? How did mortal mind "which is not an entity" come into being so that, acting independently of the divine Mind, it could fabricate deceptions and illusions? How could it usurp its place as slave and dethrone, apparently, the divine mind? This difficulty becomes all the more profound when we examine the definitions of Mortal mind as found in the glossary of *Science and Health*.

"*Mortal Mind*. Nothing, claiming to be something, for Mind is immortal; mythology; error creating other errors; a suppositional material sense, alias the belief that sensation is in matter, which is sensationless; a belief that life, substance, and intelligence are in and of matter; the opposite of Spirit, and therefore the opposite of Good, or God; the belief that life has a beginning, and therefore an end; the belief that man is the offspring of mortals; the belief that there can be more than one creator; idolatry; the subjective states of error; material senses; that which neither exists in Science, nor can be recognised by the spiritual sense; sin; sickness; death."

Unfortunately the problem is hardly clarified, and we are still left mystified and in the dark. But no matter how inadequately it and its origins are defined, nevertheless Mrs. Eddy makes it perfectly obvious that she will none of it. It is error, false belief and illusion, and all its works partake of similar qualities. It is more or less conterminous with the body, its organs and its functions, as when she says in effect that matter and mortal mind are different states of the same thing—false beliefs. The grosser substratum is called matter, the finer, mortal mind. Both in neither of them is there intelligence nor power, nor aught else that could invest it with reality. It is in the real mind, divine mind, where intelligence and truth resides. It is mortal mind, so-called, which is so liable to misinterpretation and misconception of phenomena. Our minds, receiving sensations and impressions, interpret the mental image we then synthesize as pertaining to matter and to corporeal bodies. This misinterpretation and misconception require to be banished by exercising Divine Mind which then perceives our sensations as purely mental phenomena relating to the spiritual images and ideas of the Mind of God. It would sometimes seem that, in reality, that there is implied not two minds, but only one mind with a double aspect or function. When entertaining false beliefs and embedded in ignorance, it is conceived of as mortal mind. But when it exercises true perception, insight and spiritual understanding it is called Divine Mind. In Divine Mind is included all that is real, and nothing of human erroneous opinions.

As I have said, Christian Science is fundamentally simple, though Mrs. Eddy employs a wide variety of elaborations and emphases on the simple basic theme. God, which is the Divine Mind, is the only reality. Matter and that phase of mind which perceives it as such, is false and erroneous, and so are all the states and conditions and qualities which properly belong to matter and to corporeal bodies. We could assume that sickness, poverty and sin are the properties of matter, in precisely the same way that we speak of the physical and chemical properties of an element or a compound. And therefore if we wish to solve our problems, and transcend sickness and poverty, and all similar unpleasant qualities of this non-existent matter, we must deny the truth of our apparent perception of it, and affirm the opposite—that in God there being only truth and infinite being and love, these other things can have no existence whatsoever. Any problem can be solved, so she tells us, by turning from it to a realisation of God's presence and power. The prominent aspect of the system consists principally of an easy technique which can, so it is said, be applied to all problems and possibilities that an individual may be confronted with.

The important thing is to realise from the Christian Science viewpoint is that disease and sickness are false perceptions and beliefs. They have no actual existence as true ideas in the mind of God, being illusory beliefs entertained only by man. Hence to assume that they are real, that they are valid and have a tangible existence, is to be unfaithful to knowledge of God, to indulge in sin. Therefore the Christian Scientist will not even acknowledge that these things have any existence whatsoever. It would be sinful and unchristianly for him to do so. All he must do is to "keep in mind the verities of Being—that man is the image and likeness of God, in whom all Being is painless and permanent. Remember that man's perfection is real and unimpeachable, whereas imperfection is blameworthy and unreal." And any of the manifold pathological manifestations of disease with which the physician is acquainted—such as infection, pathogenic micro-organisms, tubercles, ulcers, calcifications, and neoplastic activity—all these, it is claimed, are false beliefs, self-imposed deceptions, dark dream-images of mortal mind which must flee before the light. All beliefs in such manifestations must be replaced by an emphatic declaration of God's truth, substance, love and divine being. Such a declaration, she emphasises, renders a belief in these human afflictions wholly incompatible with the divine facts.

There is one way of looking at the process of denial which renders the idea a little more intelligible to the scientific mind. That is to say, it can be regarded not only as metaphysics but simply as psychology. For example, an artist who is engaged on a portrait he is painting becomes so creatively excited and impassioned by his work that all other distractions fade away into relative insignificance. A poet, creating an epic poem or a play, becomes so enamoured of his work, so caught up in the exalted heights of his inspiration as to lose sight of time and environment, forgetting his meals, his companions, and everything else. Only one thing exists for him—his work, his poem, his ideal conception. Only this fact occupies his attention. All else becomes forgotten, ignored, automatically denied. The artist does not deny consciously, but the result is approximately the same. He withdraws his attention from unnecessary and unimportant trivialities so as to become exclusively concentrated on the work at hand. So also with the Christian Scientist, at least in theory. The mind must so be fastened on God, on this ideal concept which is conceived to be the saviour which will redeem from sin and heal all sickness and disharmony, that the psychological concentration is aided and tremendously intensified by denying every distraction. Anything that might cause the mind to deviate one iota from the contemplation of the divine order of infinite love, substance and truth must be denied, and ignored. All psychic energy is withdrawn from all external objects to intensify and enhance his mental focussing on the spiritual world, upon God. Viewed in this light, it is seen to be an admirable psychological technique. It is very good psychology. From the metaphysical point of view, the psychologist is unable to express any kind of opinion. It is outside the realm of his criticism and opinion.

So at all times the Christian Scientist is obliged to remember that the tendency to disease is not hereditary. Regardless of what heredity is conceived to be, he is told that the only true thing about heredity is that we are children of God, partaking therefore of his divine nature of truth, love, and intelligence. With such a divine heritage, how could we inherit disease? All pathologies are superimpositions upon the mind-body system brought about by ignorance and all that follows therefrom—fear, anxiety, hate, jealousy and greed. These negative emotions, the false products of a false self, are sufficiently potent by themselves to precipitate into manifestation all the diseases and problems which the human imagination can conceive. All human difficulties, such as lack of sufficient money and food wherewith to function adequately, social and marital problems, difficult questions of adjustment to any and all situations—these are the products of the errors and ignorance fostered by the lower mind. They are not true, for they do not pertain to the divine mind of man. Can we imagine that these have any part whatsoever in God? Is it possible that a God who is infinite Good and Love would possibly cripple his own children with such foul diseases and problems as we have? It is our mental falling away from the knowledge and realisation of the ever presence of the infinite divinity of God's being that produces these problems? Our problems are not positive factors in themselves. They are solely negative manifestations—manifestations of lack—lack of God and his truth and substance and love.

Ideas such as these have evoked ridicule and derision from the scientific field. Yet in the scientific sphere there are many concepts which are eloquently illustrative of the Christian Science viewpoint. By describing the scientific opinion we may be able to grasp more clearly the Christian Science outlook. In the sphere of biochemistry, it is asserted that vitamins are groups of vital constituents of most foods in their natural states. Some of these have been isolated in chemical laboratories and synthesised. Very minute quantities of these vitamins are said to be essential for the growth, development and health of man. Several distinct vitamins have been recognised and classified under letters of the alphabet, and data has been accumulated by their experimental administration to both man and beast. When diet has been artificially restricted so that one or more of these vitamins are absent either wholly or partially, serious deficiency diseases invariably result. Typical of such diseases are xerophthalmia, or night blindness, the result of degenerative changes in the retina caused by deficiencies in Vitamin A intake. Pellagra, beri-beri, and many dermotoses are due to lack of the several factors in the Vitamin B complex, which moreover is said to be absolutely essential to normal nerve and muscle function. Vitamin C deficiency results in the dreaded scurvy—and so on with the rest of the vitamins. The astonishing thing about dietotherapy is that these diseases disappear no sooner than foods containing the appropriate vitamins are administered, or when the vitamin is given in synthetic form.

Similarly the Christian Scientist believes, and claims to have demonstrated, that any lack in awareness of the presence of God results similarly in deficiency diseases. In fact, all diseases from this point of view are the result of lack. The are evidences of an individual's inability or refusal to admit God into his life. Lack of God and his love and divine substance results therefore in a false emphasis on mortal mind with it fabrication of manifold false beliefs, erroneous intellectual assumptions, perverted perceptions, and a mass of negative destructive emotions. Just a person suffering from the aviteaminoses develops perverted appetites in food and perverted habits, so similarly a person suffering from lack of God and from an over development of mortal mind, embraces perverted views on life and short-sighted materialistic philosophies. Disease and poverty and problems are the result. Of course, we must understand clearly here that the Christian Scientist regards avitaminosis and deficiency diseases as he does all other disease states. The topic of vitamins has been mentioned only to illustrate the Eddy idea of divine lack and a deficiency in man's realisation of God.

Yet this lack of God, is only an *apparent* lack. In itself, it is an illusion, a false belief fostered by this lower mind, fathered by deception and mothered by perversion. If God is infinite and omnipresent, there can never be any lack of God, for He is present even in the mind which denies Him and ignores Him the most strongly. Man in his true nature, which persists throughout all the vicissitudes of life, is incapable of falling away from God. He is incapable of sin, sickness, and death, enjoying an eternally flawless perfection since he derives his essence from God, and constantly lives in the mind of God, and is bathed forever in the omnipresent and omnipotent ideas and substance of God. Man has never departed from God, and the metaphorical description of a falling away from God is only a convenient description. While convenient, it is however utterly false. It is as much of an illusion as if, to a hypnotised subject, it were suggested that he was slowly being asphyxiated from lack of air, even though he were enclosed in an oxygen tent.

It is this illusion that Mrs. Eddy would have us deny. By shifting the point of view over to a realisation of the fact that God is ever present and powerful in us, even when we least realise it, we will come slowly to *know* that we exist only in His Mind and nowhere else. And, when we realise him and achieve a consciousness of the omnipresence and omnipotence of divine love and truth and being, all our problems immediately will fall away. They become starved out for lack of nourishment, and a full participation ensures in the eternally divine order.

Is there poverty in your life? Then attempt to dwell mentally on God as the only substance there is, a never-failing source of infinite supply from which all things are derived, and which will meet and fill every demand that life can make. This substance is everywhere, and is the basis of everything. How can there be poverty and want and need? This need exists because of lack of realisation that God's substance and supply is there, just waiting to be grasped and utilised by His children.

Is yours a problem that is so perplexing and worrying, that the mind reels constantly with anxiety and fear, bringing with it insomnia, phobias, and a host of painful, psychological states? But God is truth and infinite wisdom! In the face of this truth and intelligence which, like God, is everywhere present and everywhere powerful, these problems will fade away—even as ugly dreams of the night fade away as waking consciousness grows stronger with the return of the light and the day. Let nothing but the likeness of God abide in the thoughts, and refuse steadfastly to let the mind, wander from that contemplation. "Let neither fear nor doubt overshadow your clear sense and calm trust, that the recognition of life harmonious—as Life eternally is—can destroy any painful sense, or belief in, that which Life is not."

This therefore is the technique of Christian Science. It consists mainly of two mechanisms—those of denial and affirmation. The adverse and the painful is to be denied so as to rob it of its efficacy and power. The harmonious and the good is to be affirmed as belonging to God, of whom man is the beloved and loving child. It is fundamentally simple to state and grasp, even though an infinite variety of changes may be rung upon so simple a theme.

Just how the method works is less simple to understand. It is quite obscure to our minds how, for example, a denial of the existence of poverty, with the affirmation of God as infinite substance, can actually produce wealth. Yet many a Christian Scientist who has practically been down and out, fearful and anxious of what life may bring, has claimed that all financial and economic problems have cleared themselves within a surprisingly short space of time. We have the supreme evidence of Mrs. Eddy's fifty "wasted years," when she was alone, penniless and sick. Yet through her application of these principles, she died a wealthy woman, loved by thousands of people and sought after by them.

The most obvious answer is that the technique of denial and affirmation is an elaborate method of auto-suggestion. Mrs. Eddy herself lends credibility to this view when she discusses in *Science and Health* a typical example of suggestibility. For example, she writes: " A felon, on whom certain English students experimented, fancied himself bleeding to death, and died through that belief, when there was only a stream of warm water trickling over his arm. Had he known this was but a belief, he would have risen above it." This story has been told and re-told thousands of times with innumerable variations, as indicating the effect of suggestion upon an individual in a state of heightened susceptibility. So also, in Christian Science, it is believed by some that the contemplation of God as the solution to all problems has in immediate quietening effort upon the mind, as though one has realised that there is someone who will help in the hour of need. This inner relaxation, with its elimination of stresses and strains in the mind, is said to be the *sine qua non* of success. It is just in such moments of complete quiet and inner peace, with its release of psychic tension, that a heightened susceptibility to auto-suggestion develops. Suggestions can then be given which will be embraced by whole mind. Lapsing into unconscious psychological levels, the suggestions will begin their subtle intangible work upon the entire personality, resolving conflicts within, stimulating the powerful drives and abilities of the individual, transforming him from an indecisive sick individual into a positive dynamic personality of whom the world will be obliged to take notice.

Possibly one of the easiest ways—though not necessarily the most accurate—to conceive how such a personality transformed by suggestions or by the Christian Science beliefs, is able to impinge upon his environment, is to imagine that everyone bears with him an electro-magnetic field comparable to that surrounding a magnet. We must conceive this electro-magnetic sphere surrounding a man as being charged with his thinking and feeling. If this thinking and feeling is negative, revolving incessantly about fear or failure, and sickness and sin, they will negatively charge his magnetic field. The individual himself maybe totally unaware of this field, even as the rest of the world is. But other people, without realising consciously the reason for it, will react towards him in a negative and repulsive way. Their own electro-magnetic fields are obliged by the process of induction and sympathy to vibrate at the same rate as does the negatively charged field. Just as a piece of metal is obliged to gravitate towards a powerful magnet when brought within its field of activity, so also do other people gravitate to the sphere of a positively charged individual. Change the thinking and feeling by a contemplation of God's presence, by affirming or suggesting that one can participate in His divine power and substance, and immediately a vital change occurs in this magnetic sphere. It becomes positive and dynamic. Those with whom one comes in contact in the course of every day life will unconsciously vibrate to the change, and their reactions alter accordingly. Then, instead of their attempting to thwart and hinder one as was their former wont, they now strive to be of service in many ways. Poverty then give place to plenty, for countless opportunities will present themselves whereby the peculiar properties of that individual will be given expression, in return for the economic privileges required. Sickness will fall away, because the suggestions will so affect the different cerebral and neurological structures that far-reaching and profound changes take place in the different cellular and visceral tissues, improving their function and structure. Social and marital and all other problems solve themselves, as these positive alterations in mental outlook occur.

There possibly are many factors other than suggestion responsible for the seemingly miraculous results which Christian Science brings about. But undoubtedly suggestion does play some part, regardless of how we attempt to explain it. And the results themselves cannot be questioned in the long run even though in the scientific sphere grave doubts are cast, to state but one type of criticism, upon Christian Science diagnosis. If the diagnosis is incompetent, doubt must be entertained as to the therapy. I feel, however, that even were the medical criticisms correct in assuming that Christian Science has affected and cured not organic disease but only functional and hysteria disorder, we should give credit where credit is due. Many a regular physician has found himself incompetent and incapable of treating a thorough-going case of hysteria. Even the psycho-analyst will readily admit that the psychological treatment of hysteria and neurosis is no easy matter, and he has to confess to many bitter failures in the course of professional practice. If therefore Christian Science assists such people, giving them a new lease on life, and a new interest and scope for their activities, then nothing in the least that we can say will alter the fact that it has accomplished much, regardless of whether the disease is organic or functional, structural or neurotic.

However, I question the medical prognosis that Christian Science is unable to affect favourably the course of organix disease. Once it is admitted anatomically and physiologically that mind is conterminous with the central nervous system, and that every tissue, even pathological and neoplastic tissue, has its own nerve supply, then given the right stimulus mental or neural impulses of a dynamic nature may be sent to those tissues. It only requires new arrangements of nerve pathways to alter diseased function. The modern psychiatric treatment of metrazol and insulin shock-therapy for psychotic states results, it is said, in new distributions of neurological pathways so that inner adjustments can take place. That it is possible to affect the involuntary nervous system by means of suggestion has undoubtedly been proven by experiments in hypnotic therapy. Whatever may or may not be the last word to be said about hypnosis, it has given us a fair idea of what psychotherapeutic treatment will do for the physical organism. The drugless practitioners of the chiropractic and osteopathic schools have their credit innumerable cures of organic lesions, cures engineered solely through spinal manipulation, resulting in improved neurological function to those tissues. Any system which therefore is able to make a powerful impression upon the different levels of the central nervous system can therefore bring about these apparently miraculous results. I see no reason whatsoever for doubting the testimony of Christian Scientists, nor can I question the statement that successful metaphysical treatment is able to produce the results it claims. All we can say, scientifically, is that we do not understand how these results are produced. Whether the results are due to suggestion, or whether other far more subtle and intangible factors enter into the therapy and transformations, is for future investigators to decide. Time alone will see these perplexing problems thrashed out, and illumination thrown on such highly complex matters.

PART II
New Thought

CHAPTER SIX
I.N.T.A.

Several years ago while in England, I had occasion to talk to some members of one phase of the Anglican Church popularly known as "high church." Whereas the "low church" was characterised by utter simplicity and freedom from elaborate ritual and pomp, the "high church" more closely resembled the form of Roman Catholicism than anything else I had previously known. And I had often wondered where lay the difference between the "high church" or Anglo-Catholicism and Roman Catholicism. A friend one day summarised this distinction for me, not too accurately perhaps, but succinctly and tersely enough. He said that in the former there was no Pope.

Now it is this difference which impresses itself upon me when the relationship between the New Though Movement and the Christian Science Church is considered. The latter is characterised not only by the most uncompromising orthodoxy so far as its metaphysics is concerned, but also by an absolute deification and worship of the person of Mrs. Eddy. She is veritably the Pope of that Church. Though now long since dead, yet her influence, her writing, and her pronouncements still persist as though she were alive today. Her books serve as the final authority from which there is no appeal whatsoever. Relatively speaking, the New Thought groups are comparable to the Protestant reform. In fact painfully so. Just as the Protestant Churches now number several hundreds of different sects, each differentiated from the other by minute doctrinal controversies, so also in the New Thought movement. It comprises dozens of different sects and cults, each one laying emphasis on some particular point as against the other. Moreover, there is no central authority to lay down acceptable doctrines or rules of procedure as in the Christian Science Church. True, there is an International New Thought Alliance. But actually this organisation is a mere figurehead. Its officers are utterly without national or international authority and their power exists only within the small component circles in which they function.

The Alliance is in reality a federation of the more important and the larger organizations teaching metaphysics outside the Christian Science Church. It is best described by the declaration of fundamental principles that it adopted at the St. Louis Congress in 1917. These principles and this declaration have been steadfastly adhered to by all the component elements of the movement in the intervening years. Therefore I can do no better than to quote the declaration in its entirety, in order to give at the outset some notion of what the Alliance is and what the movement as a whole stands for:

"We affirm the freedom of each soul as to choice and as to belief, and would not, by the adoption of any declaration of principles, limit such freedom. The essence of the New Thought is Truth, and each individual must be loyal to the Truth he sees. The windows of his soul must be kept open at each moment for the higher light, and his mind must be always hospitable to each new inspiration.

"We affirm the Good. This is supreme, universal and everlasting. Man is made in the image of the Good, and evil and pain are but the tests and correctives that appear when his thought does not reflect the full glory of this image.

"We affirm health, which is man's divine inheritance. Man's body is his holy temple. Every function of it, every cell of it, is intelligent, and is shaped, ruled, repaired, and controlled by mind. He whose body is full of light is full of health. Spiritual healing has existed among all races in all times. It has now become a part of the higher science and art of living the life more abundant.

"We affirm the divine supply. He who serves God and man in the full understanding of the law of compensation shall not lack. Within us are unused resources of energy and power. He who lives with his whole being, and thus expresses fullness, shall reap fullness in return. He who gives himself, he who knows and acts in his highest knowledge, he who trusts in the divine return, has learned the law of success.

"We affirm the teaching of Christ that the Kingdom of Heaven is within us, that we are one with the Father, that we should not judge, that we should love one another, *that we should heal the sick, that we should return good for evil*, that we should minister to others, and that we should be perfect even as our Father in Heaven is perfect. These are not only ideals, but practical, everyday working principles.

"We affirm the new thought of God as Universal Love, Life, Truth and Joy, in whom we live, move, and have our being, and by whom we are held together; that his mind is our mind now, that realising our oneness with Him means love, truth, peace, health and plenty, not only in our own lives but in the giving out of these fruits of the Spirit to others.

"We affirm these things, not as profession, but practice, not on one day of the week, but in every hour and minute of every day, sleeping and waking, not in the ministry of the few, but in a service that includes the democracy of all, not in words alone, but in the innermost thoughts of the heart expressed in living the life. 'By their fruits ye shall know them.'

"We affirm Heaven here and now, the life everlasting that becomes conscious immortality, the communion of mind with mind throughout the universe of thoughts, the nothingness of all error and negation, including death, the variety in unity that produces the individual expressions of the One-Life, and the quickened realisation of the indwelling God in each soul that is making a new heaven and a new earth.

"We affirm that the universe is spiritual and we are spiritual beings. This is the Christ message to the Twentieth Century, and it is a message not so much of words as of works. To attain this, however, we must be clean, honest and trustworthy and uphold the Jesus Christ standards as taught in the Four Gospels. We now have the golden opportunity to for a real Christ movement. Let us build our house upon this rock, and nothing can prevail against it. This is the vision of the ALLIANCE."

The great Swiss psychologist Dr. Carl G. Jung makes some fascinating remarks in his book *Psychology and Religion* upon the relative psychology of the Protestant and the Catholic, curiously apt to this present consideration. What he says in that book applies equally well to my differentiation between the Christian Scientists and the adherents of the New Thought groups. "Protestantism was, and still is," he wrote, "a great risk and at the same time a great opportunity. If it keeps on disintegrating as a church, it succeeds in depriving man of all his spiritual safeguards and means of defense against the immediate experience of the forces waiting for liberation in the unconscious mind. Look at all the incredible savagery going on in our so-called civilised world, all of which is derived from human beings and their mental condition! Look at the devilish means of destruction?...This ghastly power is mostly explained by fear of the neighboring nation, which is supposed to be possessed by a malevolent devil. As nobody is capable of recognising where and how much he himself is possessed and unconscious, one simply projects one's own unconscious upon the neighbour...All one's neighbours are ruled by an uncontrollable fear just like oneself...The Protestant is left to God alone. There is no confession, no absolution, no possibility of any kind of an atoning opus divinum...Owing to this fact the Protestant conscience has become wakeful, and this bad conscience has acquired a disagreeable tendency to linger and to make people uncomfortable...The Protestant is left to his tension, which can continue to sharpen his conscience...If a Protestant survives the complete loss of his church and still remains a Protestant, that is, a man who is defenseless against God and is no longer shielded by the walls or by communities, he has the unique spiritual chance of immediate religious experience."

The Protestant reform made spiritual freedom possible, and inaugurated a concept of growth that had not been generally possible within the boundaries of the Roman Church. Nevertheless, insofar as it robbed the individual of the adequate defense mechanisms of church authority and tradition, it made him a more sensitive being. This sensitivity had its useful as well as disagreeable aspects. Similarly with the New Thought associations. Certainly they represent the utmost in spiritual freedom—but they have also paved the way for incalculable schism. So far from representing divine unity, the spirit of the heresy of separateness was rife. Each recognises in its own way the validity of the quest for God and the conquest of sin, sickness and poverty. They have broken away from fixed doctrinal formulation as well as, for example, from formal stereotyped methods of conducting meetings and services. This difference becomes apparent following a visit to a Christian Science Church and, let us say, a service of any branch of either the Unity School of Christianity or of the Divine Science churches. In the one case there is an air of complete formalism, even of rigidity, while in the latter there is a flexibility—though I cannot say ease—which at least permits the entry of some degree of spontaneity into worship. Moreover, in Christian Science, Mrs. Eddy's interpretations of philosophy and her stilted exegesis of the Bible are accepted at the final revelation. None would dream of questioning its validity. No one may discuss it freely or volunteer independent interpretation. In the New Thought movement, a free interpretation of metaphysics characterised by a fine flight of imagination and the exercise of intuition is not only permitted by actually encouraged as the one factor which will make for progress. The entire movement represents a strong individualistic activity. New and highly suggestive interpretations of Bible stories are forwarded in the light of metaphysics and a quasi-psychological science, and use made of them in practical manner. Spiritual freedom is the hallmark of the New Thought.

There is another factor which establishes the relationship similar to the ecclesiastical one described at the beginning. In spite of the fact that the I.N.T.A. declares itself to be the historical descendent of the teachings of Quimby which in part was previously described, yet the true facts seem to indicate that the New Thought sects are really schism-of Mrs. Eddy. Though this statement will not be acceptable to many in the movement, the truth might as well be stated. From that point on, we can move forward progressively to ever greater achievement. The misconception can only act as a stubborn fixation to the past, and prove a handicap to further development. In a book recently published under the auspices of the I.N.T.A., *Mind Remakes Your World*—which incidentally can be highly recommended as a fine presentation of metaphysics—there are thirty-six chapters describing metaphysical theories and practices by as many writers and New Thought leaders. These essays bear very little relationship to the basic teachings of Quimby and his disciples, even though he is mentioned two or three times by name. There is a resemblance, but that is as far as it goes. I call attention principally to the chapters on Absolute Science, Divine Science, and the teachings of the various Homes of Truth as they are called. They so clearly and definitely reflect the Christian Science point of view and even terminology that I feel there can be no doubt of origins. In fact, the books Christian *Mind-Healing* by Harriet Hale Rix, and *Lessons in Truth* by Emilie Cady, for example, are so definitely Christian Science in tone that we can safely assume that they are systematisations and organised classifications of Mrs. Eddy's rather unwieldy tome.

Actually, a careful study of Horatio Dresser's book *The History of the New Thought Movement* reveals that many of the more popular and better known New Thought teachers derived from the Christian Science Church. Emma Curtis Hopkins for example is one of the principal teachers we can include in this category. With a number of other people, Mrs. Hopkins left the Christian Science Church after a personal dissension with Mrs. Eddy. She trained, either directly or indirectly, many students who have since come to form large and powerful organisations of their own. Charles and Myrtle Fillmore, the founders of Unity, are special examples, and I have reserved a whole chapter for a sympathetic discussion of the Fillmores, their work and their organisation. The founders of Divine Science and Homes of Truth likewise were disciples of Mrs. Hopkins. Mrs. Elizabeth Towne, the editor of the *Nautilus*, one of the most popular New Thought publications, was at one time the student of Mr. Shelton and Mr. Paul Militz, who were likewise trained by Mrs. Hopkins. The representation of Quimby in the present-day field of applied metaphysics is so very slight as almost to be negligible. Most of the work and teaching today is, without doubt, modified Christian Science. That the New Thought people today claim to be in descent as it were from Quimby, can readily be explained. It is due quite understandably to the fact that they do not wish to acknowledge their indebtedness to Mrs. Eddy whom they feel, anyway, initially derived her knowledge and technique from Quimby. Whether this latter conclusion is accurate or not may be left to the discrimination of the reader who has carefully examined the evidence of a former chapter.

Not that it really makes a particle of difference. The validity of New Thought is not in the least questioned or abrogated because of its origin. No one would question the value of the Episcopalian or the Methodist Church because in the final analysis they are schismas from the Roman Church. Each has its own place, and each caters to a different group of people with different spiritual needs. However, a study of origins does yield useful information necessary for the sake of our intellectual equipment.

From the psychological point of view, some very interesting implications can be deduced from this relationship. On the basis of known facts, we could speculate on possible reasons for people having entered the New Thought sphere instead of remaining in the Christian Science Church. The problem is not too dissimilar to speculation onto the unconscious psychic life of many sincere people who become communists. Instead of labouring peaceably to evolve the present state into the ideal democratic organisation it could be, the communists seek to overthrow it by violence. Revolution as a dynamic concept is implicit in the Marxian ideology. It is a necessary conclusion in view of their biological and dialectical outlook upon evolution.

Most of the communists I have met are people consumed with an underlying and intense hatred of their own father. This hatred has persisted from early childhood in almost total unconsciousness. The hatred is there all right, but they are not in the least degree aware of its nature or origins. Father, to the infantile mind, is the central authority of the household, running the entire organisation with a rod of iron, and possessing all things within that domain. If, for a variety of complex reasons, a revolt occurs against him, it is likely to spread to everything that may, no matter how remotely, symbolise father. The state, for example, is the supreme arbiter of justice and represents absolute authority. The State is the fatherland, and the chief executive, whether King, Premier or President, is the father surrogate himself. All these may become substitute symbols of father. When, at puberty, the dormant hatred for father is aggravated by the impetuous desire for growth, everything father represents is unhesitatingly discarded in favour, preferably of just the opposite. If father is a conservative, unconsciously the boy swings into the opposite direction and becomes a communist. If father is an atheist, the boy turns to dogmatic religion. If father is a Catholic, the authority and wisdom of the church will surely be challenged. If father already is a Protestant, then some other sect is liable to be chosen. Whatever is dear to father becomes the butt of this imperious urge to overcome that is present in the youth.

This same mechanism apparently prevails in relation to the Christian Science Church. Those who enter it desire unequivocal authority. They are people who have accepted parental authority without question; even seek it with fervour and joy. They have never found the need for discarding it. Their psychology is that of an infant, happy and secure in the love and favour of its parents. The New Thought devotees on the other hand, insofar as they enter a heterogeneous field which is totally unorganised and characterised by dissension and by multiplicity of beliefs, evince in their very choice of philosophy an unconscious attitude of rebellion. And not merely rebellion in the abstract sense, but a definite, even though unconscious, revolt against parental authority. In that sense they represent a movement than can grow, unfold and evolve. And as such it has unlimited possibility.

Such unconscious trends can be sublimated in part. But in part only. Unless the tendency to revolt is understood consciously, it too may fixate the individual to the past. If the unconscious infantile conflict remains unsolved on the conscious level, it may continue to exist as one of the "dog-faced demons in whom there is no trace of virtue," to arise at any subsequent period in life, when the threshold of physical and mental resistance has become lowered. At such a period of life, they are apt to arise and create trouble and disease. Mary Baker Eddy's phobia about malicious animal magnetism, which dogged her to the day of her death, undoubtedly was due to the mobilisation of similar unconscious emotional residues. Due to her various squabbles with those around her, the earlier infantile conflicts were mobilised as though by sympathy. Because they were unconscious, and because she was utterly helpless to resist these overwhelming psychological attacks in spite of her belief in the redeeming virtues of spirit. All such unconscious conflicts become projected upon the outside world, according to the now familiar mechanism of paranoia and psychosis.

The attack from repressed aggressive emotions, which long had existed in an unconscious state, issues from a source outside of the conscious ego. Since the average individual in his ignorance has no direct awareness of the existence of unconscious states of mind and feeling, he is unable to refer such disturbances to an inner sphere. Hence it is obvious that their source can only be understood to be in the external world. Therefore the neurotic refers such psychic pressure to people and things within the immediate or remote environment. People attack him on the mental plane with magnetism or electricity, with evil thoughts, with telepathic impulses. These phenomena are commonplace to the psychiatrist.

Mrs. Eddy's fears followed a familiar pattern and can be similarly explained. She stands as the type and symbol of large numbers of people within the metaphysical movement as a whole who have powerfully repressed their own strong and highly charged feelings that date back to the tender years of infancy. What happened to her has occurred, I know, to many another figurehead in similar movements. The unconscious aggressive tendencies, and inner rebellious attitudes that are involuntarily depicted by many of the New Thought advocates, would be far better dealt with on the plane of the infantile psyche rather than be still further repressed. To repress them means they will become projected onto the outside world. And the very emotion one refused to face within, now confronts one without. That is not to say that I advocate a crushing of the inner revolt by a return to Christian Science. It is little use employing the orthodox metaphysical techniques without adequate understanding. Psychological analysis of the classical academic type is invaluable to provide such insight. Metaphysics could be tremendously improved and transformed into an inconceivably powerful instrument for the redemption of mankind were it allied to modern psychological knowledge. The analytical techniques, rather than the methods of blind denial and ignorant suppression, should preferably be employed as a preliminary process of cleaning house. Then into the purified sphere of the mind, the God forces and higher realisation could be awakened by the usual affirmations. But then dwelling upon God as the omnipresent mind and universal love, some realisation may be achieved of this eternal presence and truth.

The origins of the new movement as such date back to Quimby and to Mrs. Eddy. However, among those who visited Quimby were at least three other people in the movement beside Mary Baker Eddy. These became responsible for much of the interest later displayed in Mind-Healing—Julius Dresser, the woman who later became his wife, and Rev. W. F. Evans. In 1863, the Rev. Warren Felt Evans of Claremont, N. H., visited Quimby after having been in poor health for several years. He had suffered from a nervous breakdown coupled with a chronic disorder that had failed to respond to current methods of medical treatment. Clearly it was psychogenic, requiring specific psychotherapy. Not only was Rev. Evans healed of his maladies, but became so deeply impressed by Quimby's practice and teachings that he studied the new method. Later, having first developed the implied philosophy in his own terms, he began to apply it.

By profession a clergyman of the New Church, he was an ardent exponent of Swedenborg's teachings. He was familiar with idealistic philosophy and was able to grasp fundamental principles and to think them out for himself. He had all the preliminary essentials so far as spiritual principles were concerned, but he had lacked a method to make practical application of that spiritual theology. Mr. Quimby gave him the impetus with the idea that "Disease being in its root a wrong belief, change that belief and we cure the disease."

From the date of his cure, Mr. Evans became known as an exponent of the new philosophy that stressed a spiritual point of view and a mind-healing system. In 1869, he published from Boston his first book on the subject, *The Mental Cure,* which was succeeded in 1872 by *Mental Medicine,* and by *Soul and Body* in 1875. It is significant to note that all three were published before the appearance of *Science and Health with a Key to the Scripture.* It is usually believed that because these three books, the forerunners of the New Thought literature, were published prior to Mrs. Eddy's work, that New Thought as such had some degree of development independent of Christian Science. This may well be true. But, as I hope to show, the more prominent teachers who became the later exponents of the different schools of New Thought were originally dissenting Christian Scientists—apostates from Mrs. Eddy. It is from their work and their efforts that the majority of the present-day metaphysical organisations and societies have their origin, most certainly not from the writings of the Rev. Mr. Evans, however commendable and salutary they may have been.

The starting point of Mr. Evans' systems was the idea of God, regarded as the source of all life in the universe. Man was created by the divine life to be an image of that life. Hence in his inmost essence he is divine, and this divinity remains untainted regardless of the vicissitudes through which he passes. The mind is not formless and unsubstantial. It consists of a real substance, that is spiritual substance, formed according to the divine ideal, and it pervades the body, being co-extensive with the physical organism. Thus the body corresponds to the interpenetrating spirit, and changes brought about in the spirit manifest in the bodily organism. There is antagonism between the inmost essence and the egoity of man. This inner spiritual conflict must necessarily reflect itself in bodily tissues. From this conflict there derives the mental and physical unhappiness and misery which man experiences.

Love, he said, is our very life. It is central, fundamental. When we act from love we act from the divine life in us. The divine love within us may become "our fountain of health." Disease, in essence, is mental not physical, springing from the conflict between the mind and the will, between the intellectual and emotional components of the self. Insofar as he propounded this view, he is scientific in a modern sense. Disease, he wrote, springs from some false idea which has attained too startling a prominence. How this prominence arose however, has been left for Freud to answer in more recent times. The restoration of the balance is the cure of the soul, hence the body too. Mr. Evans made extensive employment of Swedenborg's teachings with regard to the spiritual body, which is considered the seat of all sensation, agreeing with Quimby that the physical body in itself is destitute of feeling and intelligence. Sensation is a mental or spiritual phenomenon. Further on disease, he wrote that it is only the outward effect of the inner disturbance. The symptoms are not the disease. The body is incapable of generating a disease by itself. In one sense, all disease in origin is a kind of insanity. This is surely a salutary concept, and one which could be stressed again and again. Cure is the attainment of sanity. The production of the desired mental state of supreme sanity is not altogether possible by the mere human self unaided. Some reliance has to be placed upon the higher life, so that the mind can receive the influx of the divine and heavenly spirit. "Such...is the normal state of every soul." And we therefore can never be wholly well or sane "until we come into the divine order of our existence."

The divine impulse, somehow, is perverted within us. And our "love terminates in self, and we become the centre of the universe." Selfishness then, or as we would say today Narcissism, is at the root of our troubles. But Narcissism, or the deflection of love upon ourselves, is only the result of our once having felt unloved. Confidence in self becomes shattered by such a realisation and upon the ruin of the ego is erected this false and diseased state of self-love. "Disease is only a state of supreme selfishness."

"The sexual and conjugal love is most intimately connected with the inmost life of the spirit, and is the fountain of more unhappiness or misery than originates with any other affection, according as it is properly controlled, or left to a disorderly activity and indulgence," Insofar as Mr. Evans enunciated this truth, he was not far from our modern psychological view.

However, the true significance of the etiology of neurosis, so far as sexuality is concerned, seems never to have been divined before Freud's epoch-making discoveries. It is true that the love problem, using this term in its widest sense, is at the root of most of our evils. Most psychologists would gladly concede that were it possible to adjust satisfactorily the love life of an individual, almost all of his other problems would disappear by themselves. It is this basic insecurity with regard to love, this involvement in self-love because of childish fears of losing this most precious of all human affections, which persist unconsciously throughout life, nullifying all our works. The sexual characteristics become attached only secondarily to this larger and greater problem of love. And it is a mistaken notion to assume, as some have assumed, that Freud has pronounced sexuality as the root of our problems. It is not sexuality as such, but the fears and ignorance related to sexuality. Fear, shame and guilt, regardless of what they become attached to, are grounded in ignorance. I am always reminded, when dealing with this problem of ignorance, of the Buddhist view that there is no sin other than ignorance. Were this one factor eradicated, all other sins—of greed, sensuality, lack of control, etc.—by themselves would be impossible. The knowledge of the true self, "the essence of mind which is intrinsically pure" has been lost, and as a result every kind of sin has become manifested. In one Chinese Buddhist text, the *Sutra of Wei Lang*, the whole problem is stated with unexcelled simplicity. "The wisdom of enlightenment is inherent in the mind of each one of us. But it is only because of delusion under which the mind works that we fail to realise it ourselves and have to seek the advice and guidance of the teacher. Now you must know that so far as Buddha-nature (the Christ-consciousness) is concerned, there is no difference between enlightened man and an ignorant man. The one knows it, the other doesn't." The whole matter could hardly be stated with greater cogency or in simpler language.

This complex of fears and hates, ignorantly generated, in turn has become attached to the larger emotional problem of parental love. It is the entire mass of conflicts developed around love and infantile sexuality which are responsible for the extraordinary neurotic development that it is the work of the psychologist to unravel. It is no question simply of controlling or indulging sexuality which creates happiness or unhappiness. In reality it concerns a far more important matter. It means the eradication of the psychic inhibitions and baby fears that have clustered around the base and root of our emotional life. Control or reasonable indulgence follow automatically by themselves without further to-do, when the stream of love flows smooth and unsullied from the deep vital wells existing within the soul. It is the perverted images of infantile unawareness that become mixed with that divine flow to which we can relate our major problems.

Mr. Evans further wrote that "To believe that we are well, or that we are going to become so, excites a spiritual force within us that goes far towards making us so." Fear does the opposite, producing equally striking effects in the generation of diseased conditions of the body. However we have to distinguish between a healthy fear, which is the beginning of wisdom, and the neurotic fear and anxiety which presage trouble. Were we without the former, the whole of mankind by now would have been exterminated. Normal fear is our guarantee against disaster and death. In the face of the vast order of the universe, we would do well to have fear—awe, possibly, would be the better term. We are so small and insignificant—the processes of nature so tremendous, extensive, and powerful. The individual without this type of fear confesses immediately to his own lack of imagination and true appreciation of life.

The neurotic fear, however, is of a totally different order. It appears to be like a free-floating body of anxiety which is ready to attach itself to any situation whatsoever that may present itself. Let any unusual, or even customary event occur, and this body of fear immediately attaches itself to it, and the individual becomes afraid. In those people, for example, who suffer from any of the common phobias and anxiety neuroses, this is the most frequent reaction. The fear of crossing the street, of going down into a subway station, of ascending a tall building, of being in a small room—these are typical fears totally irrational in nature, and to explain which we have to look in other directions.

The direction we look into is the unconscious side of psychic life. There we find that the root of many fears is desire. Today we have come to understand that many wishes and desires of the early years of our lives have been retained in all their perennial freshness in the unconscious side of our minds. They have been retained in their youthfulness and potency because their force has never been expended through expression. Never have they been permitted to come into open manifestation. Their nature was not originally acceptable to the moral self. This latter side of the personality, punitive and critical that it is, has its origin in an absorption of the parental attitudes that the child has experienced. These attitudes become built up within the psyche to form an independent mental factor, the superego. It acts as the parents would have acted. To this moral self, the Freudian censor, such wishes were not acceptable. They were even obnoxious. Hence they were repressed and inhibited. But though repressed, they live on.

By the process of repression, the wish becomes dynamically converted into its opposite. Fear and wish may be regarded as two opposite sides of a single coin—equivalent yet opposite terms. This process of conversion is a constant phenomenon observed with regard to the activities of the unconscious psyche. Aggressiveness that is suppressed becomes converted into an unnatural timidity and shyness. Repressed cruelty becomes changed into mere sentimentalism. Objectionable wishes, by the same process, become converted into fear. The conversion, primarily has the effect of serving as a defense mechanism. So long as the fear and anxiety prevails, the individual is safe. He need never succumb to these powerful but objectionable desires that have been thrust from him into the outer darkness. He thus protect himself, in ignorance, from himself. But though thus defended, he is unable to get rid of the fear. The fear remains.

One of the best and most readily appreciated examples of this is the fear evinced by an occasional unmarried and elderly woman. Before retiring, every window in the house must be carefully tested, the underneath of the bed is examined, doors are open and closed, and the closets are peered into in order to ascertain that no one is hiding. This becomes a nightly observance, for the fear has evolved itself into a thoroughgoing ritual or obsession. Behind such a fear it is not difficult to perceive a wish lurking in the darkness. That is not to surmise that the woman now wishes to find a man in her room. Not at all. But it is easy to imagine an earlier period in her life when the life urges were strong and imperious and her fantasy rich and vivid. It would not have been difficult for her to have desired ardently the entrance of some fairy prince, a figment of a girl's imagination, to possess her and ravish her with adolescent love. But the moral self is adamant, regarding such adolescent fantasies with considerable misgivings. They are repressed and, in their stead, shame and guilt make their appearance. The child does not know that such emotions and fantasies are perfectly natural in those tender idyllic years. She revolts in shame and disgust from herself, so that the entire mechanism of repression is set into operation. The feelings and fantasies are repressed and forgotten, but they live on in the unconscious where they slowly become changed into fear. Fear replaces the wish, and to the extent that the wish was intense and powerful, so also does the fear become.

In *Christian Mind-Healing*, Miss Harriet Hale Rix, give an example of a woman who was tormented by fear of mice to the point where she fell victim to spells of agitation and nervous prostration. Unable to get rid of this irrational fear, she studied metaphysics, no doubt under Miss Rix's supervision. One day she determined to put her knowledge to the test and so went down to the basement, all trembling and frightened, to "beard the lion in his den." After a while of waiting, a mouse appeared and her courage sank so low that she had to run upstairs out of the basement. A little bit ashamed of her fear, she descended again, praying meanwhile for faith and courage. Again the mouse appeared. This time she stayed and began to notice its actions and the intelligent use of its paws in handling food and in cleaning its body. As she watched, thus objectively, her fear departed to be replaced, so it is said by love. It even ran over her foot, and her sense of rejoicing in the conquest of her phobia was great because she knew that "perfect love casteth out all fear."

Now commendable as such treatment is—and as active therapy it is valuable—it yielded nothing to the lady in question as to the why and the wherefore of her phobia. She was no wiser as to its meaning after her cure than before. It is the hall-mark of modern man that the asks why. No longer is he content merely to accept things on faith. The phenomena of life, whatever they are, have to be rationally correlated to the rest of his intellectual knowledge. If only we could realise that the very thing that we fear is, in reality, our saviour and redeemer, no doubt we could adopt a different and more highly intelligent attitude towards it. What good is it to have overcome a fear unless and until we know why it was that we have created it? If the outer world mirrors perfectly the status of the soul inside, we can learn much of the inner man by a study of the environment in which he finds himself. If fear is there, and the object of that fear is known to be irrational, how much wiser would it not be to take the trouble to investigate our own minds and eradicate its cause? Otherwise, no matter how successfully treated from the superficial standpoint, this body of fear which still remains intact and unbroken, can attach itself to any other phenomenon that may happen to present itself. I should be curious to know more of the subsequent events in the life of this good lady who overcame her fear of the mouse.

It is here, in my opinion, that lies one of the inadequacies of the usual metaphysical treatment for fear. The individual consciously may desire to get rid of fear or sickness or any other manifestation of disease. But we must recall that the conscious personality is but one part, a small fraction of the entire personality. The unconscious aspect of the psyche is the dynamic part of the self. It is the machine shop of both mind and body. Hence wishes that have been thrust into that dark hinterland of the mind stand a far greater chance of working into open active manifestation than those of the conscious self. If the healer does not treat the unconscious self with its powerful wish-fears, his efforts in the final analysis must fail. Changes to the conscious self may be achieved—and that noticeably as in the instance quoted. But unless change are wrought in the deeper levels of the mind, to raise up these unconscious fears and wishes, they will remain obscured in spite of conscious progress. At a late date, when general psycho-somatic resistance has for any reason become lowered, they will commence to operate again in another sphere of activity.

Later, Mr. Evans began with renewed vigour a systematic study of philosophical idealism in order to find theoretical parallels for the therapeutic doctrine he had been enunciating. In the year 1881 he published a book *Divine Law of Cure*, which evinced familiarity with the writings of Berkeley, Fichte, Schelling and Hegel. Its fundamental doctrine is that to think and to exist are identical, and that every disease is the physical translation of a fixed idea of the mind and a morbid way of thinking. Correct the manner of thinking and regenerative changes commence within the body.

It was his particular form of expression which came to mark a new vogue in metaphysical writing in subsequent years, remarks Horatio Dresser. Evans' former books stressed to some extent the spiritual side of mind-healing. In this particular book, however, he began to lay emphasis on mind in such a way that later generations not trained to reason accurately beyond ambiguity, developed a system of pure suggestion. In place of spiritual metaphysic they employed transcendental philosophy. No longer did he stress the Swedenborgian ideas about love as the life of man, nor the necessary influx of the divine. Everything depended upon man's power to turn his thoughts into another direction. Stress was laid upon attention as the determining factor in the mental life. The term "mental science" was introduced by Mr. Evans with reference to the psychological aspect of the new therapeutism, and around

1882-8 it began to be used for the whole teaching. But the term "mental" had a definite spiritual significance for those who adhered to Quimby's teaching. It did not represent a therapy of mere auto-suggestion as much as it really implied "Christian" for those who believed that the new healing was accomplished by spiritual means.

It seems to me that those who followed Mr. Evans in using the terminology of auto-suggestion and mental science, were not very far wrong. Their efforts represented an attempt to express popularly their metaphysics in terms of applied psychology, however inadequate the psychology of their time was. Today we know more of psychology than did the writers of fifty and sixty years ago. Our knowledge of the unconscious aspects of the psyche has been immeasurably enriched, and through psychological analysis we have become familiar with many of the mechanisms by means of which it operates. We can appreciate the psychological interpretation today far more than could our forebears. They were surely on the right track. We must continue on the life formerly laid down—not wishing to whittle away the metaphysic, but attempting only to render it more intelligible and understandable in terms of the scientific concepts in common usage. The terminology of the old mental science school—employing concepts of suggestion, relaxation and the subconscious mind—was infinitely more intelligible to the layman than the outworn quasi-religious nomenclature of the metaphysicians. Today all old forms of religious thinking and feeling are rapidly being discarded. By all means let us thrown off these symbols of bondage to the past—but we must retain the worthwhile content stored in those symbols. Metaphysics, as such, is definitely worth survival in our day and age. But the metaphysical language is an atavistic relic of two thousand years ago.

The President of the International New Thought Alliance, Dr. John Seaman Garns has recently made a significant utterance which is corroborative of this conclusion. In the October-November, 1941 issue of *The New Thought Bulletin*, he notes that the tides of desire to participate in the new movement for psychological integration and spiritual redemption, are certainly rising. But, he adds, "we seem to lack effectiveness at a single point. Hard-headed business people who have examined and been impressed by the marvelous dynamic of this teaching, continually marvel at the fact *that it is not spreading more rapidly.* One of these, an advertising man, said to me not long ago, 'The trouble with your teaching in so many places in which I have heard it given, is that the teachers are not talking in terms of the interests and experiences of ordinary people. They state their principle in a vocabulary which the ordinary man of the street does not understand, instead of doing what we, as advertising people *must* do, demand of ourselves that we sell our goods in terms of people's desires and of their already active motives.'...To be practical then in the application of this principle, every lesson...should state those needs in such terms that the interest of the individual would be quickened—his desire stimulated—and his power of understanding lifted to the level of the truth which we have to give."

This is excellently stated and is worth emphasising again and again. The average person is not all interested in a religious terminology, which is a medieval barbarity. Most of them rebelled against, and discarded religion in their early teens. The modern age is one of scientific concepts. If the movement wishes to survive, it must fit its teaching into an acceptable system of nomenclature that is even now being developed. Those who still persist in the employment of an outworn and archaic verbiage, evince the fact that they are themselves tied to the past of their fathers and forefathers. They give notice to all that they are unable to move freely forward in the future. What wonder then, that the large mass of mankind will have nothing whatsoever to do with the scheme.

There is a robust selective instinct in the masses. The may not be able to reason adequately, nor to put their rational processes into suitable words. That their instinct makes them shy away, frightened and bewildered, from the statement of progressive metaphysics, whether of the New Thought or Christian Science variety, should give us pause. It must make us aware of the fact that we are not fitting our ideas into the form of the modern mind. We are swimming against the tide, bucking up against a strong wind. Success, the, cannot be ours. Let us go with the tide, altering here, modifying there, though ever retaining the central thought of the system. Some of the best examples that I have ever read in this direction were two books. One was written by Robert Collier entitled *The Secret of Gold*, written in very simple English, yet enriched with a host of examples, instances and parables. The other was *Practical Psychology* by Judge Simmons. These, while not perfect, at least indicate where we can go—with success and integrity.

The characteristic of this particular period of New Thought literature was, in one sense, determined by not merely accepting Rev. Evans' terminology on its face value, but by the wide interest in the phenomena of suggestion. Years earlier, in France, Liébault and Bernheim had come experimentally to the conclusion that in order to give suggestions to somebody's mind, hypnosis was not at all necessary. The *sine qua non* of the successful administration of suggestive therapy was a relaxed frame of mind and body. Hence, it began to dawn upon a number of enterprising people that this being so, any individual by relaxing sufficiently, could give himself the appropriate suggestions. Recourse need not be had to any second person to administer the suggestions. These could be self-administered. Thus a vast literature arose along these lines, catering to people urgently in need of help.

What the people wanted was above all their physical and mental health. They were not especially interested in metaphysics as such, nor in the possibilities of the transformation of character. They simply desired to regain their bodily and inner health so as to be able to function adequately and make the most of their lives. Therefore there was a very workable conception in the very simple teaching derived from Evans' that "disease is an error of the mind." All that needed to be done was to set into operation a different type of thinking. This could be done the most readily by a simple process of auto-suggestion. Naturally this was encompassed about with a religious terminology. And from one angle, it was well to do so, for the faith and expectancy that religion awakens could prove to be the dynamic factor to hurtle the suggestions through the inhibiting barriers of the mind into the creative levels of spirit.

For the average person the new movement amounted to a method of healing that gave him back his health. As such it assumed great significance. An individual would study for a while with one of the successful metaphysicians, take a course of several class lectures, succeed in making one or more startling cures, and then start out to heal and teach in his own right. There was no authoritative textbook, no generally accepted leader. Each person went about his business in his own way. In time, the meetings that they organised were devoted to an exposition of the new healing modality. This came to take the place of the regular church services that people were wont to attend. Instead of the prayer service, a period of silence was inaugurated for healing purposes. In place of the sermon, a lecture on the simple principles of metaphysics and auto-suggestion. Moreover, the meetings were held on a Sunday, so that gradually a definite religious significance became attached to the therapeutism of this phase of New Thought.

Its metaphysical colouring tended to attract to the movement clergymen and ministers of various liberal denominations, and they, because of their training and greater ability, came to take over the meetings and provide leadership. The first of these independent societies in Boston was named "Church of the Divine Unity." Evidently it symbolised the new trend away from the old sterile theologies. Its name implied the spiritual teaching also, for they had come to understand that in their realisation of some kind of unity between man and God was renewed hope and redemption.

Much of the early defense work of Quimby as the innovator of the new spiritual technique was undertaken by both the Dressers, Julius and Annette, his wife. Not only did they write extensively, but they did a great deal of lecturing. The greater part of their object in so doing was to lay before the public the fact that it was not a revelation from God that inspired Mrs. Eddy's Christian Science, but the more evident and concrete fact that Quimby healed her of a paralysis. To them, possibly more than any other source, must we look for the real labour undertaken on behalf of the defense of Quimby. Yet, their work was not exclusively negative, that is in forcing home the realisation that Mrs. Eddy's revelation came originally from a human source. It was definitely positive in that they laboured far and wide to disseminate the fundamental principles of mental science.

We must remember that Dresser was in Belfast when Mrs. Eddy, then Mrs. Patterson, first visited Quimby asking for help. Not only so, but that after Quimby's death, Mr. Dresser received an urgent letter from Mrs. Eddy telling him that he should assume the cloak of the master and become a healer in his own right. She asked him to become Quimby's successor, obviously so that he could come down to Concord and finish the healing job that Quimby began. When he refused, it is not difficult to understand that Dresser was motivated by a sense of modesty, even of inferiority. He did not feel that he had evolved sufficiently in his understanding of the new mental science to be able to step into Quimby's shoes and heal far and wide, as had his master. Later however, when he realised that Mrs. Eddy's claim to divine realisation was threatening the prestige and integrity of his later master, he decided to do what he could to place on record what he knew to be true. Therefore he lectured here, there and everywhere. He wrote articles, essays and books on the principles of mental science. His son, Horatio Dresser, has continued in that same work, and I consider the son to be a writer of astonishing good sense, excellent literary ability, and fine idealistic principles. He too has laboured valiantly and earnestly on behalf of the New Thought.

The term metaphysics also came to indicate the relationship of the past with the present. This relationship developed because there arose an intense interest in what the teachers of former periods of time had laid down with regard to these metaphysical ideas now prevalent. Charles M. Barrows, who was formerly a school teacher, wrote a book, *Facts and Fictions of Mental Healing*. He looked back to the philosophies of India where he thought he might discover the origins of the New Thought. There is a definite relationship, as I have shown, between modern metaphysics and the Vedanta philosophy. By this date, 1887, the Theosophical Society had been in existence for many years, and since it had laid great stress on Hindu and Buddhist philosophy, such ideas, disseminated with great zeal though not with much tact, had become more commonly accessible than before. Moreover, he undertook an examination of the writings of Emerson, coming to realise that the New Thought was closely related to Emerson's passionate idealism. It was from that time that the wide interest among metaphysical students in Emerson definitely dates. Others around that time attempted to correlate Theosophy with the principles of New Thought. But not much ever came of this attempt. The original teachers of Theosophy were definitely opposed to the new therapeutism, preferring to stress a high moral and ethical outlook upon life, and an intellectual approach to philosophy.

This period also saw the birth of the first independent metaphysical periodicals. The Church of Divine Unity in Boston, mentioned before, was the first organisation to issue a periodical, *The Mental Healing Monthly*, devoted to the principles of mental science. In Chicago, Mr. A. J. Swarts, formerly one of the disciples of Mrs. Eddy, began to publish a magazine called *Mental Science Magazine*. Mr. Swarts' departure from the sanctum of Mrs. Eddy was the result of his own investigations into the origins of her revelation. He had absolutely nothing against her, and equally had no reason for defending Quimby. He was simply interested in the facts. Swarts paid a visit to Belfast, Maine. After the opportunity of reading excerpts from the popular press concerning Quimby's healing work, and to hear portions of the manuscript read to him by Quimby's son, he came to his own conclusions. He denounced Mrs. Eddy for plagiarism and for dishonesty—the metaphysics he retained, so becoming one of the early pioneers of the New Thought movement. *The Christian Metaphysician* was published around the same time by Mr. George B. Charles, while several other pioneers in the movement began *Wayside Lights* from Hartford, Conn. The Unity magazine, then entitled *Thought*, likewise made its first appearance about the same time from Kansas City, and another one called *Harmony*, edited by Mrs. M. E. Cramer, began in San Francisco. All these magazines stood for an independent interpretation of metaphysical healing, thus evincing the attitude of revolt against Mrs. Eddy. All had a common tendency freely to interpret the Scriptures, having as their object the revival of the true and primitive Christianity of the early centuries of the era, continuing their didactic work in the light of Quimby, Evans and Eddy.

Although Quimby had definitely employed the technique of silent treatment, as proved by *The Quimby Manuscripts*, one of the earliest New Thought treatise was called *Personified Unthinkables* by Miss S. S. Grimke. She interpreted metaphysics with special reference to the formulation of mental images and their possible effect on character and physique. Mrs. E. G. Stuart, the author of *The Healing Power of the Mind*, also was once a student of Mrs. Eddy, and she too brought forward into the movement the idea of the silent treatment. In 1885, she began a series of classes in Hartford, Conn. One of her own students was Mr. Leander E. Whipple who, in New York, established the *Metaphysical Magazine* in 1895, wrote several volumes on the general subject, and organised the American School of Metaphysics. Some of his ideas were typical of the day when the new therapeutism and its enthusiasm knew no bounds or limitations. Anger and ill-temper, so he claimed, when frequently indulged in, may produce muscular rheumatism. Under anger, valvular disease of the heart becomes established. In the final analysis, anger and fear, for him, were closely allied. Abnormal emotions affect the composition and consistency of the blood, hence the vital organs. The liver is disturbed in its function, and thus malarial symptoms of pigmentation are the outcome. Biliousness, typhoid and puerperal fevers follow upon some violent outbreak of temper. The right remedy for these diseases is not drugs, but, so insisted Mr. Whipple, the establishment of correct mental action. When a change in thinking occurs, the physical organs are obliged to respond to the natural action envisioned by the mind. His method follows the now familiar pattern of emphasising the existence of God as the root and source of life and realising that man is made in the image of the divine life and mind and substance. The recognition of these facts, and the attempt to substitute strong dynamic and spiritual images for sick thoughts, are adequate to the restoration of health.

From one point of view, of course, Whipple's theory is absolutely correct. It seems somewhat offensive nevertheless to many modern minds, only because of the manner of presentation. However, we know that under the stimulus of any great emotion such as anger or fear, the supra-renal glands, which are two minute bodies located above the kidneys, are stimulated. Under such stimulus, these glands release into the bloodstream minute quantities of a powerful chemical substance which we name adrenalin. The effect of this hormone is primarily to stimulate all those structures supplied by the thoraco-lumbar portions of the sympathetic nervous system. That is to say, it dilates the pupil, augments cerebral circulation, accelerates the heart, and constricts the blood-vessels, with consequent heightened blood pressure. Adrenalin may be termed the emergency hormone, preparing the body for fight or flight. A man who is ready to run, fearful of his life, is a picture of just such changes as I have outlined.

These physiological changes, brought about through the intermediary of the adrenalin hormone, are actually the result of fear or anger. These emotions may be conscious, in which case, once the stimulating outer factor is removed, these phenomena subside.

But now let us imagine that certain emotions are in a state of repression. They have not been eliminated. They are merely forgotten, and so temporarily are out of sight. Their physiological result, however, is exactly the same. Unconscious emotions of fear and anger will produce very much the same effects as will a momentary conscious reaction of fear or anger. The emotions also have a dynamic effect upon the whole autonomic nervous system which supplies the all-important viscera of the body. In consequence, there is constant cerebral congestion, chronic hypertension, a fast heart and rapid respiration, and other complex metabolic reactions. In the long run, pathology and organix change will have to occur to compensate for this demand for increased function. The high blood pressure alone—if it is a true or essential hypertension—must inevitably bring about cardio-vascular-renal disease, and from that point onward, anything can happen.

If metaphysical pursuits can somehow release these unconscious emotions which are responsible for physical deterioration—and we know they can—the glandular and neurological stimulation will cease, permitting normal physiological function. Every psychologist has known of radical changes in blood pressure in both cardiac and kidney function, within a few minutes after some hitherto unconscious problem has been brought to light and then discussed honestly and decently. Once some kind of avenue or outlet can be provided for these pent-up unconscious energies, many symptoms of themselves will subside. And this is true not merely of some physical diseases, but also of nervous and mental diseases also.

Another leader who began as a student of Mrs. Stuart, was C. B. Patterson. He adopted mental science in 1887, and established an alliance for teaching and publishing in New York City. He wrote a number of books which have enjoyed wide popularity. One of these was entitled, *What is New Thought?* Which is an adequate and well-written book—considerably above the level of much of the more recently written material. "Oneness is the great characteristic of Love," asserts that book; "whatever we love we become one with; true understanding comes with love...The ultimate end of life is to love, not to be loved, although that follows as a natural sequence, but the greatest desire, the greatest prayer of life should be to love with soul, and mind, and body; to radiate love, as the sun radiates light. In the sunshine of love, the mind knows no fear; sin and all its disastrous consequences have no place where love lives. Sin, disease, and death are only evidences of the lack of love in the life." This is a far better statement of fundamental principles than was made earlier in the Christian Science literature. Whatever may be said of New Thought, we must give high credit to the writers of this progressive movement that they have clarified many of the obscure issues raised by Mrs. Eddy, and stated them as she never could have. None of her direct followers could have done so either. Their blind adoration of the teacher, and the tacit belief that they must not criticise nor dilate upon her work, acted as a deterrent to spontaneous exegesis.

Coming back to Mr. Patterson's statements, we find him asserting that the only way to overcome a false condition of thought and feeling is through a "realisation of what we are in reality, sons of God, joint-heirs with Christ, endowed with eternal life and intelligence, a full recognition of our own innate powers and possibilities—possibilities as sons of God—powers derived directly from an Omnipotent Source." If therefore we lived with the consciousness of our true origin and divine nature, we could so affect the different parts of ourselves as to bring about a complete transformation of character.

"We could make the sub-conscious mind so that in time the sub-conscious would give back truth instead of a lie; would give us back riches instead of poverty; would render us health instead of disease; would bring peace instead of discord; yea, would give us eternal life instead of that lie of lies, a never-ending death." With that transformation achieved by a realisation of God's eternal presence within the soul as its guiding light, life would take on altogether new meanings for such an individual. "He would perceive the plan; he would bring the personal will into harmony with the universal Will so that he become a perfect instrument, through him divine Love and Intelligence would work for the upbuilding of a new, a more beautiful world—a world that would express both God's love and wisdom; and man, the son of God, would be its builder; a world devoid of everything that is transitory; a world in which there is no more night, no more sorrow and pain, no more disease or death, but a world of eternal life and light; a world that is a real manifestation of Love." It is a divine and powerful vision such as this that elevates New Thought and its literature beyond the sentimentalism and trash that has unfortunately found its occasional way into the movement.

In New York and Chicago, various phases of the movement began to appear at this time, under the leadership of teachers who rejected, as I have said, against Christian Science. They branched out independently for themselves agreeing in part with the mental scientists, and in part introducing ideas of their own. Mrs. Ursula N. Gestefeld adopted the term Science of Being, which for her was a practical idealism emphasizing mental or spiritual causality in contrast with the assumption that matter possesses independent life and intelligence. In the foreword of her book *The Builder and the Plan*, she gladly acknowledges the fact that she has utilised many of the fundamental propositions of Mrs. Eddy's *Science and Health*. She read this latter book sometime during 1884, enrolling the following month in one of Mrs. Eddy's classes for personal instruction. While she was studying, apparently she perceived some defect in Mrs. Eddy's exposition of truth principles. She asked for further light, but no adequate response, it is alleged, was elicited. "For seventeen years I have prosecuted the search for what was lacking, compelled by the sentiment 'Truth for authority, not authority for truth,' with results that have made me doubly thankful it was my privilege to have been taught by Mrs. Eddy as a preparation for the exploration of a previously unknown country." Mrs. Gestefeld's system of a metaphysics based largely upon

Christian Science, as presented in the above-mentioned book, is a well-thought out scheme, very simply and logically presented. Every phase of her mental process is represented in a short chapter devoted to a consideration of just that one topic, succeeded by a series of questions which the reader or student should pose to himself. The final chapter is devoted to pointing out the differences which exist between her own system and that of Mrs. Eddy. Throughout, no attempt is made to attack her former teacher, nor to utter derogatory remarks about Christian Science in favour of her own ideas. The tone of the whole work is on a very high moral and intellectual level.

The New Thought of this time fostered an exaggerated kind of impersonalism. Its leaders apparently reacted against what they considered to be Mrs. Eddy's egocentricity in such a way as to take only a modicum of credit to themselves when they individually began to teach. Thus, more than ever, the movement embodied protestantism, in the truest sense of the word. Likewise revolting against Mrs. Eddy, the movement rejected all personal revelation, substituting each man's quest for the authorised textbook.

But an attitude of this kind, fostered in revolt, can only produce a vigorous pendulum swing that would be psychologically equal to, if not worse than the original egotism revolted from. So much so, that the term mental science was employed by many writers in the West in a peculiarly technical sense. They said it was a kind of self-emancipation, which involved a new assertion of the self, for the one who had the courage to affirm the I. It led to a species of self-assertiveness and rugged individualism which, even today has not yet disappeared from the movement. This attitude has been one of the chief obstacles encountered in the attempt to organise all the warring metaphysical societies into a coherent and discrete whole.

In England the movement was characterised generally by the term Higher Thought, and a centre was organised having that name. Later, Judge Troward who was the author of several books, likewise named his version of the teaching Mental Science. In Boston, the name Higher Life was selected to describe the first

Church. There were innumerable variations employed. The Circle of Divine Ministry, the Home of Truth, the College of Divine Science, and the Unity School of Christianity, of which latter Horatio Dresser has remarked that "this is perhaps the best of all terms for the movement on its spiritual side." It probably is the most widely known as well as the largest of all the New Thought organisations, with Divine Science running a close second, and the Home of Truth was a good third. In all of them an element of high optimism prevailed. It is clear that the belief in the essential goodness of life, and the quest for the divinity in all things, was paramount from the beginning.

The writings of Henry Wood are regarded as among the most rational expressions of New Thought. Earlier in the history of the movement, when the mental science attitude rather than the metaphysical prevailed, his writings were most popular. His books though optimistic, are nonetheless characterised by a sobriety and quietness that is very welcome. They have that tone possibly because he had a successful business career when a nervous breakdown, so-called, overtook him. Many of the best physicians of his day were unable to help him. Today I suppose he could have been handled more intelligently than he was then. It is curious that both the Rev. Mr. Evans and Mr. Wood had nervous breakdowns, turning to metaphysics for their cure. That they did achieve a cure is indicative of the fact that their illnesses were psychogenic. That is to say, the causes of the disease were of a mental nature, hidden foci of emotional inhibition which were hidden from view in the unconscious levels of the mind.

It is a common sight, this. A man sacrifices all other interests to achieving a success in his chosen business profession and art. Then, when he has reached the pinnacle, and wishes to devote some of his energies and time to lighter pursuits, his mind breaks down and he is unable to function at all. What we have to realise is that in such a case the libido has been sublimated in a certain direction. The latter stands somehow in etiological relationship to some other earlier object which once was cherished above all other things. Usually that other object is a loved parent. In reality, a mother fixation has occurred. The whole emotional capacity of the individual becomes fixated upon that love-object, and while physically and mentally growth ensues, nevertheless the emotional life remains infantile. Constantly the personality seeks to sublimate that fixation in some occupation which, while serving as a channel for the expression of the energies which were emotionally bound to mother, yet seems superficially wholly unlike her and does not suggest her. Thereafter the individual works and slaves in that occupation, exhausting all his energies and powers in such a way as surely to suggest an individual lost in the glories of love. In fact, quite often we speak of an individual being madly in love with his work or art. And the vernacular, in these instances — does really express the truth. The individual is in love, not with his work, however, but with the infantile reality which the individual has become so wholly devoted to the exclusion of all else serves him merely as a symbol, in much the same way that a flag serves as a symbol for the country, or a cheque represents a certain sum of money that is deposited in a bank.

Having proved his deep and abiding love by succeeding in that business or art, the conscious personality of the individual finally comes to think it is time to devote himself to relaxation and the pleasures of life. But he finds, in effect, that he is totally unable to do so. It is almost as if he is driven by something outside of himself to go on, and not relax. We may compare it to having given the old man of the mountains a ride on one's back, and if fatigue develops, he forces one willy-nilly to continue, to the bitter end. Nor can he be thrown off. He clings and clings and clings. The unconscious implication is that the individual *must* go on. He is forced to slave, for once he lets up and relaxes, the awful truth hidden in the unconsciousness phases of the mind may arise to the surface. Then he may become acquainted with the true emotions that he has tried to hide these many years. It is too much of an inner ordeal. He cannot face the dread issue. There must be no relaxation. The work upon the symbol — business or art — must go on. The real truth of the mother fixation, with all its implications and correlatives, is too horrible to be accepted willingly and consciously. The psychic strain becomes too great to be borne. Few human minds can withstand such a conflict. The unconscious drive to continue, and the conscious wish to relax, is entirely too much—especially as this type of conflict usually happens when the physical forces of the body commence their decline towards the close of middle age, when the resistances of the entire personality are lowered. In sickness therefore, in the so-called nervous breakdown—which is a phase entirely without meaning—a solution to the problem is found. No individual can work when sick. Consequently the unconscious drives to continue work are relaxed, and in this compromise of sickness the conscious desire to let go is similarly fulfilled.

This is evidently the psychic background in the case of both the individuals referred to. And of many another too is this true. Since the sickness itself was psychogenic, being due to the desire to escape from the urgency of unconscious wishes that are not consciously recognised, both men found relief in the sphere of mental healing. Mr. Evans went to Quimby and was cured. Mr. Wood was treated successfully by several mental healers of his day. The similarity is worth noting. Afterwards they both worked with as much vigour and enthusiasm in their newly discovered realm as they had earlier in their former professions. A successful sublimation was achieved. Rev. Mr. Evans became the first populariser of Mr. Quimby's teachings, and it is said by some that the growth of the metaphysical movements may be laid to his endeavors. On the other hand, Mr. Wood became so deeply interested in studying the metaphysics that had been responsible for his regained health, that he devoted the remaining twenty years of his life to writing and publishing books on the New Thought. He was the first New Thought philanthropist, noted Mr. Dresser. Both men were able to find a new direction in which to sublimate their energies, which flowed out dynamically once the release was obtained. New Thought became an idealised version of the earlier infantile love, and it could be adored and laboured for, even as the earlier love could be. In fact, Mr. Wood made the remark "I have found something which the world needs and I must give it out."

We need not necessarily suppose that everybody's honest and sincere statement should be mistrusted and that we must start looking for the ulterior motives. No doubt I look at problems and people from the somewhat jaundiced eyes of the psychologist, since every day my profession requires me to deal with people who are burdened and sick of soul. Nevertheless, the modern psychological outlook enables one to pierce through the mask which all of us are required from time to time to wear. It enables us to see into the real motives for action and belief. Hence I feel strongly that modern metaphysics would go much further and accomplish even more than the miracles it has accomplished could it see its way clear to achieving a marriage of its own views with psychological knowledge. People act—but we have no reason to suppose that they ever understand why they act. The motives for human behaviour lie deeply hidden from view. It is the task of the psychologist to expose such motives so that, becoming aware of the true motives for behaviour, we can either alter our behaviour or else, through retaining certain characteristics or continuing a certain line of behaviour, change our motives. The whole race could be immeasurably happier if the utter hypocrisy of our lives were thoroughly eradicated. This hypocrisy is not merely the worldly opportunism that so many of us are obliged consciously to adopt as a way of life, but a psychological mechanism that can be traced back to infancy, to an unwillingness to confront our emotional reactions to those people of the early environment.

Be that as it may, Henry Wood found a superb outlet for his energies in the New Thought sphere, and devoted himself wholeheartedly to its cause. Not only did he publish and write books, but he gave them freely to libraries, institutions, and to anyone who might be interested. All of them ran through several editions. In the book The New Thought Simplified, probably one of his best, he not only provided a provocative and easily read outline of metaphysics, but presented a system of mental and spiritual gymnastic lessons. In these he gave specific instructions whereby, step by step, each phase of metaphysical achievement could be gained. He claimed, "Be assured that if you enter the mental and spiritual gymnasium, and earnestly develop your inner powers for six months in the way suggested, you will value the acquirement beyond possible estimate." He stated that one of the most electric ideas that ever came to him was the affirmation, "God is here." Since it had great effect on him, he laid great emphasis upon it in all his works, employing it as a dynamic suggestion in his series of spiritual gymnastics for development.

Another of the popular writers for the movement was Ralph Waldo Trine. His influence on the Truth movement dates back from the publication of *What All the World's A-seeking*. Mr. Trine possibly is one of the most inspirational of the New Thought writers. He has written not merely metaphysical textbooks, as have so many others, but literary achievements that give pleasure when read. His book *In Tune with the Infinite* is, in its own sphere, a beautiful piece of writing, a lyrical paean of joy that has pleased hundreds of thousands of people. In fact, at one time its very title was a phrase in popular parlance. I personally came to love this book after having too dogmatically rejected it earlier in my life when my own interests were too strictly philosophical and formal. Nowadays I treasure it, and keep it amongst those few books that I will never discard.

Not that the view he enunciates is so novel. It has been said before and many times. But Mr. Trine above all is a writer, and has cultivated the art of matching words to fleeting thoughts, pre-eminently succeeding in conveying an optimistic and inspirational spirit. On one of the preliminary pages of the last mentioned book he has said, descriptive of his intent in writing it, that "within yourself lies the cause of whatever enters into your life. To come into the full realisation of your own awakened interior powers, is to be able to condition your life in exact accord with what you would have it." The different chapters deal, always in excellent literary style, with the several concepts with which metaphysics has familiarised us. It opens with a consideration of God as the omnipresent life and wisdom and love, and that the great central fact of our existence is the conscious opening of our minds to this realisation. He discusses the power and effect of love at some length, never in an offensive or sentimental manner. Many have gained great insight through his consideration of the meaning of religion, and the import of its saints and seers and prophets, and the facts of wisdom and interior illumination.

Speaking of the metaphysical concept of achieving a consciousness of the ever presence of God's power and intelligence, he wrote: "There is nothing that will more quickly and more completely bring one into harmony with the laws under which he lives than this vital realisation of his oneness with the Infinite Spirit, which is the life of all life. In this there can be no disease, and nothing will more readily remove from the organism the obstructions that have accumulated there, or in other words, the disease that resides there, than this full realisation and the complete opening of one's self to this divine inflow. 'I shall put my spirit in you, and ye shall live.'"

"There are almost countless numbers today, weak and suffering in body, who would become strong and healthy if they would only give God an opportunity to do His work...Many will receive great help, and many will be entirely healed by the practice somewhat after the following nature: With a mind at peace, and with a heart going out in love to all, go into the quiet of your own interior self, holding the thought,—I am one with the Infinite Spirit of Life, the life of my life. I then, as spirit, I as a spiritual being, can in my own real nature admit of no disease. I now open my body, in which disease has gotten a foothold, I open it fully to the inflowing tide of this Infinite Life, and it now, even now, is pouring in and coursing through my body, and the healing process is going on. Realise this so fully that you begin to feel a quickening and a warming glow imparted by the life forces to the body. Believe the healing process is going on. Believe it, and hold continually on it..."

Boston seems to have been one of the important starting off points of the movement. No doubt this was because of the fact that Mrs. Eddy's own Church was thriving there and, as we have seen, frequent schisms were occurring, each party going off to found his own group. One of the first such societies, formed on the basis of a real leadership and a thorough-going organisation, was the Church of the Higher Life, started in 1894 by Mrs. Helen Van Anderson. It was devoted to the propagation of metaphysical truths, and served as a centre where friendship and brotherhood would be found. The leader resigned from his Church after a while to begin similar work in other cities. It was in this way that the work grew, and the movement prospered. Later Boston societies were the Procopeia of rather short-life, and the Metaphysical Club organised not long afterwards. This latter club constituted an important event in the history of the movement. It brought together some of the more active participants of the mental science period, those who had been responsible for the formulation of the Church of the Divine Unity and its monthly periodical. The Club was highly successful and attracted to its membership numbers of liberal-minded people. Its objects were, in part, to seek "the spark of infinitude in the seemingly finite," and the Club "seeks to fan it into a blaze that shall be the light of the world. It is therefore striving to bring into hearty cooperation all the individual potencies that have tended toward the high end which it has in view, believing that thus a resistless impulse might be given to the development of life on the highest attainable plane."

It was their type of New Thought which has since been espoused by the rest of the movement. They were eager to demonstrate that they stood not only for a method of healing, important as that was. But they wanted to insist above all upon a philosophy, an affirmative way of life, which to them was primitive Christianity, the gospel of spiritual healing of the whole man. One of the leading exponents within the movement, Elizabeth Towne, has defined the movement as "the fine art of recognising, realising and manifesting the God in the individual." Consequently the entire movement has now become recognised as an idealistic phase of liberal Christianity throughout the world.

Meanwhile in the far West, the New Thought leaders had not been idle. There, the movement came to be recognised under the term Divine Science. It recognised "the God idea of perfect unity, harmony, and wholeness, associated together in unity of spirit, for the healing of the nations, and the general good of humanity." Congresses and conventions were held as far back as 1894, although the first association was organised in 1892. In the 1899 congress in San Francisco, a statement was issued which defined Divine Science: "It is being understood that the law of the universe is the nature and goodness of the Supreme One; the thoughts and ways of all must eventually be adjusted to accord with this knowledge, and Divine Science be accepted as the basis of true education. The Science of Being includes every subject pertaining to Infinite Life and the good of humanity, the well-being of every creature. Its work is the universal dissemination of a knowledge of the Divine purpose of the Creator in creation."

The origins of Divine Science are also due to the efforts of Mrs. Hopkins. In the year 1887, she went to San Francisco at the request of several interested people, and taught a class numbering two hundred and fifty students. The name first employed out on the Coast was actually Christian Science. Later in order to avoid identification with Mrs. Eddy's organisation, the name of the organisation was altered to the Pacific Coast Metaphysical Bureau, and after several metamorphoses it finally came to be called the Home of Truth. To this day, the name has persisted to represent the metaphysical centres out West. One of Mrs. Hopkins' students was Miss Harriet Hale Rix. She, with her sister, who later became Mrs. Annie Rix Militz, were largely responsible for the propagation of metaphysical ideas there and for the foundation of the Homes of Truth. Miss Rix was the author of many books and her writings, in my estimation, differ in no wise from Mrs. Eddy's system. Her book *Christian Mind-Healing* is an excellent statement of Christian Science principles in textbook form. It contains the usual chapters on God, the mechanisms of denial and affirmation, descriptions of the technique of prayer and concentration leading to the acquisition of spiritual understanding, and lessons of the forgiveness of sin, overcoming fear and establishing faith. She wrote in her preface, that real life began for her "when the message contained in this book was revealed. It was a veritable new birth, and I owe all that I am and have to its light...In meekness and gratitude to God, and to those blessed souls who became avenues of His revelation to me, I send forth this little book, trusting that others find through it the joy of life." I have not attempted to describe the mechanisms she writes of, for my opinions are presented in various places in this book.

Her sister, Mrs. Militz, developed into the leading teacher of metaphysics in the State of California, and opened a Home of Truth in Los Angeles in 1896. These Homes have since become fairly numerous. Mrs. Militz must have been a very active worker. From Los Angeles, she went to Chicago, working there until 1902. She taught classes in Boston, Brooklyn, and New York City and twice travelled all over the world, lecturing and teaching.

One of the most important and vigorous of the New Thought publications appeared in San Francisco and was established by Henry Harrison Brown in 1900. It was called Now, and was described as "a Monthly Journal of Positive Affirmations, devoted to Mental Science and the Art of Living." Mr. Brown was the author of a book called *Dollars Want Me*, which first appeared in serial form in Now. It had an immediate success and has enjoyed an enormous distribution. Some of its ideas are so salutary and revolutionary that it is worthwhile to give a summary of the book. He commences his discussion by stating that neither health nor prosperity can exist without harmony. Where there is want, there is no peace or health. Love, truth and financial security are things that appear well-nigh indispensable to our welfare. "Money represents Supply. It stands in our thought for food, clothing and shelter; for books, pictures and companionship; for enjoyment, unfoldment and expression...But the Dollar also means opportunity for the realisation of high ideals. The individual must be free and, until the necessities of life are assured, he is not free. Thus the Dollar stands for individual liberty." This is the theme of his book, and it is well taken. His ideas fit in very well with modern notions about social security, that there cannot be nation-wide happiness until each and every component part of that society is made secure from material need. People cannot be truly happy until and unless they are freed from want. But whereas the state attempts to overcome this want by pensioning the aged, and so forth, the metaphysician seeks to raise the quality and tone of the individual's usefulness and spiritual potency. He proposes to teach man how to help himself, and not be dependent upon the state but only upon God, the one source of supply.

"Harmony is living in obedience to mental law. It is found in right thinking...This right thinking means that there shall be on the part of the individual a change of attitude towards the Dollar." How shall we achieve such harmony? Mr. Brown says: "Live true to self; live spiritually; give the first place in your thought to the eternal from which things come and then all things will come to you at need. Not Dollars first, but that mental attitude which attracts Dollars."

This is profoundly true. Though I have found it to be so in a manner slightly different to the usual metaphysical one. In my professional role of psychologist, I have often found my patients, in the course of analysis, dreaming of money and banks. It would be futile to take such symbols on their face value. They require analysing to divine their real significance. But without a doubt, when the analysis was successfully completed, it was clear that the individual had a greater facility than before for succeeding in the business world, and acquiring for himself the goods of this world which he could use and wisely enjoy. Omitting, for the moment, a number of intervening symbols and associations, invariably money is used in dreams as a symbol of love, of libido in the widest sense as relating to the totality of the individual's spiritual energy. The bank itself where money is stored has a dual significance. It is, on the one hand, a symbol of mother, whom, as a rule, the individual as a child has worshipped. Therefore the entirety of his love-life is inextricably tied up with mother love, which, though persisting in adult life, has become entirely unconscious. She is the bank, the receptacle, where the money-love has been deposited. And secondly, the bank may be used as a symbol of the unconscious psyche itself, the storehouse of the individual's spiritual wealth, his intellectual knowledge and emotional capacity. The Unconscious, as I have attempted to indicate on other pages, also bears many resemblances to the concept of God.

So long as the individual is bound emotionally to mother, he may give unconscious evidence of wishing constantly to be in that relation to her which he enjoyed as a small child—of utter and complete loving dependence upon her for everything. Hence, so long as an infantile fixation of this particular type exists, he may find it impossible to achieve any kind of social or financial security in the world because of the inner conflict that prevails. The unconscious wish is to remain fixed upon mother, the conscious wish to succeed and achieve. The conflict between these two sets of wishes breeds indecision and incompetence. No matter how much the conscious personality strives for success, the unconscious psyche seeks stubbornly to retain the infantile status. In the face of such opposing drives, the individual can do nothing. He is helpless, because he is unable to realise the true state of affairs within him. He is truly unconscious of the strains and stresses operating within his mind. When such a conflict becomes cleared up through self-understanding, there is such a tremendous release of inner energies that the individual is able to throw himself into the world's work with more than the average chance of succeeding. Thus his own attitude towards the symbolic equivalent of money, which is love, is transformed from an infantile to an adult attitude. The financial equivalent of love, in consequence, is inevitably attracted towards him once the real inner attitude towards it has altered.

"To supply human needs is the function of the universe." The universe, asserted Mr. Brown, following an ancient Hindu sage named Patanjali, exists only for the sake of the soul. Nature builds and destroys ceaselessly in a continuous and never-ending cycle. It is only man who wishes to modify these drastic manifestations of nature, and put them to useful employment for his own betterment. Through man, Nature becomes conscious. Everything in nature ministers to the needs of man—money included. "All power is in man. Dollars are machines with power delegated to them by man. They are useless without man." On the other hand, poverty is primarily the result of states of mind, as was indicated above. If one is born into a poor environment, that infantile pattern of poverty impresses itself upon the sensitive and impressionable mind of the child, and unconsciously can be retained as the ideal pattern to be followed and realised. Poverty, our author asserted, "can be cured only by the affirmation of Power to cure...Affirm this and patiently wait for the manifestation."

The first step to be applied, however, is that which is demanded in all metaphysics—become aware of God. Most metaphysicians here follow Mrs. Eddy rather than Quimby in their concept of God as infinite and omnipresent Substance. We have no record of any person applying to Quimby for help because he was down and out, threatened by financial difficulties which he could not solve. But Christian Science, in many people's minds, represented just that direction in which to turn when all other sources of financial betterment have been employed and exhausted. And credit for this enlarged application of metaphysics to every conceivable type of problem must be given rightly to the work of Mrs. Eddy. The metaphysicians conceive of God as the omnipresent Spirit, the one power and presence, whose aspects or qualities or attributes are those of mind, power and substance, present everywhere at all times and at all places. Therefore "first become one with the Power, become the Power, and these desired things will come. The ordinary process of business, the customary method of thinking, is to be reversed. Think from inward Power, think from Being.

Again and Again he insists upon a much needed realisation that "money has only delegated Power." It is man who give money the value that we automatically and commonly associate with it. The native of Timbuctoo would value beads or a cheap mechanical gadget far in excess of a thousand dollar cheque signed by J. P. Morgan. The native red Indians sold Manhattan island for a mere song. Money could have no meaning to them. It is imperative to alter our attitude to money by realising that in reality we do not need money for ourselves, rather that money needs us. So long as it is not used, it is valueless. It can only be fulfilled by our utilisation of it. "Come to me that you may be used. I do not need a dollar. Dollars need me." This is the truly revolutionary attitude that he seeks to inculcate in his readers—and an amazing thought it is too. "You do business with thoughts only; dollars are but materialised thoughts. Each dollar in any man's hand represents his thought in material form. Send out at all times with your dollars the thoughts you wish to return to you, for what you sow in your dollars, you reap in dollars that either do, or do not, come back to you. Put the thought of Success, Happiness and Health into every dollar that passes out and it will return so laden." "Things for man and not man for things! Whoever realises this Truth cannot want. All nature wants him, is constantly bidding for him, and even lying in wait for him."

Insofar as this is an attempt to change the normal conscious attitude towards money and security, it is pre-eminently successful. Any method that will destroy our customary moulds of sterile thinking releases the inner powers. Obviously, psychological analysis is not the only way of eradicating this over valuation of conscious thought at the expense of the inner spiritual, but unconscious, values. As metaphysics endeavors to alter customary and habit-bound forms of thought, it tends to set free the inhibited unconscious feelings and powers. Insofar as it succeeds in doing this, it is an invaluable technique. The first result in all cases must be a sense of release from tension, a throwing off of the heavy burden that has been carried on the back for so many years, leading to sterility and frustration.

The further and full history and ramifications of New Thought are entirely too extensive adequately to be dealt with here. All that I have attempted here, as with all other phases of metaphysics considered in this book, is to give a bird's-eye view of major historical factors and high-light of metaphysical teaching. The student who is interested will find a wealth of material in the writings of Horatio Dresser, especially his work *A History of the New Thought Movement*. On the instructional and practical side of the subject, the various works mentioned in this chapter could be consulted to good advantage.

One of the ugliest phases of the movement, in curious contrast with it high idealism, is its blatant commercialism and it vulgar advertisements, both of which represent not too pleasant states of mind. In many of the New Thought journals, one discovers advertisements which promise that the advertiser, a healer, will solve your problems and pray every day for a month for the restoration of your health or success for a dollar or so. This sort of thing is by no means uncommon. It is based upon the metaphysical proposition that in the spiritual consciousness there is no limitation represented by time and space. It is not incumbent upon a sick person to attend the healer or practitioner for treatment. When the healer prays, ostensibly lifting up his mind to a contemplation of the universal mind and power, he strives to feel and believe that the enquirer who has written, and mailed him a dollar, for aid, is a perfect child of God. Hence he cannot be sick, poor, or encompassed about by any kind of difficulty. Possibly there are merits to the idea. I am sure that it has been frequently been made good use of. Unity, the Homes of Truth, the Divine Science Churches, and many other metaphysical organisations, all maintain special departments dedicated to silent and absent healing. Of their work, I have no criticism to make, for they are conducted in absolute sincerity and honesty and faith, and they attempt to give full service to the best of their knowledge and ability. But when an idea flagrantly is abused by the most vulgar and coarse advertising, one can only feel that the movement needs to clean house before it can command the full measure of respect and esteem that it craves.

Correspondence courses are frequently employed by a large number of the organisations that are integral parts of the International New Thought Alliance. The integrity and sincerity of some of these organisations is beyond reproach. The courses they offer in Bible interpretation and metaphysical fundamentals are sound enough. These are not questioned here. However, that is only one phase of the situation. To examine some of the New Thought publications, however, on this single topic of correspondence courses, is enough to induce rather vigorous reactions in the alimentary tract. They are nauseating to a degree. Many books on metaphysics which teach the subject thoroughly and well are offered to the public through the normal commercial avenues at reasonable prices. Not so, however, with some of these correspondence courses which sell, some of them, for extraordinarily high fees. And the material, after all, can be found in any one of a hundred easily obtainable and cheap books. I suppose these extortionate prices for extravagantly claimed courses are paid by students who are eager, but unfortunately gullible enough to fall for any offer made, no matter how fantastic the price or ridiculous the claims.

"Becoming a Doctor of Psychology and Metaphysics. Get the degree of Doctor of Psychology or Doctor of Metaphysics. Teach the secret of unfoldment, contentment, happiness. Solve mental problems. Learn how to obtain spiritual power. Experience truth's revelation. Chartered College gives individual help. Write for free book."

This is an advertisement typical of many found in the metaphysical magazines. This, assuredly, is the correspondence school racket at its worst. We have all along known that it exists. But it is lamentable that these things should be found in a movement really dedicated to the higher truths. The movement is a fine progressive religious trend, seeking to establish itself on a high ethical and spiritual basis. Until the movement cleanses itself of these elements, even refusing to permit such inferior paid advertising in it publication, a large question-mark will always be held against its integrity by those who are without its organisations.

CHAPTER SEVEN
Neville

Near Broadway on 49th Street in New York City is the Old Actor's Church. Should you go there on Wednesday, Friday or Sunday night of any week, either winter or summer, I can promise you more than a pleasant evening. It will be a highly instructive evening. You will hear Neville's discourse on Truth. A young man, not more than 36 years of age, he is a dynamic, handsome and most charming personality. He has a winning smile—thoroughly and completely disarming. His presentation of truth is forceful and sincere. Charged with feeling, and reflecting his own integrity and purposefulness, he communicates himself readily from the pulpit.

Four to five hundred men and women flock to the Old Actor's Church on each of these nights that he talks. How much of his evident popularity is due to his charm and how much to his dynamic orations, is not for me to say. Some, however, have hazarded an opinion. Some suspect it is the former. Nevertheless this judgment does not in the least detract from the value and worth of what he is impelled to teach. His method and content of teaching are entirely too good and provocative readily to appeal to so many and to such different varieties of people. However that may be, his readers and listeners must be the judges. He does get a crowd—and he satisfies most of them.

Neville is not a native American. He comes from the Barbadoes, British West Indies, having been born in a planter's family in the year 1905. Evidently he felt a cane-sugar plantation was no place for him. A wider sphere of action for imaginative flight and spiritual understanding were necessary to him. His spirit craved other than a small island off the mainland of the United States. So at the age of 17 he came to this country to study Drama.

"A Man's Faith Is His Fortune," he wrote at a much later date—it was the title of a book of his. Evidently he had unbounded faith in himself to have set off youthfully on the unknown possibilities of a career in an unknown land. His confidence has stood him in good stead, since it has brought him through, to a position where he has become a public figure. No doubt there are greater heights of achievement and fame awaiting him in the future.

The year 1925 found him beginning his theatrical career at the Hippodrome, which not so long ago was torn down, removing from New York one of its old landmarks. The destruction of this building was also a milestone to Neville's life. It coincided with his departure from the world of theatre. He entered a totally different public life. Yet it was a life which at the same time bore certain resemblances to his old dramatic career—as we shall see.

He has had a wide and varied experience for a young man, this Neville. In 1925 he sailed for England with a dancing partner, and travelled widely in that country. It was there that he became openly interested in the study of the occult and mysticism.

Whilst in England, he met Arthur Begbie who introduced him to the world of psychical research, giving Neville his first taste of the spiritualistic seance. It left him, I should say, a little bit flat, but nonetheless, he knew afterwards, that he was definitely embarked upon a long journey. Of that he was sure, in spite of his dislike of the atmosphere and the procedure of the seance. Shortly after his return to America in 1926, to continue his theatrical career, his interest in mysticism became keener, coinciding with a waning interest in theatre.

I want to emphasise that Neville was a success in the dramatic world. He did not retire from the stage to metaphysics because he was a flop. Not at all. His salary from the theatre at times ran to $500 per week—a sum not usually earned by failures. This is important to know. It will help dispel the popular notion that only failures and "life-dyspeptics" go for metaphysics.

It was around this time that he became associated with one of several so-called Rosicrucian bodies. I should like to write at length on this subject of Rosicrucians and Rosicrucian organisations. However, I shall have to leave that for another occasion despite the fact that it is a fascinating subject for research, and a lovely topic for a disquisition on the foibles of human nature. Anyway, he not only became a member of this body and studied with it, but embarked upon a definite spiritual and moral discipline, imposing upon himself a regime of abstemious living, sexual continence, and a vegetarian diet. It was enough surely, to break a stronger person than him. From a husky strapping fellow of 176 pounds, he rapidly fell in weight to about 135 pounds. Not only was his efficiency impaired, but he became subject to fainting fits, and had long spells of weakness and languor. At the same time, probably because of the dietary and this irrational mode of life, and undoubtedly because of the neurological disturbances which would accompany such a procedure, a number of psychic experiences occurred to him, including involuntary astral projection and momentary clairvoyant glimpses.

His was a successful theatrical career. I repeat this and emphasise it. He had featured in six Broadway plays, and had travelled all over the country from one theatre to another, and his income ran into several thousand dollars per year. But because of his mystical predilections, and his declining interest in the theatre, he finally withdrew from the theatrical career that he had so laboriously struggled to build up. It became a closed episode of his life. Yet the experience of the theatre gave his something that enabled him in later years to succeed in his newly-chosen work. His personality and his teaching are both highly dramatic.

We are not to imagine that various events in a man's life are out of relationship with one another. A Barbadoes plantation, dramatic school, theatre, professional dancing, and teaching metaphysics—while these seemingly point to a discrepancy in the continuous line of his life, that appearance is only due to our lack of insight. It is one of the characteristics of our age that we seek for superficial consistency, failing to realise that there may be deeper levels of reality, hidden from view, where the true line of continuity may be seen. A man's life is in reality a continuum. Regardless of the number of breaks that may appear in the line of his life, a true continuity does exist. We must not imagine for one moment that growth and development persist anywhere in nature in a straight line. The process of growth involves the idea of a spiral, of an apparent occasional backward trend, of appearances and disappearances, of surges and retreats, of endeavors and new endeavors. The Hegelian dialectical concept may well be the true story behind all human endeavor. There is a forward movement succeeded by its utter negation. Hard upon this, however, there is a manifestation of an entirely new order. Such a cycle persists throughout the whole of nature, and man is certainly no exception to the world order. If we bear such a concept in mind, we will be enabled to understand far more readily the intelligent direction of our lives—and in particular, the work and life of Neville.

In this Rosicrucian body, Neville remained for many years as a student and probationer. But his was finer stuff than this. This cult with its narrow pseudo-occult-religious dogmatism, its lack of imagination and real spiritual achievement, left him cold within. For him there was really nothing there. Life initiated him into its mysteries far more successfully than this occult order. Gradually, he drifted away from it, finding his way, in response to an inner need, into the private sphere of an eccentric Ethiopian rabbi named Abdullah. Here he studied the Qabalah, a Jewish form of mysticism, and obtained illuminating insights into the books of the Bible. As he himself says in *Your Faith Is Your Fortune*, "The Bibles are psychological dramas representing the consciousness of man." And again, "If man were less bound by orthodoxy and more intuitively observant, he could not fail to notice in the reading of the

Bibles that the awareness of being, is revealed hundreds of times throughout this literature." He developed an utterly new approach to the whole problem of man and his relationship with the pulsating world of spirit around him. Entirely satisfied for the first time, he became a devoted disciple of this giant Ethiopian rabbi. His imagination became tremendously stimulated, envisioning life in an entirely new way.

No longer was he confined to the sterile formalistic occult philosophy of this moribund Rosicrucian body. Now he conceived of God and man being entirely one. And it altered the whole coarse of his life. The core of man's being was God—even though man in his blindness and ignorance did not know it. Outside of man there was nothing that man had not himself created. The entire world was a picture world, projected from within. The Ethiopian soon restored balance to his eager groping mind. Overboard went his fanatical vegetarianism, his continence, and his crankiness—and he became that rare anomaly, a human being. And he is very human this Neville, very human indeed. With the development of this phase of his personality, he was able to loosen his hold upon the hem of Abdullah's skirt, to become a teacher in his own right.

It was in February 1938, then, that he commenced his very successful career in New York City. At first he met in a small room in a public building in New York, where dozens of petty little lecturers held their sway, nightly. Merely a handful of people attended his lectures at the beginning. But as his ability grew, and he gained confidence in talking and expounding, so his audiences grew. Now, as I mentioned above, you may go to the Old Actor's Church three nights a week, and find a tremendous and enthusiastic audience. He has not yet achieved nation-wide fame, but no doubt this will come in time.

In his talks on metaphysics, he reveals the Bible as a psychological rather than a historical document of the law governing the expression of life. He has a genius for interpretation, and unconsciously employs an exegetical technique that would surprise many a psycho-analyst and professional interpreter of dreams. For example, he takes Dumas' novel, *The Count of Monte Cristo*, and interprets it as would a psycho-analyst a dream. His interpretation of the story reveals that Edmond Dantés is really Everyman, adrift on the stormy sea of life, trying to steer himself into some haven of security, and attempting to find a refuge against the storm. The old priest with his wisdom and understanding, whom Dantés discovers in the prison, really represents man's awareness of being, that ancient unconditioned self, locked up since time began within the bosom of man. And at the end, after Dantés escapes in the sack intended for the body of the old priest—now dead, because Dantés possesses his insight—and finds the buried treasure, he is able fully to express himself, and impose his will upon the world. "Edmond Dantés becomes the Count of Monte Cristo. Man becomes Christ."

In another place, he analyses the nature and character of the Apostles. He concludes that they represent the twelve qualities of mind which can be controlled and disciplined by man. When discussing the story of the disciples' feet being washed by Jesus, he states that "the foot symbolises the understanding which must be washed of all human belief or conceptions of itself by the Lord."

The story of Daniel, again, is the story of every man. Those lions that Daniel found in the den are the lions that beset our pathway through life, the problems of money, health, and relationships with other people. These beset all of us. Most of us, in the face of such predicaments, become so preoccupied with the problem, so brow-beaten by poverty, sickness, or marital difficulties, that we are unable to find a solution to them. The problem obsesses us. It fascinates us. Daniel decided to turn his back upon the lions, resorting to prayer. That is, he turned his gaze inwards, to his I AM consciousness, his real self which alone is capable of solving such problems. And so Neville concludes his exegesis by insisting that here too is our way out, and that what worked for Daniel, will work for us too.

I ought to mention at this juncture that during the course of his lecturing career, Neville has written and published a considerable number of pamphlets dealing with specific points of his system. Some of them explain his attitude towards particular themes and problems of the Bible. His applications of this theory extends to every phase of Biblical theme, from that of the world's creation to the Crucifixion of Christ, from the meaning of circumcision to the significance of each one of Jesus' twelve disciples. Latterly these essays have been gathered together and incorporated into a single volume entitled *Your Faith Is Your Fortune*. It is upon that volume that I have drawn extensively in order to present what I understand Neville to mean.

However, just as sometimes one feels that the psycho-analyst uses more ingenuity than insight in elaborating a meaning from an involved dream, so occasionally one feels that Neville is hard-pressed extracting psychological meaning from certain sections of the Bible. That is the difficulty in using, for the thin end of one's psychological wedge, a book which is so crammed with heterogeneous and diverse stuff that is clearly not psychological. However, he presents in a simple and practical manner the advantage of realising the identity of man's own consciousness with God. As he himself writes, "I AM the eternal Nothingness containing within my formless self the capacity to be all things. I AM that in which all my conceptions of myself live and move and have their being, and apart from which they are not."

Neville's choice of the phrase I AM to imply that underlying god-like essence in man, is dependent upon several reasons. The most obvious is the self-assumed name of God, which was given to Moses before that fateful visit to Pharaoh—I AM that I AM. This phrase is also repeated throughout Scripture in the same abstract sense.

But apart from this, Neville uses it because if we would define ourselves at all, we must use I AM before we can further qualify it in any way. Before I can say what I am, I must first have said I AM. Before I can assert that I am a man of such and such an age, of a certain race, residing in a certain country, of a certain profession and status, I must say I AM. Not that I am this or that, but that simply I AM. I can condition or formulate this limitless expanse of abstraction by enclosing it within the limitations of sex, age, race, country, profession, etc. But it still remains there, unconditioned, uniformed and unlimited. So also is the basic self of man. It can express itself though a variety of masks, play an infinite number of parts, adopt a maximum of possible roles. But it remains nevertheless, unconditioned and unformed—I AM.

In reality Neville is an atheist. It is conceivable that both he and his audiences would be shocked to learn of my conclusion. Yet he himself clearly and definitely states that outside of man, there is no God. "If man would give up his belief in a God apart from himself, recognise his awareness of being to be God, he would transform his world from a barren waste to a fertile one of his own liking."

Here he allies himself in philosophic principles with the one Buddhist reform. Gautama was a rebel against orthodoxy, against Brahmanism, against the Hindu church. And in passing, let me say that there is more than one correspondence too between Neville's formulation of God, and let us say, Vedanta philosophy, I refer the interested reader to Swami Vivekanada's book Gnana Yoga for a first-rate presentation of Vedanta, which will certainly bear comparison with the ideas contained in *Your Faith Is Your Fortune.* In the chapter on Christian Science, I have given a resumé of Vedanta philosophy.

The Buddha had realised that so long as man relied upon God and the church with its priests for help of any kind, man leaned upon an already broken reed. In fact upon a reed that had no tangible existence. It was a palpable life. If help was to be obtained, in order to solve any of the urgent problems that press upon one in the world of everyday life, only one thing could be relied upon—man, and his inner consciousness. That is the ultimate reality. All else may be explained away, may be challenged, may be denied. This alone remains.

By realising this fact, one is enabled to draw upon secret reserves of strength, of inspiration, find a hidden source of salvation which could be demonstrated and applied to every experience in the hard cold world of reality. This fundamentally is Buddhism and the creed of Buddha. God, or the Wisdom of enlightenment, is inherent in the mind of each one of us. It is the "essence of mind which is intrinsically pure." Unfortunately it have become obscured. The problem is to clear away this obscurity, this delusion under which the mind works, to discover the light of true consciousness which exists beneath.

And so with Neville. Atheist that he is like Buddha, in denying validity to some extra-cosmic personal god—an aged senior with beard, capriciously pulling strings in some far-off corner of the universe—he states categorically that in man is an unconditioned consciousness which is uncreated, unmade, unformed, and unbound—God. If one can only find God in oneself by an ecstasy of feeling, in interior states of prayer and meditation, one also becomes free like God. Poverty, sickness, and need fall away. They are only the products of conscious thinking and feeling, the products of the mind that has divorced itself from its divine roots. These things are the result of denial—the denial that man's consciousness in its deepest levels, in what we call the subconscious level, is God and able to create and destroy man's world. It can destroy the present world in which we all live, of sickness, sorrow and need of one kind or another. And it can create happiness, health, and fullness of plenty of every conceivable kind, on every plane of existence.

Many people, by accepting and applying the principle that he has disclosed to them, have experienced what they at first thought were miracles. This is no new doctrine and its implications have been known and taught since time began. But they are new to some people. They have heard it for the first time. And, credit must be given to him, Neville "can put it over" extremely well, with simplicity and with force.

On the other hand, some other people find themselves intellectually in sympathy with his teaching, yet discover that they are unable to "make it work." They struggle and struggle, and still no results are forthcoming. These fall by the wayside, attacking him and his system—even becoming vindictive. Some of these suggest that when some of Neville's disciples obtain satisfactory results, they do so only because they have been hypnotised by Neville.

The sort of person who can make this sort of statement, has not in the least understood the fundamental psychological factor in Neville's teaching, nor the fundamental fact about Neville himself. It is a very simple fact. Neville is a dancer.

I have watched Neville dance. He is superb. He has a magnificent body. I have already remarked that he has charm and is very handsome. When he dances, his muscles move with that lithe suppleness which one associates with the trained athlete. His every movement suggests power in repose, the effortless ease of a cat, with its undisguised sensuality and force of movement. As an artist, he knows the value of alternate relaxation and tension. Above all, he knows the dance. His metaphysics and his system, are a dance—a dance of words, a dance of mind, a dance of feeling. And unless you can dance with him, his system is likely to be unproductive. His system is in reality strictly personal—an offshoot of his own personality. To make it work as he has done, you too must become like him.

An artist in every fibre of his being, he has the capacity to sink himself whole-heartedly and imaginatively in the task at hand. He is an artist, and has passion and fire on hand at every moment. The artist in him is truer than his desire to expound publicly the system he does expound. He has the ability spontaneously to apply his own teaching. It is quite another story, however, to teach the practical elements of his system to those who are not artists, who have not his imaginative or emotional capacity to engage in this ecstatic dance of the mind which evidently means so much to him.

Possibly, in his audiences, there are individuals here and there having the necessary artistic and mystical temperament—identical, really—not only to absorb the truth as Neville presents it, but make immediate application of it. To "demonstrate" successfully, as the cliché goes. The average person with his commercial prosaic mind, his unimaginative sterile attitude to life, uninspiring employment and home, is incapable of realising that inner-spiritual being, which Neville implies by "I AM." Such a person cannot evoke that intensity of feeling, that temporary madness that Neville demands of all those who would apply his teaching successfully. A fiery white-hot passion is but a phrase to them. Consequently, in being unable to whip themselves into such an emotional frenzy, which can be focused in certain pre-determined directions, his words fall on barren ground.

Yet, in one sense this is not their fault. Life has dealt hardly with them, I do not blame them in any way. I am full of sympathy for them in their plight. Of all the metaphysical systems which I am acquainted, Neville's is the most evidently magical. But being the most magical, it requires for that reason, a systematised training on the part of those who would approach and enter its portals. It requires a dynamic alteration of viewpoint—a revolutionary turning around of the mind. An entirely new and radical attitude to life and living must be developed, not merely intellectually, but emotionally. Above all, it demands that the student must learn the gentle art of relaxation—not by turning the back on body and ignoring its demands, but by learning the simple technique of so doing. Neville knows the art of relaxation instinctively. He is a dancer, and a dancer must, of necessity, relax. Hence I believe he does not fully and consciously realise that the average person in his audience does not know the mechanism of relaxation, does not know how to "let go." It is true he speaks of relaxing. "Close your eyes and feel yourself to be faceless, formless and without figure. Approach this stillness as though it were the easiest thing in the world to accomplish. This attitude will ensure your success." But for the average person, this is hardly adequate. A little more detailed scientific instruction is imperative.

Not only so, but the average individual does not know how to evoke powerfully his feelings and emotions. He does not understand the means whereby he can arouse this passionate intensity so necessary to complete identification with or recognition of the Unconditioned faceless, formless consciousness of which Neville speaks.

To some extent it is possible to succeed more easily with women than with men. Women are essentially more emotional than men. The average male is entirely repressed from an emotional point of view. From early boyhood he is taught, either directly or indirectly, that it is "sissyish" to show his feelings. By early adolescence, his feelings are pretty well hidden. So that when he achieves true adulthood, he has no feelings at all. His emotions are totally repressed into the dark hidden depths of his unconscious life, and he is completely and thoroughly inhibited. Even his mind must suffer from such violence. Never must we forget that the emotional life is the mainspring of every other phase and aspect of our lives. What wonder that we become ill and impotent and needy, both physically and mentally?

This is the problem of the average adult approaching all forms of metaphysics—the problem of the male primarily, but to some extent true of the female too. In the face of such repression, where violence has been done to the emotional life, and all feelings have been inhibited, a serious question arises. What course of practise may be engaged upon that will evoke from out of the depths, the emotions so necessary to the cultivation of this passionate intenseness which conduces the spiritual experience and the ability to "demonstrate"?

Neville, if not totally adequate to this situation, is at least wise. Whether he did this deliberately or intuitively, it is not possible to determine. But his step certainly serves a useful purpose. He knows that the average person approaching his lectures has had a religious training of some kind. This may have been forgotten and strayed from. But invariably it remains in the individual's unconscious in some form or other. Emotional intensity is of necessity associated with this early infantile training in religion.

There were the first prayers that mother taught us all when we prayed in love and reverence with her. Early experiences in Sunday school and the first feelings of awe and wonder and love that arose with them—such memories are retained, never forgotten, and are stored within. Hypnotic experiment reveals the tenacity of even the most trivial events in our minds. Neville therefore casts a magical cloak of religion about his system, advocating the study of the Bible as revealing this psychological drama of which he speaks. In using the Bible, he draws directly upon the level of consciousness which goes far back into time for most of us— to infancy when the emotions were still powerfully active in our small childish worlds. In drawing upon this level, which he does through the use of the Bible, he draws by association upon all the power and energy which are tied up in that stratum of our minds. This he stimulates and whips into dynamic activity, so that it will accomplish the purpose of which his system speaks.

Whether this technique is wholly successful—or even desirable—is another story. Occasionally it works; very often it does not. Sometimes the listener is so completely inhibit and repressed, that even the stimulus of the Bible is unable to awaken the magical power of the unconditioned consciousness to achieve what he wills and to make manifest that which he envisions.

Of all the popular teachers of metaphysics, Neville possibly is the most broad-minded. Some many months ago when I was engaged in some practical experimental work with hypnosis and suggestion, I extended an invitation to Neville to be present. After the experiment was over, I put it to Neville that the crucial factor in all metaphysics and New Thought was auto-suggestion. We had just witnessed a hypnotic demonstration in which an individual performed certain physical and intellectual feats which, in his waking state, would be quite impossible for him. Through meditation and prayer, the devotee of metaphysics is also able to perform many things he could not have done otherwise. It seemed to me that there must be some connection. In the case of hypnosis, hetero-suggestion is responsible. In metaphysics, self- or auto-suggestion may be the underlying factor.

Now, it did not strike Neville as at all contrary to his principles of truth that this should be so. In fact, he accepted my idea willingly, remarking that man has become, by reason of defective early training, hypnotised out of his knowledge that he is God-like in nature. Therefore, what could be more reasonable than to employ suggestion, not as a means of superimposing additional ideas on an already heavily-burdened psychological apparatus, but to awaken and to evoke from within what is already there, and has been there for ages—dormant, latent, and unseen. Hence his system really amounts to little more than this—when all the extraneous details are eliminated, and the cloak of the Bible and terminology are flung off. It seems that he demands complete relaxation, in order to become aware of the deeper levels of the mind, the Unconscious. When in that ecstatic state brought about by the contemplation of phrases and versicles in the Bible, you must drop into the Unconscious the suggestions or desire that one wishes to be fulfilled. "Such simple acceptance of your desires," he says in his recent book, "is like the dropping of fertile seed into an ever-prepared soil. When you drop your desire in consciousness as a seed, confident that it shall appear in its full-blown potential, you have done all that is expected of you." This, in effect, is a perfect statement of the rationale of auto-suggestion.

In another place, he speaks of the efficacy of faith, as an important adjunct to successful demonstration. For example, he writes, "The beliefs in the potency of drugs to heal, diets to strengthen, moneys to secure, are the values or money-changers that must be thrown out of the Temple...The thieves who rob you, are your own false beliefs. It is your belief in a thing, not the thing itself, that aids you."

Here is a very wide agreement with modern psychological knowledge. Every doctor knows that fully half of his patients would respond equally well to a regime of sugar-coated pills as to specific medical therapy. Even surgical operations have the effect only of providing the patient with what he longs for unconsciously, and thus enabling his to get well. It is suggestive value of these factors which is effective. Psychoanalysis has much to teach us about the hypnotic or suggestive value of any therapeutic agent. It is effective, provided the patient's emotions can be shifted or transferred away from the formation of symptoms. The phenomenon of transference is just as ever-present in the lecture hall as it is in the consulting room or clinic.

Daily and hourly we give ourselves countless suggestions and we permit others to do the same for us. Life for many people consists of suggestion and counter-suggestion. Every few minutes over the radio, in the subways and street cars, in newspapers and magazines, suggestion is thrust at us until we succumb to its insidious appeal. Modern selling and advertising seems to consist almost exclusively in how cleverly one can suggest to the members of the general public, that they must purchase things not wholly necessary to them.

It is not faith that renders effectual the drugs and medicines and so forth that the advertisements blare out to us. They inform us that these things are effectual and because of long continued emphasis, we come to accept those suggestions. When we are in trouble and use such advertised articles, they succeed not because of any inherent virtue they possess, nor because of faith. But they succeed only because the advertisements have suggested to us that they will succeed.

Though emphasised by Neville, faith and belief seem to be a façade for our lack of understanding why suggestion sometimes works and why at others it fails. It is not faith in the old religious sense that is effectual as it is necessity and the feeling that one is in *extremis*. When the rules of applying auto-suggestion are closely adhered to in every way, success must inevitably follow. Therefore, we say such a person had faith. Moreover, we must remember that faith is an emotional quality. It evokes an intensity of feeling which is one of the indispensable factors in the successful unconscious reception of the suggestion or the desire or the mental image. Faith has no scientific validity in itself. It is simply convenient as an emotional excitant. And when all other things all fail and despair has set in, then faith stimulates the whole nature to respond to the next healing or saving situation that will arise.

So far as Neville's teaching goes, the theory is inevitably bound up with the practice. In philosophy is the means by which demonstration may be manifested. God is the beginning, end, and middle of the theory and practice. And since this is so, we can do no better than to consider a bit more carefully what he means by God.

The book *Your Faith Is Your Fortune* attempts at the outset to present the supreme problem with which all philosophies, religious or otherwise, are confronted. If God is infinite, omnipresent, eternal and omnipotent, how does He bring that world into being, and what part does that world play so far as He is concerned? Christian theology based upon the Bible, attempts to solve that by a miraculous creation from nothing. God created the world and everything in it—and that is that. Insofar as Neville is influenced by the Bible and Christian teaching, he follows more or less the same miraculous theme, adapting it however, to his particular conception of God. "The world is your consciousness, objectified," relates equally to the original creation of the world as it does to the constant renewal and creation of our own particular worlds. "The conceiver and the conception are one, but the conceiver is greater than his conception." God is the conceiver and the whole of creation is his conception. Naturally, God is greater than his conception, which though part of him and of his own substance, is yet identical with him.

"In the beginning was the unconditioned awareness of being, and the unconditioned awareness of being became conditioned by imagining itself to be something, and the unconditioned awareness of being became that which it had imagined itself to be; so did creation begin."

This quotation from one of his pamphlets *Before Abraham I Was* really sets forth in a nutshell the whole of Neville's teaching. Implicit in this single sentence is contained everything that he believes in. In conversation with him and in his writing, he states, re-states, and emphasises this concept in a dozen different ways with all the fluency and eloquence and feeling at his disposal. The rest of his teaching is merely explanatory of and dilatory upon this one fact. In stating his idea of how the world and everything in it evolved and came into being, we are not to imagine that he is contenting himself with mere metaphysics. Neville is not abstract—nor is he a philosopher. We learn from him nothing new of dialectic, of logical world-processes, nor of ontology. He is not interested in expounding an elaborate cosmological theory. Let me emphasise again, the fact that he is an artist—and the artist's imagination continuously flows forth into creation and activity. So with Neville. He is pre-eminently a practical person. It is his fundamental belief that this primal consciousness, man's unconditioned awareness of being—at once unbound, unformed and free, which conceives or imagines itself to be something other than it really is—mirrors itself in our very act and thought, every hour and every minute of every day of our life.

Before God could conceive of something other than Himself, or fashion within Himself some conception or other, He had first to be moved by desire. Hence the emphasis placed upon desire by Neville. For him, it is the saviour and redeemer. Desire for him is holy and creative, providing the dynamic impetus to the whole of life and living. It is of the nature of Godhead, which will save us from our limitations, break open the bars of our prison, and make us whole once more. "Look upon your desires as the spoken words of God and every word a prophecy of that which you are capable of being. Do not question whether you are worthy or unworthy to realise these desires," he says. "Accept them as they come to you. Give thanks for them as though they were gifts..." And again "Every problem automatically produces its solution in the form of a desire to be free from the problem." Thus we see the all-important rôle that desire plays in his system. If the desire is intense enough, and can be reinforced by sufficient feeling and reach a high enough voltage, it must necessarily manifest itself objectively.

If God can be moved by desire sufficiently to evolve conceptions which can, as it were, clothe themselves in form, so also can man, for God is only the consciousness of man, his awareness of being himself. Man is that primal consciousness—man is God. Not as he commonly knows himself, but deep down in his heart, unconsciously. As man knows himself, he is obviously limited in manifold ways. His desires rarely fulfil themselves, for his is essentially impotent. In his unconscious self, however, in the "Secret Place of the Most High," he *is* unconditioned, formless, faceless and uncreated, and his desires come true. They are always mirroring themselves outwards, projecting themselves objectively—whether he is aware of it or not.

It is essential to stress this differentiation which I believe Neville has failed to do sufficiently. Man is not God, save in the deepest levels of his soul. Man can come to this realisation when he is very quiet and still. Only when the motion of the thinking mind, which is the superficial self, has been stopped altogether, can man know in that silence that "I AM is God. "He will know that his consciousness is God and that which conscious of being, is the Son bearing witness of God, the Father."

When Neville speaks of consciousness in this way, he would have done better to have used another more specific term. Better might have been the word Unconscious, or even the Subconscious mind, and to have reserved the word consciousness for what he calls the Son, that which man is conscious of being, or calling into manifestation. Unless we differentiate in this way, we run headlong into an inescapable but highly unpleasant conclusion—that we are mad. In our mental hospitals there are hundreds and hundreds of inmates who insist, quite consciously and deliberately that they are God. It is a pathetic experience to see and hear them. We must not say that their statement is any different from ours because their minds are unbalanced, that they are insane. We must avoid this pitfall more rationally. We must define our thinking terms more carefully. Neville's system contains this clarification, if not explicitly, then implicitly. It only needs to be brought out more definitely.

We are not God in our waking conscious state. But there is some part of our personalities of which normally we are not conscious, which can be called God or "I AM." This saves us from the horns of the horrible dilemma that we too are insane. By this differentiation we are enabled to retain some degree of sanity and balance.

The entirety of our life is rooted in the Unconscious "I AM." Truly, as the Bible says, "In him we live and move and have our being." Without God, or its psychological equivalent, the deep consciousness of Man, the Unconscious, we have no life whatsoever. We only believe that we are masters in our own house, that we are independent, and that we do not need God. But that is because we like to flatter ourselves. We are vain and egotistical. The truth is that we are dependent to a startling degree upon the proper functioning of the Unconscious psyche, and we must therefore see to it that our roots are in the right place. The various events and experiences that occur to us and the things that come to us in the course of daily life, are the result of its outpicturing, the projections of this Unconscious psyche which we harbor within. Even the contents of our conscious thinking and imagination, spring from and depend completely upon the activity of the Unconscious. All thought and ideation and the predispositions to certain types of experience, are constantly being evolved within us, unconsciously. God and the Unconscious are words, then, that bear an equivalent meaning—and irrespective of what it really is in itself, this much is true, that we cannot live apart from it in any way.

We know very little about the Unconscious—and only a little more about the way it works. But we assume that in some way the conscious thinking self evolves out of, but still has its roots in its inchoate darkness. In the child, we can see this growth of an ego occur at an early age, watch speech and understanding develop, and see mind grow where before there was only irrational irresponsibility. Life and the Unconscious existed long before the child could say "I" and when this "I" disappears, as it does for all of us during sleep or coma, life and spirit or God, still continue—

as our observation of other people and our own dreams inform us. We assume that this process taking place in the individual, is a rapid-fire recapitulation of a psychic process which occurred thousands, possibly millions of years ago, in the development of humanity, when mind gradually and ever so slowly made its appearance on the evolutionary scene. Mind once evolved out of the unconscious, and even today is still dependent upon it. Man's present conception of himself has evolved out of his unconditional awareness of being which, if called upon, can alter that conception in strange and wonderful ways.

God and the Unconscious are one. These terms imply the same reality. And as all things flow from God as his conceptions, so in the same manner, the form of our environment emanates from the Unconscious. As God created the world through the formulation of his own imaginative concepts, so also the Unconscious creates its own world. "Your world is your consciousness objectified." The tragedy of today is that we do not know this. We are out of tune with the infinite, having ignorantly lost our contact with the unconscious world of inner reality, the true source of life. Today, therefore, we are a people tragically cut off from our roots, from our creative and spiritual roots—and the upshot is that we are impotent and worthless and ill.

The law of creation is "first conceiving, then becoming that conceived—all things evolve out of No-thing. And without this sequence, there is not anything made that is made." If therefore our world, which is the particular environment of any one of us, is distasteful and hateful to us, we first must remember that it is the reflection of ourselves. "The world is your consciousness objectified." How to change it follows logically upon the thesis of creation. "Waste no time trying to change the outside," stresses Neville. "Change the within or the impression; and the without or expression will take care of itself." If our environment is unfavorable, it presupposes the fact that at some former time we must have conceived it. Either knowingly or unknowingly we must first have evolved it as a possibility within. We must have mirrored it into being from our of ourselves, and identified ourselves with it.

To create a new world, it is useless to alter the pieces of the puzzle outside. New conceptions must be formulated within, conceptions which the conceiver can handle, as it were, to form into new objective realities without. How does one make these new conceptions? How does one employ this faculty that is ours as the conceiver of all things?

Consciousness or God, is the magical faculty which has all power, and can miraculously alter, change, create and destroy forms, ideas, and beings. "The foundation of all expression is consciousness. There is only one power and this power is God (consciousness). It kills, it makes alive; it wounds; it heals; it does all things, good, bad or indifferent." Consciousness dwells within that which it is conscious of being. I AM man is the Lord and his temple." It is imperative therefore, to call upon the aid of the deep self, upon God. He magically can re-arrange all the component parts of the body, the environment and the surrounding world which is his Temple, to coincide a little better with the heart's desire. Only God has the vision, the power, to foresee and arrange how events may develop. We can provide the goal by formulating the wish, but the manner in which it will occur and how, is entirely beyond us. That is completely in the hands of the Unconscious. Its wisdom will know best how to dictate the course of future events.

How this could possibly be, is indicated by Jung in one of the psychological essays in his book *Modern Man in Search of a Soul*. There, discussing the nature of the Unconscious, he says that it contains certain primordial instinctual patterns that have come down to us from the past. These patterned mark definite processes of development and evolution. Moreover, he adds, "If it were permissible to personify the Unconscious, we might call it a collective human being combining the characteristics of both sexes, transcending youth and age, birth and death, and from having at his command a human experience of one or two million years, almost immortal. If such a being existed, he would be exalted above all temporal change; the present would mean neither more nor less to him than any year in the one hundredth century before Christ; he would be a dreamer of age-old dreams, and, owing to his immeasurable experience, he would be an incomparable prognosticator. He would have lived countless times over the life of the individual, of the family, tribe and people, and he would possess the living sense of the rhythm of growth, flowering, and decay."

I do not feel it is an exaggeration, then, or a conviction that in any wise borders on superstition, to assume that the details of the working out of the wish may safely be left to the superior experiences and wisdom of our inmost self. The real problem seems to be not that the Unconscious is incapable of fulfilling the wish. More to the point is how to enlist its power on our behalf, how to employ it?

"You cannot serve two masters or opposing states of consciousness at the same time." Neville is adamant on this score. "Taking your attention from one state and placing it upon the other, you die to the one from which you have taken it and you live and express the one with which you are united." Like Daniel we must, insists Neville, turn our backs upon the lions confronting us and forget them—in order to pray.

This is the first step then—to turn one's back on the evidence of one's senses. To ignore the world which one's mind and all the faculties of one's being perceives. We have already seen that he claims the world to be merely the outside picture of an inward spiritual state. It remains therefore, to ignore the immediate problem that one finds ahead of him—whether it be one of money, of sickness, of love, position, or whatnot. Leave it alone, Neville urges his disciples, and turn the attention away from it. Such neglect will cause it to deteriorate, to die, whilst the newly-directed attention is focussed on the construction of new conceptions which will out-mirror themselves in new worldly conditions. Put the old out of mind altogether. Reformulating one's being on an entirely divine basis, affirming oneself to be basically God, will instigate such radical alterations in the environment as one desires.

"...When this expansion of consciousness is attained, within this formless deep of yourself, give form to the new conception by claiming and feeling yourself to be that which you, before you entered this state, desired to be. You will find that within this formless deep of yourself, all things appear to be divinely possible. Anything that you sincerely feel yourself to be while in this expanded state becomes, in time, your natural expression."

We must, as I have described above, switch our minds away from the consideration of the immediate problem. Neville says that, instead of saying, "out of sight, out of mind," we really should reverse the phrase by saying, "out of mind, out of sight." This concept is peculiar not merely to Neville, but so far as I know, is common to all the metaphysical and modern religious movements of today. It is not a valid concept, however, on any logical or scientific ground. But it is, in effect, just this contradictory illogical phase that commends it to the metaphysicians. For they say, after St. Paul, that the wisdom of this world is foolishness with God. But it does not follow that this world's folly is God's wisdom. So that the modern way of dealing with any kind of problem, staring it right in the face and attempting to find out the hidden psychological meaning for its existence, is totally disregarded on the hypothetical ground that once the attention is removed from it, it must disappear. "This manifestation will remain in sight only as long as it takes the force with which the conceiver—I AM—originally endowed it to spend itself."

Before suggesting that I think this procedure is highly illogical and baseless, I ought to state that I am very much in sympathy with a great deal of the content of mysticism. I am also well aware of the limitations and inadequacies of the thinking principle, and that the services of a higher or different faculty must be called upon to lead us out of the maze into which the use of the mind alone will land us. Nonetheless, the conscious thinking self has a definite role to play and it remains for us to extend the field of its operations so that ultimately it may include within its sphere most of what hitherto was called unconscious.

The idea of "out of mind, out of sight," is one of those common metaphysical fallacies which on the surface sounds so penetrating and seems so true. To get something out of mind is surely to eliminate it from sight. But there is no indication that the mental content thus disposed of, has actually been eliminated altogether. We may not be aware of it—but once an ostrich has buried its head in the sand, it too, is totally unaware of anything that may be in its vicinity. Such reasoning as this was valid in the days before depth-psychology came into being, when it was really thought that to take one's mind off certain thoughts and feelings, really destroyed them. Nowadays, however, we know that people can so handle various emotions and ideas, as to become totally unconscious of them. We may deny, consequently, that we ever entertained such thoughts and feelings. We have repressed them utterly—that is to say, forcibly forgotten them. So severe and intense is the repression and forgetting that many of us really and truly believe that we never had them. On the other hand, though these thoughts and memories are now unconscious, they are no less realities than if they were fully present and real, but a very great deal more potent—sometimes disagreeably so. They have been hidden in the darkness of the unconscious levels of the psyche, which is the kinetic factor in our lives, that which is in reality "the power house behind the throne." It is the machine-shop of the body and mind. These repressions, rather than conscious states, are the true psychological contents that out-picture themselves in the creation of adverse social, economic and family conditions that we loathe so much and try to eliminate from our lives. These are the dynamic conceptions which we so blindly feed to the magical self underneath, the conceiver of all things who, as a result, can only turn these conceptions into realities. Says Neville, "God, your awareness, is no respecter of persons. Purely impersonal, God, this awareness of all existence, receives impressions, qualities, and attributes defining consciousness, namely your impressions." I will extend his idea, by saying that the Unconscious is no respecter of ideas. It is impersonal, and will turn into realities whatever ideas are thrust into its sphere, good, bad, and indifferent.

There is danger in turning our backs on problems, however much desirable it may appear to do so. There is entirely too much clinical evidence available today, confirming the fact that it is the whole content of repressed ideas and experiences that become projected into the world of reality, forming our sicknesses, social problems, and all else beside. The problem confronting one is itself an out-picturing of oneself. We can learn much of ourselves, about the true self within, from a study of the unsolved problem confronting us. It ought to receive a great deal of study and meditation, to stimulate us to ask "why" many times, before we begin to use these metaphysical methods to eliminate them. Sometime we would do better to swallow it and accept it—bitter pill that it may be. Nasty medicine often does us more good than simply to have refused to take it.

It is an offense against our own integrity and intellectual honesty first to assume that what is present in our external world picture is but a projection of the mind, and then to ignore utterly that visible projection from within. It seems more rational, before attempting to make new spiritual images within, to inquire why previous pictures were created that would produce such untoward effects that displease us so. What meaning have they? What is the significance of this problem, this environment, this situation? Meaning there must be—otherwise the whole structure of our existence falls around us like an inchoate mass of cards. Our spiritual work hence must be so to enlarge our understanding of life and of ourselves that we divine a meaning in every single and isolated phenomenon. As the Unity leader, Charles Fillmore, write in his book *Christian Healing*: "The material forms that we see about us are the chalk marks of a mighty problem being outworked by the one Mind. To comprehend that problem and to catch a glimpse of its meaning, we must grasp the ideas that the chalk marks represent; this is what we mean by studying Mind back of nature.

Man is mind and he is capable of comprehending the plan and the detailed ideas of the supreme Mind."

Apropos this technical consideration of ignoring facts, or of denying them, because they are only reflections of inner conceptions which the conceiver of all things has thrust into the outer world, Neville also gives us a commentary upon one of the little stories in the Bible. He calls our attention to the Book of Numbers where, it is said, that "There were giants in the land and we were in our own sight as grasshoppers, and we were in their sight as grasshoppers."

Explaining that in the light of his particular system, he says: "Today is the day, the eternal now, when conditions in the world have attained the appearance of giants. The unemployed, the armies of the enemy, business competition, etc. are the giants which make you feel yourself to be a helpless grasshopper. We are told we were first in our own sight helpless grasshoppers, and because of this conception of ourselves, we were to the enemy helpless grasshoppers.

"We can be to others only that which we are to ourselves. Therefore, as we revalue ourselves and begin to feel ourselves to be the giant, a center of power, we automatically change our relationship to the giants, reducing these former monsters to their true place, making them appear to be the helpless grasshoppers.

Convincing as this sounds at first sight, unfortunately, it is not altogether as true as it sounds. I know men who are considered by the world to be very great men. They have achieved much, having position and power and money. Yet within themselves they are consumed by a gnawing inferiority, feeling themselves the helpless grasshoppers of which Numbers speaks. However, no one knows it. No one knows or even suspects their helplessness, their internal conflict, their never-ending doubt and self-torture. They and they only, are aware of it. It goes on all through the hours of the day, continuing in their dreams at night. But never is it suspected even for one moment by their friends, their most intimate friends and colleagues. It is a secret that none must ever share. Never does the world divine it, because they never divulge it.

Like many other public speakers, even successful actors, I am sure Neville has frequently, especially at the beginning of his public career, felt considerably nervous and frightened just prior to delivering a lecture. So far as the audience was concerned, he appears not in the least frightened or nervous, but calm, collected and poised. I myself have experienced this so many times that it is no longer funny. And a friend of mine, who has delivered thousands of lectures, including radio addresses, invariably becomes nervous and fearful, to the extent that his physiological functions are temporarily interfered with. Yet he is successful, and he is no grasshopper to the world, however much of one he may at times seem to be himself. Some even consider him one of the giants.

Things are not always what they seem. It is not always true that we can be to others what we are to ourselves. I may be worthless and valueless to myself, yet of inestimable worth to hundreds and thousands of people. Life cannot be reduced to a few simple formula capable of application to the world at large.

Nor is it altogether true that as we evaluate ourselves anew and feel ourselves to be giants, do we actually become giants. Many a braggart and egoist has strutted like a turkey-cock about the world, even in the small familiar sphere of our own lives, telling us of his own importance and what a giant he is. This is impressed upon us daily, almost hourly. Yet, all we feel about his evaluation of himself, is sorrow and pity for such a poor fool.

Nevertheless, Neville's underlying idea is essentially correct. But there is a misunderstanding of levels upon which we must apply his principle. His system demands, as I have suggested above, a better definition of terms, a more exact usage of words. It is not our conscious evaluation of ourselves which means very much. It is what we feel about ourselves deep down in our hearts—and that, unfortunately, is not known to most of us. What we feel in the unconscious side of the psyche—what Neville calls our awareness of being—that is what people will feel about us. I may feel a worm unconsciously, but no matter how much I may consciously over-compensate for this unconscious inferiority and suggest that

I am a giant, the world will know me for a worm. On the other hand, while my conscious evaluation of myself may be very low, my real and unconscious appreciation of myself, as revealed for example in dream, may be terrific—in which event sooner or later the unconscious view will win out, and I will actually become to myself and to the world one of the giants. Those around me in my environment may then feel that I am potentially more than I express, and may really say of me that "He is a gigantic personality if he could express himself—as one day he will."

Apart from those theoretical considerations, Neville's technique is fascinating and psychologically instructive. It will be more graphic to consider it in connection with a certain problem. Though I select a specific type of problem, let it be understood that Neville himself believes it to be applicable to any contingency that may arise—and that its limitations are really unknown.

For example, suppose that having attended his lectures and learned something of his principles, you find yourself confronted by a certain problem. A bill has just arrived for $500 on your house. All your money is gone, no loan can be arranged from the bank or friends—and you just do not know where to turn. You are worried, beset by anxiety and ready, if not to commit suicide, then at least to pull out every hair of your head—an awkward situation to be in, especially if you are getting bald like the author. What to do?

I can almost hear Neville suggest that you should sit down, or lie on your couch, in a comfortable position, close your eyes. Begin to murmur over and over again "I AM, I AM." Not I am this or nor I am that. But just quickly affirming your own awareness of being, the fundamental fact of your consciousness. As relaxation of both mind and body ensues, you will sense a feeling of floating in space. Try and feel through the constant repetition of this deific phase that you are unconditioned, faceless and formless, the primal consciousness which is the true self underlying the normal activities of mind and body. Develop this state of consciousness until you feel that you are identified with it. With the acquisition of this awareness, imagine that the $500 which you simply must have, is *already* in your possession.

"To be conscious of being poor while praying for riches, is to be rewarded with that which you are conscious of being, namely poverty. Prayers to be successful must be claimed and appropriated. Assume the positive consciousness of the thing desired.

"With our desire defined, quietly go within and shut the door behind you. Lose yourself in your desire; feel yourself to be one with it; remain in this fixation until you have absorbed the life and name by claiming and feeling yourself to be and to have that which you desired."

In this relaxed and exalted mood, you should then switch your mind over to the nature of your desire. It will not do, when so elevated emotionally, to affirm "I want $500," for that would only emphasise your lack, your need of money. This emphasis would constitute a further suggestion which would manifest itself inevitably in the perpetuation of the material condition. And it is just this that needs to be overcome.

You must remember that Neville defines God as our unconditioned awareness of yourself. When defining yourself, you must first of all state "I AM" before following it up with our name, sex, colour, age, nationality and so forth. Now, in this highly relaxed state of being in which you have affirmed yourself to be God, the unconditioned I AM consciousness, it must follow that the next stage is to condition this abstract unlimited awareness of being in a certain predetermined way. It is useless from a practical point of view to state that a certain sum of money is required. But it is good technique to affirm emphatically that "I AM abundance," or that "I AM substance, the infinite supply from which all demands shall be met." A complete identification of the primal being with the desire is imperative. This conditions the initial formless consciousness so specifically that it immediately becomes modified according to the terms of the suggestion or affirmation. And, in accordance with Neville's formulations, this suggestion is the seed that will be vitalised by God to grow into an actuality for all to see.

How would you feel if you had this money now? How would you feel if the problem were now ended? Depressed—or elated?

Then try to encourage this sense of ecstasy, of jubilation in having this money. Feel keenly that a check for $500 has immediately been written, and your mind rid of this spectre which had been haunting you and assuming such terrifying proportions. Feel yourself in the presence of your dearest friend, asserting your problem to be solved, and that you have the money to pay this bill. Imagine and feel piously that he too participates in your jubilation. He shakes your hand vigorously, embraces you, so happy has he become that anxiety and worry are shaken from your shoulders.

"All things gravitate to that consciousness with which they are in tune. All things disentangle themselves from that consciousness with which they are out of time...Consciously define yourself as that which you desire...Claim yourself to be that which you want filled full."

Neville asserts that if we would only encourage such states of consciousness, steadfastly eliminating worry and fear and trepidation, encouraging this sense of joy and happiness, external conditions must of necessity change themselves. "Consciousness being Lord and Master, you are the Master Magician conjuring that which you are now conscious of being." If therefore you have become conscious of having and being the money which will set you free from your problem, some event would occur to externalise this inner vision. How it would occur is not known to any of us, but a materialisation of the spiritual state would ensue—not in some supernatural manner, like manna falling miraculously from heaven. There would be no violation or cessation of natural law. But in some way, through the people already known to us, possibly through some means already at hand, an offer would be made which would produce that $500. Many people have claimed to have applied this principle and found it to be practicable—almost in spite of themselves.

His treatment of the problem of time is very interesting in this connection. Let us assume that this $500 which we discussed above, had to be produced within the space of a few days. It is Wednesday now. By Sunday that money must be forthcoming—or else! What is to be done about it? What procedure should be followed?

At first the procedure would be identical with that described above. Not only is that money to arrive, but it is already here. Suppose that this money were to arrive from out of the blue on Sunday—well, the, imagine how you would feel on Sunday. Here you are tense, fretful and consumed with anxiety. Your mind has been crowded with the contemplation of the dire possibilities and complications of sheriffs, dispossess notices, an so forth, in the meanwhile. In due course Sunday arrives, and someone hands you $500. What would the state of mind be? Use every ounce of imagination and feeling that you have. Fantasy freely on the pleasure, the relief from tension, in actually holding in your very hand that $500. Imagine waving that check gleefully right under Neville's nose. $500—in your possession! Now all our problems can go to the devil. You are saved.

You and I have said time and again, 'Why, today feels just like Sunday,' or '—Monday,' or '—Saturday.' We have also said in the middle of summer, 'Why this feels and looks like the fall of the year.' This is positive proof that you and I have definite feelings associated with these different days, months and seasons of the year. Because of this association, we can at any time consciously dwell in that day or season which we have selected."

In other words since we associate definite emotional tone-values with certain days or seasons, we can easily conjure up imaginatively those days or seasons in our minds. Sunday has for most of us a well-defined set of images and feelings which can readily be evoked for the purpose of our exercise.

"If today were Wednesday and you decided that it would be quite possible for your desire to embody a new realisation of yourself by Sunday, then Sunday becomes the point in time that you would visit. To make this visit, you shut out Wednesday and let in Sunday. This is accomplished by simply feeling that it is Sunday. Begin to hear the church-bells; being to feel the quietness of the day and all that Sunday means to you; actually feel that it is Sunday. When this accomplished, feel the joy of having received that which on Wednesday was but a desire. Feel the complete thrill of having received it, and then return to Wednesday, the point in time you left behind you. In doing this, you created a vacuum in consciousness by moving from Wednesday to Sunday. Nature, abhorring a vacuum, rushes in to fill it, thereby fashioning a mold in the likeness of that which you potentially create, namely, the joy of having realised your defined desire."

By dwelling now, on Wednesday, on the sense of ecstasy and freedom that you would have on Sunday when the saving shekels arrive, you project yourself forward in time. And since time, according to most metaphysical teaching, is but a creation of man's consciousness, a form of his thinking and feeling, time itself may be superseded and future events anticipated. For "Now," as the Bible says, "Now is the appointed time." Not tomorrow, not Sunday—not even next year. Right now, at this very moment, one may save oneself.

Such states of consciousness demand not merely mental concentration and steadfastness of purpose, and indomitable will and courage, but an ability to feel, a high capacity to evoke at a moment's notice an enormous potential of emotion. Whether the average person can do this is another matter. Certainly some people can do it. Neville, I am sure, can do it. But he is an artist, a dancer. He has been enabled by his training, by his life's discipline, to assume a definite role. He can adopt a certain part, acting it out as though it were true. His is the ability and capacity to achieve identification with mental images, with a personality other than his own—that is an intrinsic part of his emotional make-up. That is why such states of consciousness are open and available to him—as naturally they are to similarly trained and similarly constituted people.

But John Doe is not, I am afraid, capable of such unrestrained flights of feeling and imagination. His mind has become entirely too restrained for such flights into the empyrean. I do not say that in the last analysis that such feats are impossible to the average person. But I do insist that training is necessary—training in the art of "letting go," in the discipline of feeling, and in the analysis of psychological states. This takes such time and effort that there are few willing to embark upon a way of life that implies the expenditure of much time and labor. But if they do not wish to do so, then such states of consciousness and such spiritual achievements must remain mere dreams, fantasies, visions of another world completely beyond their reach.

Though my sympathies are largely with Neville both as to many of his conceptions and technical procedures—yet I feel that several factors are absent from his method. He is absolutely correct in placing emphasis on "feeling." By means of this intensity of feeling, all things become possible. But the problem is to provoke such an intensity, a storm, a madness of emotion by means of which a communion with the unconscious self may be established. This certainly has not been adequately dealt with.

Moreover, Neville advises relaxation. One must relax to the point of "floating," and losing awareness of one's body. But how shall we achieve such deep relaxation? This is not easy for most of us. What instruction does Neville give?

"You take your attention away from the problem and place it upon your being. You say silently but feelingly, 'I AM.' Simply feel that you are faceless and formless and continue doing so until you feel yourself floating.

"'Floating' is a psychological state which completely denies the physical. Through practice, in relaxation and willingly refusing to react to sensory impressions, it is found to develop a state of consciousness of pure receptivity."

I feel inclined to wager large odds that most who hear him or any other teacher of metaphysics, have not the least notion as to how to relax. There is nothing metaphysical in relaxation. By following a few simple rules which operate in accordance with known physiological and psychological laws, a deep state of freedom from neuro-muscular tension can be induced. I propose dealing with this thought on a later page, and suggest an elaborate technique for adequate relaxation.

Moreover and far more important—what shall we do about developing this intensity of feeling? Merely to relax will not do it. One can relax, lose complete consciousness of the body, "float" beautifully away from awareness of sense and mind—and still be as cold-blooded as a fish. Neville's method is sound enough. But the difficulty is that few people are able to muster up this emotional exaltation or this intellectual concentration which are the royal approaches to the citadel of the Unconscious. As a result of this definite lack of training or technique, the mind wanders all over the place, and a thousand and one things totally unrelated to "I AM" are ever before their attention.

I believe that the ancients had superior methods. Confronted by the same problems, and by the same lack of training, they evolved methods which have stood the test of time. To some people they prescribed a long course of psychological training, having as its logical objective the development of a tremendous power of mental concentration. This training we have come to know as Yoga. To others not temperamentally capable of this, or unwilling to engage upon such a discipline, arduous to the extreme, they worked out other methods.

Anything that will tend to exalt the mind and feelings, is useful. Music, color, poetry, perfumes—anything that will intoxicate the mind and senses within certain limits, is utilisable. It is more difficult to describe invocation, another method they employed. It is simpler to explain it by quoting several examples of them in these pages, so that the reader can develop some idea of their content and power and ecstasy.

The writers of these invocations were well acquainted with what we can call the "I AM" principle, for they employed it throughout. But not alone, as we shall see. This subject, therefore, I will reserve for another chapter, when I shall attempt to describe it as some length.

PART III
New Thought

CHAPTER EIGHT

History

It was during the spring of 1941, shortly before I began active work on the writing of this book, that I became acquainted with Unity. I had made a point, in New York City where I was then residing, of listening to the radio early in the morning. On one occasion, whilst idling with the tuning dials, I pushed a button without any deliberate intent—and WMCA came through. A man was speaking in a nice, quiet, soft voice, though a little monotonously. It sounded somewhat inspirational. Not too exciting perhaps, yet what he had to say intrigued me and held my attention. Ever since that day, and for some considerable time, part of my morning has been devoted to a faithful listening to the Unity programme—to my edification, good fortune, and personal inspiration. Even during the war years when I served in the army, I attempted whenever it was possible to tune in on that station.

My astonishment would have been great had I then known that this programme was but one of many sponsored by Unity all over the country. Unity had gained the distinction years ago, of being the first organisation in the country to use the radio for religious broadcasts. Originally, Station WOQ in Kansas City was the only Unity School's broadcasting station. It was not originally owned and operated by Unity—that came later. It was authorised to broadcast music, entertainment and weather and market reports. But during 1924 Unity purchased the station, moving it to their own administration building. Some ten years later, the station was discontinued because its wave-length required for more general and commercial purposes. Many Unity students feared that this loss would prove a serious handicap to the institution. Their fears proved groundless. Other station facilities came to be rented. Today twelve broadcasting stations located in various cities in the United States carry Unity programs regularly, extending all the way from California to New York, and from Michigan in the north to Louisville, Kentucky in the south. I understand that there is even one in Auckland, New Zealand.

To me, the story of the phenomenal rise of Unity to prominence and wide organisation is as fascinating a story as ever I heard. Were not the facts well authenticated, one might well believe that the whole thing should be dismissed as fantasy. Quite apart from its ethics and formal teaching, the organisation with its many ramifications and diversified aspects, is enough to excite wonder. It has grown from a family of a man and wife. From the depths of dire sickness, they cured themselves by means of a metaphysical message. The outgrowth of their personal miraculous healing has now become a corporation that owns extensive buildings, executive and administrative offices, and a large farm of several hundred acres. It includes a publishing house that issues over a million magazines a month and millions of educational books a year. Not only so, but it maintains a correspondence that necessitated the writing and mailing of three million or more letters in a single year.

Unity centres and classes are now established all over the globe, in the principal cities in the United States, Canada, England, Hawaii, and Africa. These centres offer instruction in the Unity teaching to all who are interested, the majority of them being open daily for teaching, healing, devotional services, and the sale of Unity literature. Unity maintains a field ministry that is far-reaching, and the benefits disseminated through the ministry of the Unity leaders and students are inestimable. Thousands of people in all walks of life are daily given new understanding, new courage, and new faith.

In discussing the way his work has grown, Charles Fillmore who was one of the original founders of Unity, asserts modestly but earnestly in a book called *Unity's Fifty Golden Years*, written by Miss Dana Gatlin, that "We thought we would just help our neighbors and the people locally, but it must be that Spirit needed us, because the work spread and grew marvelously. This is the method by which Unity has succeeded. Every person who is helped by Unity passes the news on to others. Every mail brings new inquiries, every meeting new faces..."

Not particularly inspiring are figures, facts, and statistics. In this country maybe we are too prone to use such facts in an over-dramatic way. But sometimes they help to illustrate an idea. For example, I could state that if all the letters comprising Unity's annual correspondence of three million or more letters were placed end to end, they would form a chain extending ten times around the world. Or that if all the paper used for the literary productions of the Unity plant were divided amongst the population of New York City, each person would have almost half-a-pound of paper for himself.

Does this sort of thing tend to edification? No, figures by themselves are not very illuminating. Yet in this particular instance, they do help to convey some sort of notion of the growth of an idea. It is an idea that once inflamed the imagination of the founders of Unity. And it was their impassioned enthusiasm about this simple idea that enabled them similarly to inflame the imaginations of hundreds of thousands of other people. The movement swept this country, and spread abroad to other countries in the world. Millions of people have bought and still buy its literature, and thus have been affected in one way or another by its teachings. A large percentage of them have undoubtedly been enabled to improve their lives in a vast number of ways. Some survey of its history is imperative therefore, to give us an insight into the origins and nature of this one idea to realise how it affected the minds and lives of two people, who in turn vitalised the minds and lives of an unknown number of others.

The beginnings are humble—as great beginnings always are. No dramatic events, no fanfare of trumpets, no world-shaking announcements in the newspapers, Charles Fillmore was born on August 22nd, 1854, on an Indian reservation on the Sauk River, near Saint Cloud, Minnesota. His father was a trader with the Chippewa Indians, his mother a Canadian of English and Welsh ancestry. As a result of a fall on ice when he was a boy, injuries were sustained which in time, though diagnosed merely as rheumatism, developed into a tubercular infection of the right hip. Abscesses formed, extending not only to the bones and ligaments comprising the hip articulation, but also to the surrounding area of the legs, and the arms too. Soon his right leg became several inches shorter than the left, and to all appearances, he seemed doomed to chronic invalidism. He got around with the aid of crutches and cane. The right leg withered, and he had to wear a steel extension with cork soles built up three and a half or four inches so that the afflicted leg would measure up in length with its mate. The result of this was a far-reaching curvature of the spine, including, amongst the appearance of an insidious crop of other symptoms, partial deafness.

Later on, he studied metallurgy, and while working as railroad clerk at Denison in Texas, he met a school teacher named Myrtle Page, whom he married in the year 1881, in Clinton, Mo. They had the usual troubles that beset a young married couple, financial and domestic, until a certain climax developed. Mrs. Fillmore's family had been subject to a history of tuberculosis. Early in her own life, she had contracted pulmonary tuberculosis, and eventually the tubercular lesions so fulminated that nothing availed her. As a last resort, the Fillmores considering returning to the mountains where the purity and dryness of the air might be palliative. The medical prognosis was that she had but six months to live. It was not a very happy or promising picture.

In 1886, the tide of their lives was turned by their attending a metaphysical lecture given in Kansas City. Some friends had heard some similar addresses, and hence strongly recommended their attendance. A certain Dr. E. B. Weeks, who was a representative of the Illinois Metaphysical College, founded by Emma Curtis Hopkins, came to their home town of Chicago, promoting a course of lessons which stressed as the keynote a modified Christian Science. Myrtle Fillmore was considerably impressed. One idea above all others stood out in her mind like a vital flame. While lecturing, Dr. Weeks had asserted as a basic part of her creed that "I am a child of God and therefore I do not inherit sickness."

You must remember that Myrtle Fillmore's family was tubercular, and her own pulmonary tuberculosis had existed from early girlhood. She probably thought she was tainted because of her hereditary strain, and was therefore doomed if not to an early death, then to a life of constant suffering and pain. This one idea which altered, as it were, the perspective of her notions about heredity, came as such a shock psychically, that it startled her out of the rut of sick thinking and feeling. It changed her entire perspective of life. As a result, she began to improve in health, and the tubercular infection became arrested. The healing began almost at once. Within a year she was in excellent health to such an extent that she was healing her neighbors. She attended other lectures in the same series, and listened intently to what Mrs. Emma Curtis Hopkins had to say when she later came to Kansas City to start some classes.

Myrtle Fillmore died on October 6, 1931, nearly ninety years of age. Forty-five years earlier, medical science had given her up to die. Through sheer faith in a metaphysical idea she abrogated and nullified that death sentence, giving lie to the medical prognosis. She spent the subsequent years of her life in active service, not passively and resting as becomes a good tubercular, but helping others through the exercise of that simple faith in Christ's teachings to which she attributed her own healing. This one fact alone is enough to demand that her message be listened to. We must learn what she has to say because her ideas, her message, are symbols of a healing and saving and transforming nature. Not only must we listen. We must try to understand. Her ideas and terms each of us must translate into other terms intelligible to us, associating them with other concepts in our mind, until the whole mind is divinely transmuted into a mentality that, like the symbol, has the power to save and transform.

The faith that she had which so influenced her to heal herself and dedicate the rest of her life to healing and helping others, can be easily summarised. It is very simple and very brief. Dana Gatlin, one of the popular Unity writers, has expressed it directly in these words: "The transforming idea was this: that God is Spirit or Mind. In Divine Mind are infinite ideas of life, love, substance, intelligence, Truth. Man has access to these ideas through his own individual mind. Thus he has direct contact with his source. God is the source of his life, and his life is unfailing, eternal. The history of Unity is a record of faith. Without faith—absolute persevering faith—Myrtle Fillmore would never have been divinely healed more than fifty years ago of a medically 'incurable' ailment. Without absolute faith she would never have been inspired to help her friends and neighbors through the medium of prayer."

During these various adventures of discovery and of transformation, we must remember that Charles Fillmore was a chronic invalid, seldom free from pain, as he himself testifies. At first his wife's preoccupation with metaphysical principles did not interest him especially. It is strange how very often the woman is more intuitive than the man of a family. Apparently it was Myrtle to whom credit must be given for the primary impetus which was eventually to result in Unity. Charles, no doubt, later on did much of the organisation and executive work so necessary to the successful administration of such an enterprise. This is not to say, however, that the spiritual and metaphysical side of the work subsequently did not claim him. It did to a very large extent. He is the author of several books and a large amount of journalism. The subsequent success of the Unity School must, in very large measure, be attributed also to him and his work. But it must be noted that as his wife improved as a result of her adherence to her newly found understanding of her divine inheritance, he too began to be absorbed in the same study. With gratifying results, he applied the healing principle to his own case. His chronic pains ceased and he slowly grew stronger and healthier. Even the hip joint began to show signs of healing to such an extent that within a few years he totally dispensed with the steel extension that he had constantly worn since he was a child—the leg had begun to lengthen. "I can now truthfully say," he writes in the introduction to Dana Gatlin's fascinating history of Unity's fifty years of living, "that I am on the way to perfect healing, although eighty-four years of age..." That was in 1939—and he, some fifty years ago, cripple and invalid—almost licked before he had started.

His conversion, for so we may call it, produced radical changes within him. For as he persisted with his prayers and meditations and introspections, he became aware of the dynamic quality of spiritual power which began to pour through him. As he claimed his kinship with God, even his identity, in accordance with the principles of his newly-found faith, he began to participate in all that was God. And the power that poured through him was God's power—so dynamic as to be capable of awakening "physical sensation at the nerve extremities." He then realised that he was beginning "body regeneration as taught by Jesus Christ. Neither physiology nor psychology offers a nomenclature describing it. The first sensation was in my forehead, a 'crawly' feeling when I was affirming life. The I found that I could produce this same feeling in the bottom of my feet and other nerve extremities by concentrating my attention at the place and silently affirming life. I spend several hours every day in this process and I found that I was releasing electronic forces sealed up in the nerves. This I have done for nearly fifty years until now I have what may be termed an electric body that is gradually replacing the physical."

The sensations of the experience described by Charles Fillmore are not to be thought of as fantasy or outside the realm of ordinary human experience. As I hope to show later in this book, any normal person may for himself experience what to Charles Fillmore was salvation and the impact of the divine upon his body. Physiologically many explanations may be devised to render intelligible what actually occurred. Possibly the easiest and most readily acceptable—which does not in the least nullify his spiritual conception of it—is that concentration upon any part of the body will cause, through the stimulation of those nerve fibres called vaso-motor nerves, a transmission of vasodilator impulses along the nerves, causing a relaxation of the muscular coats of the blood-vessels. The arterioles and systemic capillaries undergo a relaxation, with the result that they hold and transmit a larger quantity of blood than is usual. Blood is life and the carrier of life. The serum of the blood conveys to the area meditated upon, an increase supply of red corpuscles and a greater concentration of the white corpuscles, the body's policemen, as well as the immune bodies for which bacteria seem to have an innate dislike. A fight thus goes on—and if there is hope, optimism, and a high spirit, the body wins. Or if you prefer, the rule of God holds predominance, and the error of disease is cast out. Slowly, infection will be driven out, to be replaced by bubbling and radiant health. It is a perceptible and verifiable result which can come to anyone through the following of certain rules—rules and processes which, while not essentially religious, being mainly psychological and physiological, may be considerably enhanced and augmented by a truly religious attitude.

Anyway, Charles Fillmore, so improved in health that it was distinctly noticeable to all around them. They became a focal centre, from which radiated good-will and the same message of faith and healing which had proven helpful to them. From that humble beginning, their ministry of prayer and Unity teaching resulting from those early experiences, now girdle the earth through its periodicals, teachers and centres. Hundreds of thousands of persons have received instruction through them that makes religion of practical daily help. Unity now maintains—in contrast to the solitary working of those two original founders over fifty years ago—a force of nearly five hundred active workers at Kansas City alone. They are engaged in spreading "the vital truths of life that Jesus Christ taught in order that humanity may be enlightened, enriched and blessed."

Their example became an inspiration to those around them. Myrtle Fillmore found that through her prayers and her idealistic life-attitude, she was able to help the people around her.

Through her prayers, her children and her neighbors and their children were healed. Many of the diseases and infections to which mankind has believed itself susceptible, were present all around her, and by her faith and her words of encouragement and inspiration, these accretions which befoul human life were thrust into the outer darkness.

Persons would appear from all over the country, descending upon their establishment in order to obtain divine healing and help of all kinds. All this was a terrific strain on the Fillmore's resources. But the house they occupied at that time was large, with several upstairs rooms, and everybody was taken in. For example, from California came a deaf boy who thought he was a prophet. It is a pity that we are not informed by the literature of Unity what happened to this deaf would-be seer. How sad, if through being cured of his deafness, he became just an ordinary boy and lost the power to prophesy! Sometimes the world is the loser when an individual discards some neurotic tendency and becomes "normal" and well. Sickness, often enough, is effectual to produce artistic and spiritual masterpieces which no other stimulus could evoke.

She must have been quite an extraordinary woman, this Myrtle Fillmore. Not only was she responsible for the renewed inspiration of those around her, giving them a re-invigorated faith in life, but common-sense undoubtedly was one of her richest endowments. Her letters to inquirers about Truth are very sober and commendable, revealing that she was able to bring metaphysics down to earth, interpreting life and its manifold problems along psychological and definitely human lines.

For example, in a letter to a woman who attempted to employ the Unity teachings to recover from a serious burn, Myrtle Fillmore writes this woman in effect, that not only will the sense of her identity with God effectively heal her when she has become ill or hurt, but more than this. The inward realisation of the indwelling presence and power should produce an unprecedented mental alertness, a co-ordination of feeling as well as thought, so that the sensorium and central nervous system will report more quickly to the brain when danger is nigh. Because of this stimulated sensory and motor activity of the entire neurological organism, these so-called "accidents" will not and cannot take place. God indwelling the soul, should make for increased accuracy of thought as well as accuracy of movement. An integration of the discrete elements of the personality should occur, so that no longer would these warring elements lead the individual into predicaments which in the last resort, are self-induced and self-devised in ignorance. Intuitively then, because of this inner unity, one will always do the right thing. God will be doing the work—the human part serving as the instrument, the machine, by means of which the work is done. God, working in the heart, must produce laudable and satisfactory ends, in the encompassing of which no dangerous or untoward event can occur.

In another letter, which she wrote to a business man, complaining of unsatisfactory business conditions for which he wished to employ the Truth teachings, she wrote very eloquently and aptly: "Building a business is more than purchasing certain canned goods and beans and sugar, matches and soap, and putting them on the shelf. You must put life into every part of the store, and then radiate this life towards your customers. Make them feel that you are there to give them the best possible service and food, and that you really love your work. To increase our earning capacity and our income, we must keep increasing in our ability, and adding to our funds of knowledge and loving interest. Prosperity is daily growth, and the manifest returns come as we keep the way open. 'Then give to the world the best you have, and the best will come back to you.'" Many business men today would do well to listen attentively to such advise.

This, I think, is sanity par excellence. Here is evidence that metaphysics breeds not superstition and extreme fanaticism as is commonly supposed, but a cultured and mature and adult attitude towards every problem that may come. Prosperity, she says, is daily growth. It is a marvelous concept—so lacking in the usual vaporous platitudinous outpourings of metaphysical writers and teachers. She was a practical psychologist in her own way, no doubt because of her teaching experience, as well as from having been the mother of three children. At headquarters, she had a way of stopping and patting people on the shoulder as she passed them. It would be a different person every day, but before very long she had made the rounds of the whole staff, uttering words of encouragement and good cheer to them all. In everybody, and in his work, she seemed vitally interested, making that person feel that both he and his work were of immense importance. Naturally this bred an atmosphere of perfect harmony and cooperation, and demonstrated better than all else how her faith would influence mankind.

The Fillmore's oldest son, Lowell, has an interestingly vivid story as to the manner in which his mother was always ready to pass on the message, to assist anyone who approached her portal. He narrates that "one day an agent came to sell picture frames and moulding, and he had a suitcase filled with samples of frames to show. Mother always let everybody in, and he spread his things out on the floor. I wanted to see what he had, and mother told him, 'This is my little boy.' He spoke to me and said, 'Well, *my* little boy will never see again.' Mother talked to him and told him that it was God's will for everyone to see, and after a while, he asked mother if she would come to see his little boy who had cataracts on his eyes. So mother went to see him, and she said his eyes looked as though they were covered with something like the white of an egg. The second time mother went to see him, he could see well enough to come to the door and let her in. In just a little while his eyes were completely healed."

This is how they began, speaking here and there, encouraging and inspiring now this person, now that. Obviously there were limitations to just how much they could do alone in this personal way.

Inevitably, expansion had to come to them. It is worth emphasising again now that Unity School has a printing plant that monthly issues seven periodicals. Numerous books presenting the Unity teaching, besides leaflets and booklets, comprise their list of publications. All this is the development from the time when because of her own healing and inspiration, Myrtle Fillmore began praying for the help and guidance of others, and when Charles Fillmore, crippled but inspired with a high purpose, tireless and fearless, was holding meetings and lecturing, buying small variegated lots of paper on which to print his magazine.

And so it was, that in order to reach a larger number of people and to spread the expanding work, they instituted a magazine called *Modern Thought*. It was a pretty general periodical in those days. It reviewed almost all of the metaphysical teachings then extant—not confining itself to the formulation of their own particular beliefs. The time was not yet when they would be able to formulate their system distinctly as apart from others. Unity was growing—both as a system of thinking and praying, and as an organisation. Neither Charles or Myrtle Fillmore had the least experience in professional writing or in publishing. They had no idea when they began, whither they were being led. They took a chance on it. Charles Fillmore liked writing, and his liking was accentuated by the fact that now he had found something vital and engrossing to write about. "I had never thought of editing or writing until I got this idea," he says, referring to the magazine. "But I saw that Christianity was not something just to be believed. It had to be lived. It was a science."

The magazine circulated widely, reaching an ever-increasing number of people. Its influence spread wave after wave, fanning outward like the ripples in a lake after a stone has been thrown in. The ripples reached the edge of the lake and a contrary movement is started backwards toward the centre. The magazines were the centrifugal ripples, and calls for help from readers were the ripples moving center wise. So numerous were these inquiries and demands for spiritual help that in April, 1890, these two people formed the Society of Silent Help, which has since developed into the present Society of Silent Unity. For quite some considerable time, just the two of them sat together in meditation and prayer on behalf of those requesting help. Later on, two or three other people joined them and sat with them. Silent Unity expanded tremendously. Recently there were one hundred or more Silent Unity workers at headquarters in Kansas City, praying for the salvation of others, attempting to help them solve their problems and overcome sickness and lack and misery.

In February, 1893, *Unity* magazine announced that the group, now a well-established organisation, was receiving as high as fifty letters a day. It was maintaining two separate hours, specially set aside from the routine of the day, for the one purpose of prayer for the benefit of those seeking "to demonstrate over negative conditions," as Dana Gatlin put it. Fifty letters a day. Fifty people in trouble. Fifty tortured cries for help, re-orientation to life and alleviation of sorrow of different kinds. It may not sound a great number, but it takes a venture like this to make you really aware of human misery. Only then can you appreciate how eagerly men and women will clutch at the nearest promise of aid to gain respite from their woes. In one year recently, Silent Unity received over six hundred thousand requests for help. The requests cover a multitude of things—sickness, poverty, moral and marital problems, and so forth.

These requests for help come to the headquarters not only by mail, but also by telephone. Unity today maintains one of the largest switchboards in Kansas City and can be directly reached any hour of the day or night. In her book dealing with Unity's half-century existence, the author Dana Gatlin writes: "The thought of that telephone room at Silent Unity has brought a tide of calmness, assurance, courage, faith, to many distressed persons, nearby and far away, when caught in a sudden dilemma or serious trouble." Help therefore, is a serious thing as envisaged by these Unity people. It is no casual service, extended when the next little bit of leisure shows up. They must have untold faith in themselves, their metaphysics and their methods, to maintain social services of this kind.

At various times of the day, those who have written to Unity sit quietly by themselves wherever they may be, and turn their minds inward. Momentarily they switch their attention away from the wake-a-day world, attempting to become aware of another more spiritual side of life altogether, through the agency of prayer. The result of this? Well, Clara May Rowland, the present director of Silent Unity, states that during her connection with the department, she has read letters "testifying to the healing of almost every known physical ailment, including cancer, tuberculosis, blindness, deafness, and so on..."

The method that is practised by the silent workers of Silent Unity, is one calculated to lift their minds above concern and preoccupation with the problems of those whose appeal for help. As a group, they strive to elevate themselves to an immediate apprehension of God as the only presence and healing power there is. In this divine consciousness they feel they are able to transcend purely phenomenal conditions, no longer picturing the individual as one who is sorely in need of help, but truly an individual "as God sees him: pure, whole, alive, and alight with the glory of the Father's presence." Unity's history states that they prefer the word 'omnipresent' to 'absent' in speaking of our prayers for healing; for they are given in the realisation that Spirit, which is the one and only healer, is omnipresent. "The Spirit of God is here with and in us and also with and in those to whom we are ministering. In Spirit, there is neither distance or separation. We speak the word, and the Holy Spirit in the individual does the renewing, healing, restoring work in him."

It is a little difficult for the average person not yet fluently conversant with metaphysics and who has hitherto managed to escape the fascination found in such systems, to appreciate the *modus operandi* of the group originally calling themselves the Society of Silent Help. It works upon the theorem that upon the spiritual plane, space and time are not existent, are transcended. Space and time are, philosophically speaking, categories of thought, forms created by the mind and imagination, not consciously maybe, but nonetheless unconsciously. The concept of unconscious mental activity given to us by modern psychology, and verified beyond all shadow of doubt, enormously aids us in the understanding of psychological creative activity of which we may be totally unaware.

The object of prayer and aspiration is exaltation beyond that level of mind where space and time exists as realities. In the heights of spiritual illumination they are recognised as fictions—as much fictions as neurotic symptoms that are realised for the first time by a person undergoing analytical treatment. Psychic paralysis, hysterical dermatoses, neurotic indecision and anxiety, and gastric incoordinations—all of those can be deliberately manufactured by the parapathiac for certain quite well-defined, though not consciously realised, purposes. They are neurotic fictions with which he invests himself. Psychological analysis has as its goal the self-realisation of these fictions, and consequently their elimination. Similarly, prayer has as its object the utter transcending of the plane of duality, of time and distance, so that he who prays, comes to realise his identity with God, or that divine Mind which is common in all things alike. "On the plane of spirit space is as if it were not, and those who go into the upper chamber of their minds," aptly observes Miss Gatlin, "will be as if they were gathered together in one place as were those at Jerusalem on the Pentecostal day, and 'all will receive the gift of the Holy Spirit.'"

This, then, is the technique behind absent or omnipresent healing. It is not necessary for the patient or one desirous of help, to be in the physical presence of the healer. Office attendance is not conceived of as necessary to those in spiritual harmony. Where sympathy exists, physical impact is hardly important. Two lovers can sit for hours side by side, with hardly a word spoken, not even a glance at each other. None of these delicate but eloquent gestures of love need necessarily pass between them. They are silent. Yet a world of sympathy and inner communication exists for both of them. Space and time are thrust completely from their minds—and they exist in eternity, with mutual understanding, love, and identification. So also we must assume with the act of prayer and so-called absent healing, as employed by Silent Unity. Its wonderful success is a fairly well-nigh incontrovertible demonstration that to be present physically in the office of the healer or Unity's headquarters is not an absolute imperative. By prayer, the healers lift their minds beyond all temporal considerations, endeavoring to realise their own Godhead, and in this exalted mood of divine consciousness, pray for the spiritual rehabilitation of those who have made appeals. The ultimate object of this group of silent healers in the background of the Unity organisation is to realise the presence of God so intensely that every illusion, both of mind and body of all those who come under its power at the hour of prayer, shall be swept away.

This Silent Unity work evidently comprises one of the most important and integral parts of the Unity's mission. Not only does it cater to individuals alone, attempting to extend aid in overcoming all human problems, but it attempts moreover, to aid the world itself. Whether successful or not—who knows, in spite of signs and indications to the contrary? One is reminded of the activities of some of the Catholic religious orders who are engaged in constant prayer, meditating and praying especially whist the world is at sleep, at pleasure, or wasting itself in sin. Unity's procedure is somewhat different, though the motive is not too dissimilar. Every morning at eleven o'clock, a prayer for world peace is broadcast by radio, being thus sent forth everywhere in the air as a benediction for all mankind. This is but one of many examples showing Unity's intense evangelistic spirit, and its initiative and modernity in spiritual matters. Every individual everywhere is invited to unite with Unity's broadcasting in declaring the word of faith uttered in the prayer that "Liberty, justice, righteousness and peace are now established in the name of Jesus Christ."

Miss Gatlin also informs us that "at twelve o'clock noon, a prosperity prayer service is held. The prosperity class thought is spoken audibly, repeated silently, and meditated upon until every soul is quickened with the realisation of God's inexhaustible substance. Then the prospering word is sent forth into the busy world in the assurance that whosoever is receptive to and accepts it, is richly blessed. Every Silent Unity worker and every loyal member speaks the word for prosperity at the noon hour in the full belief and conviction that when man learns to understand and accept providence there will be no strife, greed, want or war."

It is this phase of the work that really constitutes the heart and soul of the Unity organisation. Prayer conceived as the mystical identity of man and God, as the dynamic mechanism of spiritual progress, as the means of really living, is the backbone as well as the breath and pulse of all the society's endeavors and activities. "Prayer is the crux, core, and sinew of Unity activity today." Just as Myrtle and Charles Fillmore, in the early days of their newly-found orientation after having heard the addresses of Dr. Weeks, discovered that the entire trend of their life's direction was altered by prayer and a high aspiration and purpose, so today, is a similar emphasis placed upon Unity's work. Faith in God constitutes the motive power—prayer being the drive.

How the name Unity came to be specifically appropriated, is a very interesting story by itself. We must remember that at the beginning of their work, the Fillmores' metaphysic was of a pretty general character. The early publications were devoted to a consideration of nearly all the metaphysical ideas current at that time. There was no concentration on the particular system that later they evolved and espoused to the exclusion of all else. But a year or so after the group had begun its meetings in Kansas City, the Fillmores were preoccupied with this problem of what name to give to their system. Not that they were wanting to form a system and an organisation to set them apart from others. The system slowly formed itself as their knowledge and experience grew. And so did the organisation, as they labored altruistically, devoting themselves to the alleviation of human suffering and despair. But it was inevitable that they should formulate all their ideas in a system and an organisation that was unique to them.

Before a name could be evolved altogether adequate to their needs, their beliefs had to be more specifically moulded. The vast mass of metaphysical material which had made its way into their ken by way of lectures, reading and meditations, had to be sifted, criticised, and assimilated—then organised and defined. All of this gradually occurred.

It was in the spring of 1891 that the name came. While sitting, meditating in the silence, an idea flashed suddenly into the mind of Charles Fillmore. It was "Unity." And of it, Charles Fillmore relates that "The name came right out of the ether, just as the voice of Jesus was heard by Paul in the heavens. No one else heard it, but it was as clear to me as though somebody had spoken to me." So forcibly did this name strike him that he exclaimed, "That's it," with probably a similar degree of intensity as did Archimedes when he ran down the streets of Carthage in his nightshirt, shouting, "Eureka." The name Unity seemed to describe exactly what he wanted. His beliefs and his metaphysics were totally devoted to achieving that conscious realisation of his identity and unity with God, the All of Life. So completely did he feel that this was the name which henceforth was to characterise his work, that he told other people about it. So Unity came to be adopted as the name of the organisation itself. The name of the Society of Silent Help was then altered to the name it now bears, the Society of Silent Unity.

On all the literature issued by the Unity press there will be found a most beautiful symbol. Its form varies, depending upon the format of the book, the pamphlet, or the stationery. But whatever the piece of printing is, invariably this symbol will be found, and is now more or less the sign and symbol of Unity. It is the winged globe or sun disc. As is well-known, this is primarily an Egyptian symbol, being found on the ruins of some of the ancient Egyptian temples, monuments, steles, as well as on papyri and vignettes. Though its earliest use undoubtedly was in Egypt, some assume that it occurred in differing forms in the religions of other races. The Fillmores looked upon it as representing the relationship existing between the component parts of man's spiritual constitution. It is an integral symbol, a symbol of the unity of God and man, appropriate therefore to the high purpose of the society.

There are several other aspects of Unity activity that I should like to call attention to, prior to describing in some detail the salient points of their teaching as promulgated through the writings of the Fillmores, Dr. Cady, Miss Dana Gatlin, and some of the other popular Unity writers, in addition to a publishing plant, large administrative offices, the services of Silent Unity. Unity conducts a correspondence school, a social work organisation devoted to the distribution of free literature, and a very extensive farm and Country Club.

It was in the year 1909 that the correspondence courses in Christian metaphysics were begun. Correspondence courses are one of the peculiar characteristics of this vast eager country of ours. In any single European country distances and travelling facilities are nowhere nearly comparable to those here, and any individual desirous of obtaining religious or metaphysical training, had only to travel for a few hours to the nearest centre in order to get to his source of information. It was not and still is not always so easy in America. With a teacher in Philadelphia and a student in Spokane, Washington, wanting desperately to obtain metaphysical teaching, the journey, the expense, and the time would be very formidable obstacles. This was very early recognised and many educational organisations took steps to aid such people, particularly eliminating the formidableness of such obstacles. Unity in accordance with this trend, had long contemplated the advisability of such a correspondence course in the principles of its philosophy, but somehow can never be ignored. It is an emphatic appeal for assistance, to ignore which would be criminal and cruel. Anyway, it had that effect upon the Unity leaders. In this way, lessons came to be prepared and were mailed out to all those making inquiry for such courses.

That these lessons have been successful, so far as concerns the dissemination of Truth principles, there is no doubt. People have read them and studied them and have been benefited by them. In fact, one might say that the widespread dissemination of Unity principles, and the formation of so many centres in almost every large city in the country, may be placed directly to the credit of this scheme.

How was this work carried on? What was the financial arrangement for the payment of such courses? Correspondence schools all over the country teaching different subjects, all place a considerable price upon their courses. The course costs such and such a sum of money, to be paid for either outright or else on the installment plan. Not so with Unity. To have done this would have been an affront to their metaphysical principle. It had always held there is an unlimited and infinite supply from which all their needs would eventually be met. Hence it was decided that the cost of the lessons would be met by the usual metaphysical method, the free-will offering plan, voluntary contributions. Many persons preferred to help that way, and each gave what he could afford. Those who could spare little, gave little, but with thanks and gratitude in their hearts. While those who could afford more, gave more—but both were benefited equally, none was discriminated against and each received the same service and attention.

Some people have developed the mistaken notion that because Unity is such a large organisation, comprising offices, printing plant, farm, correspondence school, etc., that it is a materially rich institution. Others even believe that it is heavily endowed, possibly by some rich Bible society, or a patron whose wealth is being poured into the Unity activities. However nice this would be for Unity, it is unfortunately not so. It is not an endowed institution, "but trusts to the divine law to have its daily needs provided for." The organisation has never solicited anyone for funds. Naturally, however, it makes known the fact that its existence is wholly dependent upon the generosity of those who have dealings with it. Therefore it welcomes free-will offerings and voluntary contributions of every sort. No pleas or appeals are or have ever been issued for funds.

The Unity periodicals never carry any paid advertising, and this fact cuts them off from a vast source of income which must therefore be obtained from a very extensive circulation of its variegated literature. Many of the books and magazines are published at such a low price that very little profit is made on most of them, and in some instances, there is actually a loss. Though not organised for individual profit, it does sell books and magazines which are distributed far and wide. Some of the popular magazines which can sell at their present low price because they carry such a vast quantity of expensive paid advertising. An enormous revenue is thus obtained which, in spite of low selling price, high administrative expenses and large royalties paid to authors and writers, yields a very fine profit. The price of the Unity magazines is entirely nominal—their deficit being made up by the voluntary contributions from those who have found in Unity that which their hearts desire. Each satisfied student and each person who has perceived Unity's message to be the Truth for him, enabling him to realise the constancy of infinite supply, power, and purpose, such a person inevitable invites Unity to partake of his worldly goods so that the stream of Truth may wander further afield. So we see that Unity does not need to be a heavily and richly endowed institution. It does not require the legacies and endowments of this world, however useful these might be. It is heavily endowed in another direction. It has placed its trust in spirit, in its receptivity to strong, positive ideas, in the promptness with which its acts upon these ideas, and in the ever-present bounty of God, which it feels comes into expression at the proper time and through the proper channels to meet whatever the need may be.

Another branch of the many-faceted organisation of Unity distributes free literature wherever it happens to be needed, to people in prisons, in institutions, hospitals, and to the shut-ins. Not even the blind are excluded from this service. A great many different types of Unity literature have been translated into Braille. Thus those who are deprived of their physical vision, may yet be enabled by the study of Truth, to open the eyes of Spirit and overcome their physical frustration. It may enable them to transmute a physical disability into a spiritual asset. All this is done through a group of Unity workers who adopted the mane of the Silent 70. Their inspiration for such a name was obviously that verse in the

10th chapter of Luke, reading, "The Lord appointed seventy others and sent them...into every city and place."

The department of the Silent 70 possibly was one of Unity's earliest developments in the path of spiritual service. The first suggestion of such a service to give spiritual instruction to people shut away from the world, for any reason, appeared many years ago in some of the notes of Charles Fillmore in the magazine. This was the year 1889. It occurred rightly to him that those who are sick, distressed and crippled, either in body or in soul,—these are the ones most of all need Unity. He wrote in effect that criminality is a persistence of infantile trends, a formulation with which modern psychology is wholly in sympathy. Nowadays, in enlightened institutions, the problem of delinquency is considered as an emotional fixation to habit formations developed in earlier years of the person's life. Physical and even intellectual development of the individual may have occurred, but the emotional make-up of the criminal, for example, is infantile. And so Charles Fillmore thought that they are in no way more responsible than children. He believed that it was circumstance and not choice, that forced one to go down the dark avenue of criminal endeavor. Circumstance, and the person's own lack of growth and unfoldment.

In one sense, however much we may dislike this concept, a similar conclusion is true of the person who is sick and diseased. Modern psychology has much to say on this topic, and it is stimulating indeed to find that Unity had thought similarly in general terms many years earlier. People are sick because they connive to escape from certain real but unpleasant situations. The truly mature person does not turn his back on experience of any kind. All is grist in his mill. Every experience is to be undergone and transmuted. It is by such means that he grows. But the individual who does not feel strong enough to cope with certain realities, feels impelled to escape from them by slipping back, unconsciously, to former methods of habit reaction. Not wishing to go to school, a child develops a bellyache, or a headache, or some other convenient kind of pain, which thus serve to buttress up what he desires to gain from his environment. Surely at the beginning, these are little more than imaginary. But such tricks eventually serve to develop habits which after a while become automatic; they can be resorted to without thought.

In one sense this is the disastrous consequence of forming habits. We must all have habits because we simply cannot afford to waste our precious time devoting conscious thought and attention to the myriad trivial events of life that come before us. All habits therefore, have meaning and motive. We develop types of reaction or habits, conditioned reflexes, which enable us to deal with certain situations unconsciously, without thinking deliberately. What we must be certain to do therefore, is to develop good, sensible, rational habits. So that when we do react unconsciously, that reaction will of necessity be the *right* one, one that makes for growth, not regression. That person who is sick, is one who, unconsciously, has fallen into the deep pit of bad habits—habits, the meaning of which he is now completely unaware, habits by means of which he has slipped back into infancy. Thus we find a person who is an adult in body and mind, with the emotional habits of a five-year old. How else could there be but conflict, and from conflict disease?

So Charles Fillmore believed that it is useful for the criminal and the sick to study philosophy, to become aware of the causes from which effects have followed. This is sound psychology, for by proper education and unfoldment, the evils and false conceptions of life, which have unthinkingly been brought about, may be thought about and by reflection be got rid of. Every inmate of a prison, for example, said Fillmore, should come to feel that he is not being unjustly punished but helped and educated, and that his keeper is in reality a brother. That those in authority are really interested in making him a better man. This may or may not be true. In some ways it is common knowledge that many a prisoner is a far better man than the warden who guards him, and that there are far worse criminals without than behind prison bars. But if the prisoner can bring himself to alter his point of view, the entire sentence may become so transmuted that he leaves it, not bitter and humiliated and ruined for the rest of his life, but definitely enriched and able to look at life from an angle which he would never have dreamed of before.

This work of the Silent 70 is an excellent field for social service. It is a splendid example of what Unity is doing in the ethical and social field. One thing for which I must give Unity credit, is the high ethical approach of its teachings. It intrigues me enormously. Metaphysical it may be, but it is very largely pre-eminently sound.

This high ethical approach to various problems was borne in upon me, I might mention in passing, by a passage from one of the lessons of Dr. Emile Cady on Truth. She had been discussing the fact that if one will turn to God, the spirit fiercely burning within one, all one's desires will automatically realise themselves—even as God's desire to create the world, realised itself too without effort. She deduces from that, that all desires are holy. They are Spirit already prompting man to evolve, to unfold. The mere fact that one wishes certain things, means that the aptitude for use is there too. If the things were not already possessed spiritually, one could not by any means desire them. She anticipates a question that could well be asked.

"Suppose I desire my neighbor's wife, or his property; is that desire born of God? And can I see it fulfilled by affirming that it is mine?"

She answers her own question brilliantly with deep insight into human needs, and here it is that we must admire the ethical approach that Unity has adopted. It does not stress the evilness of desire, or attempt to state that certain desires are good and others bad. All desires are good and holy, but one's goals need definition and understanding. "You do not and cannot by any possibility," she says, "desire that which belongs to another. You do not desire your neighbor's wife. You desire the love which seems to you to be represented by your neighbor's wife. You desire something to fill your heart's craving for love. Affirm that there is for you a rightful and an overflowing supply, and claim its manifestation. It will surely come, and your desire to possess your neighbor's wife, will suddenly disappear.

Sixteen miles southwest of Kansas City is a farm of five hundred acres. U. S. No. 50 passes by its very entrance. It is an amazing farm—if you will stop to consider that this is but one of many departments of the Unity School. Again I will resort to statistics and figures to convey an idea of just what this five hundred acre farm is like. I quote Mr. Rickert Fillmore. "There are now fifty-three operations carried on daily at the Farm. We have our street department, police department, fire department. The chimes in the tower were built by our own man who has had wide radio experience and is an expert. Our own engineers put in our light plant. Our waterworks system, with filtration equipment, is capable of supplying a community of four thousand persons. In our dairy we make our own ice cream. There are spraying and pruning crews for the two hundreds acres of apples, cherries, plums, peaches, grapes and other fruit. We have our own automobile repair shop, for in the many operations of the Farm, there is a lot of machinery involved." The modern swimming pool there is considered to be of the most beautiful in the environs of Kansas City. There is more-over a good nine-hole golf course and two tennis courts—all under the supervision of the Unity Country Club. Obviously the value of recreation has been adequately recognised, for metaphysics without play would certainly turn out a lot of very dull and uninteresting teachers, hardly capable of understanding and coping with people and their problems.

Rickert Fillmore, one of the sons of the founders, is evidently the guiding genius back of the development of the farm. He had a definite artistic trend and some training in that direction too. He worked with professional experts in the designing and execution of the landscaping. Even the buildings on the Farm, and they are beautiful indeed, were designed by him in collaboration with architects who sufficiently perceived his vision to execute his ideas.

Embodying a vision, and being devoted entirely to the needs of workers in the metaphysical field, one must needs surmise this farm to be a most usual institution. Apparently it is, for it has gradually developed an atmosphere which sometimes impinges itself on visitors. "Metaphysicians from all parts of the country have sensed it," Charles Fillmore tells us, "and observed its harmonious effect upon them. We have carefully noted their separate testimonies as to its quality, and they all agree that they have here a sense of freedom and peace."

Surely an enormous expenditure of money was necessary for the acquisition of such property and for the development and construction of the farm and its buildings. I have already discussed in part, the attitude of Unity toward money for lessons and services. That same attitude prevailed here. They went ahead and did what they saw fit to do, what they wanted to do with what they had. Throughout, they trusted in their own spiritual realisation, recognising that when the time was ready the necessary funds would be forthcoming. They kept the supply open, their ideals high, consequently their needs were always met. Never did any difficulty arise. The farm grew from a few acres bought in 1919, to the magnificent five hundred acre institution I have described, as a result of faith, and financed in exactly the same way.

The same condition was true when the present large administration building on Tracy Avenue was started. In this connection, Rhetta Chilcott, who started work at Unity headquarters in 1914 as a routine office worker, and who is no the office manager, give us these interesting facts. "We did not have any funds on hand for the purpose, but we started to put up the building, and through faith and prayer, we demonstrated enough funds each week to meet our bills and our payroll which we took care of each Saturday..."

With the arrival of Dr. Emile Cady, one of the really important turning points in the early development of what we can call the militant evangelism undertaken by Unity, occurred. Now that it had embarked on a wide program of dissemination, it was an event of the first magnitude for the growing organisation when she entered the widening sphere of the Fillmore's influence.

One day, Myrtle Fillmore ran across a small book entitled, *Finding the Christ Within Ourselves*. It had been written by Dr. Cady Myrtle Fillmore was so impressed with its sincere, lucid and forceful presentation of this mystical process which bore so many points of resemblance to the scheme which both she and her husband had espoused, that all excited, she passed it on to her husband to read. Both then realised that here was another voice in the wilderness. No longer solitary isolated workers, striving with living water to moisten the parched sand of the desert, for here was another worker. And an inspired and capable one at that. Naturally, the inevitable ensued. They wrote to her—that was in 1892. Curiously enough, they never met her personally until about 1927, when they both paid a visit to the eastern seaboard.

A warm and profound friendship and association developed almost instantaneously—the two musketeers became three. Dr. Cady was begged, invited, and cajoled to write for the magazine. After some persuasion—for apparently she was a modest, retiring, and unassuming woman—she complied with their requests to produce a series of articles that subsequently were collected in book form *Lessons in Truth*. This exposition of metaphysical principles is very simple and directly presented. It complies with the basic rules of all good didactic writing—combining euphony with simplicity and lucidity. It is a powerful book, giving wide evidence to a most understanding personality, one who without doubt had experienced some measure of the mystical religious experience of which she had written. *Lessons in Truth* was immediately adopted as Unity's textbook for beginners and inquirers, and still continues to be used as such. It has enjoyed a wide popularity, and has been translated into French, Italian, German, Norwegian, Dutch, Swedish and Spanish, and was also printed in Braille for the blind.

A special week has been set aside each year as Cady Week, during which an intensive study of this book is commenced by all Unity students everywhere.

Inestimable numbers of people all over the world would appear to have been aided by her in their rehabilitation and re-orientation. Testimonial letters still pour in—even after all these years. From here and from there they arrive. From all over the world. And from the length and breadth of this country they come, testifying to a new and higher direction given to their lives through the inspiration gained from *Lessons in Truth*.

CHAPTER NINE

Teaching

Although a consideration of historical factors and evolutionary antecedents belongs properly to another chapter where considerable space has been given to such topics, little need be said her save that all modern metaphysical systems owe a very great deal of their content to Christian Science. That debt is very often an unconscious, or maybe an unacknowledged, one. But the historical antecedents are nevertheless easily demonstrable in most cases. In the case of the Fillmores, their original source was Mrs. Emma Curtis Hopkins of the Illinois Metaphysical College. She was directly concerned at one time with Christian Science, as evidenced by Horatio Dresser's history of the New Thought movement. Similarly with Dr. Cady. I know nothing or very little of her personal life and background. But that knowledge is hardly necessary. We have her writings to go by. And they betray a very powerful influence that surely derives from Mary Baker Eddy.

Hence, in trying to describe the Unity teachings, we must begin with that central idea upon which the entire practical and philosophical structure is based, as in Christian Science—God, the Universal Mind, Life and Love. One very important difference exists here, a notable one that may evince an entirely foreign and unsuspected line of descent. While Christian Science denies the validity of the external world in terms other than as a series of ideas held in the mind of God, and that to ascribe to them an actual reality in matter is to subscribe to sin and error, Unity is willing to admit the reality of matter as apart from spirit. Not matter as the layman would be inclined to accept it—gross, unyielding, inert, and ponderous. But a substance, on the other hand, which is fine, plastic, volatile and imponderable, a root substance of so fine and subtle a texture that it is non-existent to the physical senses, but is constantly perceived and moulded by mind in its thinking. "One of the axiomatic truths of metaphysics is that 'thoughts are things.' That the mind of man marshals its faculties and literally makes into living entities the ideas that it entertains is also a foregone conclusion," asserts Charles Fillmore in a book entitled *Teach Us To Pray*. And but a page further on in the same work, he states that "every experienced metaphysician knows that man's mind moulds from an omnipresent element whatever takes form, shape, and intelligence and becomes part of his thought-world." What we think, voluntarily, creates picture or forms, sooner or later, with the passing of time, and with a dependence upon emotional intensity, must become precipitated into matter and visibility.

It betrays a familiarity with certain theosophical views, borrowed perhaps from eastern Sankhya philosophy which postulates a qualified dualism in manifestation, in opposition to the Monism of the Vedanta which is curiously akin to Christian Science. There are two principles constantly operating in nature, Purusha and Prakriti, Spirit and Matter. Spirit as intelligence and consciousness, matter as the invisible substratum of the objective world, ensouled by spirit. Both, in the final outcome are dual manifestations of God, aspects so to say of his infinite being and activity. Insofar as Unity accepts this idea of spiritual substance manipulable by mind, and which must therefore precipitate itself concretely and objectively, there is here an important point of departure from Christian Science.

Like Christian Science, it attempts to find biblical authority for each of it propositions, and to substantiate its ideas relating to this spiritual substance it employs the text in Genesis which speaks of the "dust of the ground." To quote once more from Charles Fillmore's book mentioned above: "Just as God has been from the beginning so Spirit-substance has been from the beginning. This substance is in fact the Mother side of God, the feminine element in God's nature. It is the universal medium in which we plant all ideas of supply and support." This is, as I suggested above, the Sankhya theory, more or less. Our author proceeds by stating that "The 'dust of the ground' spoken of in Genesis represents the radiant substance, the fruit of the initial thought in the expression of the substance idea. Under the influence of man's mind radiant Spirit substance continues to be manifested in form and shape. For example, the sunshine is incorporated in the products of the vegetable world; these being appropriated by man through mastication, digestion, and assimilation, it becomes part of his body, Light and electricity are forms of radiant substance."

God, or the Universal Mind, is the beginning, middle and end of Unity. We are not to suppose, according to this system, that God created the world at some far distant moment of time, and then left it to run like a machine all by itself. God is constantly passing into manifestation, constantly creating and renewing, and all things at every moment of their terrestrial and spiritual existence depend wholly upon Him. All the wisdom and love and power that we see at any moment in the universe is God—the potencies of God projected through a visible form. So that, every minute of every day of our lives, we are attempting unconsciously to express something of God, that unchangeable inexorable divine principle at the source of all existence. If this is so, the Unity teaching is that we should do so consciously. This would totally alter our point of view, our attitude to life, making us not merely cogs in a mechanistic universe, but efficient co-workers with God in the maintenance and operation of the worlds.

Our own human spirit is the standing forth of God into visibility, the Father in us. At this central core deep within the heart, everyone can say "I and the Father are one," and speak absolute truth. Each individual manifestation of God, each person, contains the whole, not for one moment implying that each individual is God in his entirety, but that each one is God manifested in different quantity or degree. "We all have direct access through the Father in us—the central 'I' of our being—"writes Emilie Cady. "to the great whole of life, love, wisdom, power, which is God. What we now want to know is how to receive more from the fountainhead and to make more and more of God manifest in our daily life." God as infinite wisdom lives within every human being, is her assertion in *Lessons in Truth*, only waiting to be led forth into manifestation. This is true education, a word derived from *educare*, to lead forth.

Man is derived from God, constructed from the same substance of God, comprising the same spiritual elements, and always existing within the broad all-inclusive vision of God. It is only man's poor thinking rooted in a faulty early education that has evolved from centuries of inaccurate thinking, that permits him to believe that he is in any way separate from God. In this way we are steeped in a race aura, as it were, of an organised, systematised series of error, believing in separateness from God and from man, dwelling in ignorance of that which in reality is far nearer to Him than hands and feet. Far nearer, for that entity which is man becomes aware of hands and feet, is God.

Creative Mind is conceived as omnipresent, infinite, eternal and omniscient. We cannot conceive of anywhere where it is not. It is ubiquitous—here, there and everywhere. No part of the universe is exempt from its presence and power. Nor can we conceive that a time will come when it will cease to be. Rather that time itself shall have ceased to exist, with God only remaining as sole spectator. All wisdom, all knowledge and all power are concentrated within it. And since it is infinite and omnipresent, all power and all wisdom are concentrated within every minute particle and point in space. Man is one of those infinite point-centres in space.

Therefore all wisdom and knowledge and love lie concealed within man himself, within every microscopic point in his constitution. Yet, although the divine mind is present within the mind of man, it lies beyond his consciousness until he makes deliberate effort to exalt himself to a particular pitch or level.

Omnipresence and omniscience "is that spiritual realm which can be penetrated only through the most highly accelerated mind action, as in prayer," Charles Fillmore tells us. In trying to communicate the idea of our relationship with God, Dr. Cady expresses herself in *Lessons in Truth* thus: "Imagine if you will, a great reservoir, out of which lead innumerable small rivulets or channels. At its farther end, each channel opens out into a small fountain. This fountain is not only being continually filled and replenished from the reservoir but is itself a radiating center whence it gives out in all directions that which it receives, so that all who come within its radius are refreshed and blessed. This is exactly our relation to God. Each one of us is a radiating center. Each one, no matter how small or ignorant, is the little fountain at the far end of the channel, the other end of which opens into all there is in God."

Unity teaches that God is both transcendental and immanent. So universal and so sublime is God, so perfect as to transcend any human similitude, any human concept of our minds, that we may feel we cannot reach Him. But He also is immanent, involved in His creation, resident therein, as it were, dwelling in the heart of every atom. He is the creator of the universe, the dweller within the universe, abiding totally apart from it as the same time.

Our minds are so constituted that to contemplate the transcendental nature of God is to remove something vital from our lives. He becomes a cold concept, a philosophical principle, something so far removed, so distant and so aloof from all our very mundane concerns, that it can mean nothing of any consequence to us. But once He is conceived as a powerful flame burning vigorously, though unconsciously to us, within the mind itself, we are immediately concerned. God becomes something extremely personal and important, not merely a philosophical speculation which is of no value to any of us. "He is principle, impersonal; as expressed in each individual, He becomes personal to that one—a personal, loving, all-forgiving Father-Mother. All that any human soul can ever need or desire is the infinite Father-Principle, the great reservoir of unexpressed good. There is no limit to the Source of our being, nor to His willingness to manifest more of Himself through us, when we are willing to do His will...We shall realise that Being is not only principle so far as its relation to each one of us is concerned; that we as individuals do actually become the focus of universal Spirit, of the all-pervading and all-wide Logos and that through us the universe is formed."

This conception of God as principle and Person, as transcendent and immanent, is vital to Unity teaching. But let me quote further, and we will see what Emile Cady has to say on the same theme. "There is no real reason why we, having come to recognise God as infinite substance, should be by this recognition deprived of the familiar fatherly companionship which in all ages has been so dear to the human heart. There is no necessity for us to separate God as substance and God as tender Father; no reason why we should not, and every reason why we should, have both in one; they are one—God principle outside of us as unchangeable law, God within us as tender, loving Father-Saviour, who sympathises with our every sorrow. It is as though infinite wisdom and power, which outside are Creator, Upholder, and Father, become transformed into infinite love, which is Mother, with all the warmth and tender helpfulness which that word implies, when they become focalised, so to speak, within a human body."

This is the important contribution that Unity has to make to modern metaphysical thinking. Not only do we have our roots in the divine source of all that is, but that God too abides in our hearts and minds constantly, that literally we partake of His nature and power, that we are actually the children of God. "You are nothing less than a child of God" affirms Charles Fillmore, and you will recall that this was the saving, redeeming word that assisted his wife over the hurdle of a poor prognosis with regard to pulmonary tuberculosis. "And to you is intrusted the creative power. When you realise this you can go forth forgiving men their sins as you have forgiven your own." Our human intelligence is so accustomed to the sound of words heard from earliest infancy that more often than not we accept the words unthinkingly, without due reflection. Do we ever stop to think, really to comprehend what it means to be, as St. Paul put it, "an heir of God and joint co-heir with Christ"? It means, as Emerson says, that "every man is the inlet, and may become the outlet, of all there is in God." It must mean that all that God actually is and has, is in reality for us, every man and woman of us, if we only knew how to claim the inheritance that is ours.

This, then, becomes our major problem. As human beings, bred in a civilisation which rightly or wrongly emphasises the art of being practical, we must learn in what way we may realise not only that we are inlets, but how we too may become the dynamic outlet of power, abundance, and inspiration. That is to say, realise in our every thought, word and act, that we express God—and all that that word means. At once we are confronted by the fact that there is so much worthlessness in our lives. We seem to express so much fear, anxiety, impotence, and inferiority. Life contains such a great deal of the unworthy elements of emotion for so many of us, that it seems an impossibility that we should ever become the outlet of God into the world around us. Evil, fear, poverty and sickness—these are the horrid demons that lurk in the darkness around us, beckoning that we should enter their threshold to be devoured.

Lesson in Truth attempts to show how we may deal with such problems in this manner: "There are four great error thoughts which nearly every one holds...First; there is no evil. There is but one Power in the universe, and that is God—good. God is all good, and God is omnipresent. Apparent evils are not entities of things of themselves. They are simply an absence of the good, just as darkness is an absence of light. But God, or good, is omnipresent, so the apparent absence of good (evil) is unreal...Second: There is no absence of life, substance, or intelligence anywhere...Third: Pain, sickness, poverty, old age, death, cannot master me, for they are not real. Fourth: There is nothing in all the universe for me to fear, for greater is He that is within me than He that is in the world."

In other words, one of the ways in which we are advised to deal with these destructive monsters encountered in the course of daily living, so that we may come to realise the omnipresence and indwelling presence of God, is by means of a technique of alternating denials and affirmations. We attempt to deny that they have any efficacy at all, no power to hurt us, by first affirming the opposite to be true. Since God is infinite, omnipresent and omnipotent, all His divine qualities must be immediately resident in every one every moment of time. It is not the human part of man that can vanquish the adversary. Man is too weak and too shortsighted, and too much an integral part of the systematised errors and organised illusions to which we have become subject. But by invoking the power of God latent within him, man may gain a mastery over every circumstance of life, and every phenomenon Whatsoever to be encountered in the world.

We must remember that Myrtle Fillmore was a tubercular, with a tuberculous heredity. When she first became acquainted with metaphysics, one dynamic idea above all others reached her ears: "I am a child of God and therefore do not inherit disease." In this statement, which she subsequently adopted as her own creed, and upon which all later Unity techniques came to be based, we can see she both denied and affirmed. She denied her human heredity of pulmonary tuberculosis, by affirming that since she was a child of God, which kinship she now claimed, it was no longer necessary, or even possible, to continue being sick. Forthwith, as we saw, she became strong and healthy—establishing a victory over her own diathesis, the environment about her, and the mycobacterium tuberculosis, even to the point of labouring forty-five years beyond the span of life allotted to her by medical prognosis. All problems, in the light of Unity teaching, may be dealt with in precisely the same manner.

With great detail, there is one chapter in *Lessons in Truth* which expatiates on this method of defeating human problems through the psychological mechanisms of denial and affirmation, and we learn much of the metaphysical attitude toward this approach. "Denials have an erasive or destructive tendency. Affirmations build up, and give strength and courage and power. People who remember vividly, and are inclined to dwell in their thoughts on the pains, sorrows, and troubles of the past or present, need to deny a great deal; for denials cleanse the mind and blot out of memory all seeming evils and unhappiness, so that they become as a faraway dream. Again, denials are particularly useful to those who are hard or intolerant, or aggressively sinful; to those who, as a result of success, have become overconfident, thinking the mortal is sufficient in itself for all things; to the selfish, and to any who do not scruple to harm others..."

The theory of the denial technique is made clear, though in certain respects I question the validity of this sort of thing. It encourages a sort of spiritual cowardice, an escapist attitude towards life. Instead of dealing honestly with a life situation and solving the problem, why deny its existence and have done with it? It is too easy, for what I cannot conquer, that will I run away from by denying its existence and tangibility.

Elsewhere, in connection with one of the other systems which recommends a similar method of denying the evidence of the senses, I have voiced some doubt as to the wisdom of such denials. Far wiser would it be to understand. Denial is so easy, much too infantile. It is too similar to the "sour grapes" attitude. If there is a tendency for the mind to dwell too fondly on the past rather than to surge forward with vigour and confidence and expectancy to the unknown future, there undoubtedly is a very good reason for it. To obscure that reason is wholly irrational. It would be just as senseless in medical therapy to treat a patient suffering from a headache by dosing him massively with aspirin, or a similar analgesic. Far wiser would it be to diagnose accurately, to enquire into the reason why such headaches exist. Are they due to gastric distress, hypertension, migraine, neoplastic activity, or simple eyestrain? Having discovered why they appeared, then attempt to remove the causative factors. And so on with all else. The symptoms of inner conflict may be obscured and masked. The causes may remain latent, but they need only a new stimulus to manifest in some other direction. In psychological practise, it is a commonplace in the treatment by symptom therapy of hysterics and anxiety neurotics, to find a new outcrop of symptoms appearing just as rapidly as the old ones are removed. The problem for the wise metaphysician or the medical physician is to find out the reason for the production of symptoms, and adequately treat the causes.

Some while ago, I interviewed a man fairly prominent in one of the major metaphysical movements. Undoubtedly, he was a highly successful business man. His offices were magnificent works of art, with mahogany panelling, luxurious office furniture, and thick pile rugs, which make one shudder a little when contemplating the cost. I am sure too that his knowledge of metaphysics both as a system and as a practical art were unexcelled. In attempting to expound principles for my edification, he narrated a dream that he had had but recently—not realising that one of my major interests was dreams. It appeared that he was in Europe, in the war zones, when some German soldiers approached him. Snatching a rifle from a corpse at this feet, he levelled it, pulled the trigger, intending to kill. Unfortunately it did not fire. His training was defective, for he did not know the successful operation of a German rifle. So he hastily discarded it, picked up a bayonet nearby, and slashed the nearest enemy soldier to ribbons.

His motive in telling me this dream was to indicate that in this dream battle every phenomenon was absolutely real. Just as real to him in the dream state as events and phenomena in the waking state are real to us now. He was trying to prove to me that the metaphysical doctrine of the illusory or error nature of the material world was justifiable in terms of the analogy. Matter is just as unreal when looked at through the eyes of spirit, as the dream state is transient and error when recalled in the waking conscious mood. At the moment I am not at all concerned with the conclusion of his analogy—which conclusion is, in any event, totally unjustified and poor logic. All that the analogy reveals is the relative nature of reality. Both states of consciousness are real—each on its own plane. It would be fatal to jump off a skyscraper tower because in a dream it could be done successfully. The laws of each reality state are valid on its own particular realm, and it would be mistaken and sad judgment to confuse these planes.

The principal point I wish to labour at this moment is that here is a successful metaphysician who would owe his success, materially and spiritually, to the application of metaphysical principles. Undoubtedly, earlier in his day—he had been in the movement for over twenty five years—he had been subject to aggressive emotions of hate, fear, anger, and enmity. And in accordance with the terms of the philosophy as he had understood it, he had attempted to deny them. So successfully had he denied them, that they really disappeared from view. He was no longer consciously bothered by them. But where had they gone? Had they really disappeared? Had they actually been eradicated from his psyche?

Evidently his systematic denials had not by any means eliminated them. Only a suppression had been engendered, as is indicated by his dreams. These aggressive emotions, or negative thoughts, had been pushed down to deeper levels of his psychological being, whence they could arise only involuntarily through the medium of dreams. I cannot bring myself to believe that this species of suppression is in any way related to true spiritual development. Real integration can only ensue through an actual eradication of such tendencies by means of an enlightened understanding, not through a criminal and wilful obfuscation by denial of the inner psychological and spiritual forces at work. We know enough—not too much, certainly, but enough—about the psyche and its operations today to realise that the products of human thinking and feeling gain in intensity through being repressed. Such emotions and ideas pass through what may be called a latency period after being repressed, during which time they become dynamically associated with a host of similar psychological factors, thus acquiring energy and power. So that, after the lapse of a certain length of time, they are transformed from a static complex of ideas and feelings, and undergo an emergence out of the psychic depths into the conscious mind or into the psycho-somatic system. There they manifest as organic or neurological disease, or else as functional defects in the visceral organisation.

Spiritual development implies an all-round generalised growth of the personality. Every constituent of man's being must be encouraged, tended, and regulated so that the *whole* man, not merely a portion of him, undergoes a thorough evolutionary process. The whole man must be made fit to live a healthy social, intellectual and spiritual life. If God is the whole, including all things, an since He is imaged in man, we would do well to pay attention to wholes and totalities. It is irrational to follow such a process of wilfully denying any aspect of life, or of problems that have arisen because of our ignorance and stupidity. Better to eliminate the stupidity and ignorance that we wallow in, then to deny the existence of the challenge which the problem constitutes. It seems so completely wrong-headed to follow such a procedure. And while we do, that spiritual growth which is the ideal we strive towards must remain simply an unattainable idea, far removed from our grasp. Forever will we carry with us the usual crop of neuroses, psychoses, and physical disease which are the outcome of one species in denying. Any kind of denial of the fullness of God's earth and ourselves must eventuate in many and varied difficulties.

Having said so much against the denial process, we must admit in all honesty that there is a certain psychological significance to its method, if it be applied with intelligence and deliberation. If the motive behind the application to this process is a conscious or unconscious desire to escape from life, because one feels unequal to it, then we are deliberately invoking trouble. On the other hand, having lived fully and intensely, having fulfilled our obligations to life, accepting every situation with grace and courage as it has come, then a logical transition can develop, in which the process of denial has its rightful place.

We know that if the attention be diverted from externals, an introversion of libido takes place. By libido we mean the sum total of spiritual energy manifesting in man. That is to say, no longer is there a wastage of spiritual energy in the objects of mind and sense. A damming back, an accumulation of this invaluable power takes place in that hinterland of the mind which we call the Unconscious.

The Unconscious is the source not merely of our minds during infancy, but also in the present-day of every idea and concept that we regard as having value. A continual process of evolution and creation is occurring every moment of our lives from the depths of the psyche. New values, new attitudes, new intuitions, present themselves to our minds from "out of the blue," as it were, having been nurtured in the darkness of the unconscious levels of soul. Hence, if we can stimulate this nurturing and creation within by a process of withdrawing energy from outer objects, giving it new direction inwardly, we shall have gone far towards bringing the Unconscious into a closer degree of proximity with our conscious selves. This will be a true unification of the self, true integrity. And it is this proximity, and integrity, this appreciation of the creative self within, that really constitutes growth. For this reversal of one's psychic being, taking place with the introversion, means an enlargement, a heightening, and an enrichment of the personality. Psychologically, the significance of this introversion is to give a new orientation towards life. It is to become conscious of oneself, not only of the conscious aspect of the self, but of the Self, the psyche, as a unit. All sides of the personality become implicated, and all that is periphery—and that means that which is without, the externals—is subjected to the command of the centre. An inner movement takes place, and movement is another term for mastery.

This inner movement instigated by the process of denial, which thus attempts to direct libido inwards into the dark side of the psyche by removing it from objective values and undesirable psychic processes, is further aided by the process of affirmation. Vitalised by the storing up of libido, the unconscious is psychically predisposed to re-orientation. This is so obviously a process of auto-suggestion that the point need not be laboured too much.

"Affirmations," continues Dr. Cady in *Lessons in Truth*, "should be used by the timid and those who have a feeling of their own inefficiency; those who stand in fear of other minds; those who "give in" easily; those who are subject to anxiety or doubt, and those who are in positions of responsibility. The people who are in any way negative or passive need to use affirmations more; the ones who are self-confident or unforgiving, need denials more.

What, then, is to be affirmed? We have already seen what should be denied. Dr. Cady pointed out before that, in the main, there were four major notions that should be subjected to denial. In the same way she indicates four great sweeping affirmations which include a series of lesser ones. These are to be affirmed constantly. I quote from her:

"First; God is life, love, intelligence, substance, omnipotence, omniscience, omnipresent...Second: I am a child or manifestation of God, and every moment His life, love, wisdom, power, flow into and through me. I am one with God, and am governed by His laws... No matter how sick or weak or inefficient you seem to be, take your eyes and thoughts right off the seeming, and turn them within to the central fountain there, and say calmly, quietly, but with steadfast assurance: 'This appearance of weakness is false; God manifest as life, wisdom, and power, is now flowing into my entire being and out through me to the external.' You will soon see a marvelous change wrought in yourself by the realisation that this spoken word will bring to you...Third: I am Spirit, perfect, holy, harmonious. Nothing can hurt me or make me sick or afraid, for Spirit is God, and cannot be hurt or made sick or afraid. I manifest my real self through this body now. Fourth: God works in me to will and to do whatsoever He wishes me to do, and He cannot fail."

Undoubtedly affirmations of this type, sincerely uttered by one who is thoroughly imbued with the religious philosophy described, would work wonders. A complete transformation of the individual should not be at all impossible. If the individual really believed the affirmations, concentrated upon them as suggestions in moments of quietness and stillness, and were able to become completely enthusiastic about God working in him, then it would be quite impossible really to determine where lie the limitations of man. To adopt the point of view of the affirmations would completely transform the point of view. And, when all is said and done, that is all that matters. Just as soon as our viewpoint to life is changed from one of sterility and ineptitude to one expressing spontaneity, whole hearted acceptance, and high value, then we begin to grow. And growth is the object of our sojourn here. It is growth which all desire and strive after.

"Almost instantly you will feel better, more optimistic and hopeful," writes Miss Dana Gatlin, in an inspirational mood, apparently echoing personal experience. "You will look better and act better, and the outside world will note the change in you. Daily your confidence will increase and a new inspiration, new leading, from the Father. You will meet your spirit—gladly, enthusiastically, praisefully, with never a thought of failure...All this happens when you recognise God as the one presence and power, when you let nothing stand between you and Him, when you believe in Him supremely and trust him fully."

"Now, let us arouse ourselves," exhorts Emilie Cady with contagion-like spreading of enthusiasm. "Denial is the first practical step towards wiping out of our mind the mistaken beliefs of a lifetime—the beliefs which have made such sad havoc in our lives... The only way by which you could cleanse your mind of the impression and make the untrue seem unreal, would be by repeatedly denying the old belief, saying over and over to yourself as often as the subject came up in your mind: "This is not true. The sun does not move; it stands still, and the earth moves." Eventually the sun would not even seem to move...If you repeatedly deny a false or unhappy condition, it not only loses its power to make you unhappy, but eventually the condition itself is destroyed by your denial...Almost hourly little vexations and fears come up in your life. Meet each one with a denial. Calmly and coolly say within yourself, "That's nothing at all. It cannot harm or disturb me or make me unhappy." Do not fight it vigorously, but let your denial be the denial of superiority to it, as you would deny the power of ants on their little hill to disturb you. If you are angry, and cannot be angry; it is not true; and the anger will leave you."

I prefer to use Dr. Cady's own clear forcible language in the description of what to do in moments of trial. "If there comes a moment when you are in doubt as to what to do, stand still and affirm *God in me is infinite wisdom; I know just what to do*. "For I will give you a mouth and wisdom which all your adversaries shall not be able to gainsay nor resist." Do not get flustered or anxious, but depend fully and trustingly on your principle, and you will be surprised as the sudden inspiration which will come to you as to the mode of procedure." Repeat the words many times, not anxiously or with strained effort, not reaching out and up and away to an outside God, but let the petition be the quiet, earnest uplifting of the heart to a higher something right within itself, even to the 'Father in me.' Let it be made with the quietness and assurance of a child speaking to its loving father."

Before passing on to a consideration of another phase of Unity teaching, let me present one last series of quotations from Emilie Cady's book on the subject of affirmations and denials. "Affirm your possession of the good that you desire; have faith in it, because you are working on law and cannot fail; do not be argued off your basic principle by anyone and sooner will the heavens fall than that you fail to get that which you desire...If you are naturally inclined to be timid or shrinking, practice of the following will help you overcome it: As you walk down the street and see anyone coming toward you, silently affirm such words as *'I am a part of God in visibility; I am one with the Father; this person has no power over me, for I am superior to all personality.'* Cultivate this habit of thinking and affirming whenever you approach a person, and you will soon find that no personality, however strong and aggressive, has the power to throw you out of the most perfect poise. You will be self-possessed because God-possessed."

It is in this last sentence that we have the clue, I believe, to the enormous spiritual potentiality that is in Unity. We have here not merely a system that is exclusively concerned with healing the sick, overcoming poverty, and eradicating anger, fear and anxiety. However important all these things are, and none will gainsay that, they are trivial compared to that most important of all goals, the realisation of identity with God. It is stressing the value and supreme worth of mystical or religious experience. If Unity could emphasise this side of its teaching even more than it does at present, we could have a recrudescence of a Christian mysticism compared to which there has been nothing in the whole history of Christianity. The objects of mysticism are active through various technical processes of prayer and meditation a realisation of God, and the soul's union and manifest identity with God. This divine realisation is to be sought not only that sickness, poverty and death may be overcome, but for its own sake. Self-realisation is its own justification, and God-possession brings its own rewards. In one sense Unity even now teaches it. In an editorial article in the June 1894 edition of Unity magazine, Charles Fillmore expressed himself significantly as follows: "To maintain the religious dignity of the doctrine we advocate, we must hold to the pivotal thought that it is a spiritual ministry, and not a new system of healing. The healing that follows an understanding of the doctrine is not good in itself, and should not be proclaimed as good—it is the effect of the good."

I should like to see this doctrine of a spiritual ministry enunciated until the time would come when universally Unity would be understood as not simply another system of modern metaphysics— one amongst many—but that it stands for the highest in Christian mysticism. Its aims and goals are to teach students of the world over could give expression to their highest and noblest aspiration to climb the heights to God. I should like to see, under its sponsorship, a recrudescence of that golden age of the Roman Catholic Church, when great souls like Meister Eckhardt, St. Francis of Assisi, St. Ignatius of Loyola, St. Theresa and St. John of the Cross and many another flourished. The Russian orthodox Church also had its great mystics, though I am not too familiar with them save through English translations of portions of the *Philokalia*. But we know that their stature is in no sense inferior to those of their brethren in the Roman Church. These were the great spiritual adventurers. These were the great pioneers, the map-makers of the world of spirit. All their energies and their lives, were devoted to seeking God, to the establishment of an identification with Him. Because of them, the world is a far better place. In fact, our spiritual health—the little that we do have—may all unknown to us be totally dependent upon their excursions and their adventurings into the divine Unknown. If Unity is able, by orienting and directing those who come to its portals for aid, to imbue them with loftier spiritual goals than the mere eradication of disease and poverty, it may yet go down in history as an authentic and authoritative source of a fine and ideal mysticism.

The founders, I am sure, have realised this, and so I want to stress the idea in quotations from their works. For example: "When our thoughts are established in love, a divine synchronisation takes place. Divine Mind has a fixed rate of vibration to which, through Jesus Christ, the mind of man is synchronised to the frequency of a broadcasting station. In order to tap Divine Mind we must bring the rate of our vibration of our mind up to the standard, for it is only when the mind is vibrating at its most accelerated rate that God can make Himself known to us."

When does the mind vibrate at its most accelerated rate? According to Unity, the mind reaches its acme of divine activity during moments of prayer and aspiration, when it attempts by dwelling upon god to achieve union with Him. During prayer, we obey the biblical injunction and, going into the closet of our minds, shut tight the door behind us by concentration. There, in the secret chambers of the soul, we attempt to realise God, by first stilling our own turbulent thoughts and emotional activity, knowing that when all is quiet and the fire of aspiration keenly burns, God will in all simplicity come in. "This 'inner chamber' of the soul has been variously named by Scripture writers. It is called the 'secret place of the Most High; and the 'holy of holies,' and Jesus named it 'the Father… in me' and the 'kingdom of God…within you.' What we need to know above all is that there is a place within our soul where we can consciously meet God and receive a flood of new life into not only our mind but also our body." Thus says Charles Fillmore. And Emilie Cady adds in effect, that the one who dwells in the secret place of the most high is promised, according to the words of one of the Psalms, immunity from the pestilence, the fowler's snares, the terror by night, and the arrow that flies by day. And this secret place—what is it, and where is it? "It is a secret place," she explains "Because it is a place of meeting between the Christ at the center of your being, and your consciousness—a hidden place into which no outside person can either induct you or enter himself."

"When you have learned how to abandon yourself to infinite Spirit, and have seasons of doing this daily" in that secret place, the rendezvous with the most high, in the deep places of the soul, Emilie Cady states that "you will be surprised at the marvelous change that will be wrought in you without any conscious effort of your own. It will search far below your conscious mind, and root out things in your nature of which you have scarcely been conscious simply because they have lain latent there, waiting for something to bring them out. It will work into your consciousness light, and life and love, and all good, perfectly filling all your lack while you just quietly wait and receive."

So far so good. But now we approach the really masterful idea expressed in *Lessons in Truth* that truly elevates this book above all others, and shows the fine degree of insight and illumination that had come to Emile Cady herself. For she writes in that book: "Whoever you are that read these words, wherever you stand in the world, be it on the platform preaching the gospel, or in the humblest little home seeking truth, that you may make it manifest in a sweeter, stronger, less selfish life, know once and forever that you are not seeking God, but God is seeking you. Your longings for greater manifestation is the eternal Energy, which holds the worlds in their orbits, outpushing through you to get into fuller manifestation. You need not worry. You need not be anxious. You need not strive. Only let it. Learn how to let it."

Here is accomplished a complete revolution in human thinking through a single idea—Let God do it! It is the effortless way of life. Possibly this is the hardest way of all for us. From earliest infancy onward, we have been trained that we must act, that we must work, that we must strive. Striving has become so engrained in our natures that even when we would, to stop striving seems an impossibility for us. Hence the way of divine inaction would be a valuable corrective to our top heavy modern over-emphasis of the life of will and activity. It does not mean that we must sit down on our haunches and do absolutely nothing. Very far from the truth is such a notion. It does mean, however, that the centre or the source of human activity must be shifted away from our selves, and be realised to emanate from a wiser and more divine actor. Both in action and in attitude, our idea must be to look upon the world not from our present point of view but from the divine point of view.

How would God look at my particular problem? What would He think or do regarding it? I need money. I have acute cholecystitis, or maybe I am having difficulty with my job. Maybe also, all sorts of domestic wrangles have arisen with my wife, my children. What attitude would He take? And just what would He do about it?

To look upon one's problems from this angle implies a thorough-going abnegation of the human ego. Surely it suggests a willingness to let something else, vital and strong and all-inspiring, come into our lives. And we do not have to strive to achieve this psychological condition. God himself is supremely anxious, so to say, to enter the mind, to shine within like some precious hidden lamp, just lighted, to illuminate our darkened and sorrowful way. Just as the sun rises every morning without our having to beseech it to shine and give us light, so, the Unity teaching has it, God is within every moment giving forth light—if we would only see it and realise it. All His light, wisdom, power and abundant supply of everything is waiting for us, and only we hinder its entry into our environment, physical and psychological.

Let God do! It is so much easier. And we comply with the ultimate law of our own being when we do so. The very spirit within us, though unknown and hidden, is God himself shining like some interior sun. And the mere fact that we desire certain things is ample evidence that a divine pressure is exerting itself within. It is God operating within the mind, urging us emotionally and instinctively in certain directions. All we have to do is fully to recognise this and accept it—that God as desire is always forging ahead at the door of our minds with an infinite supply of all that we want and need. What we desire is not only for us. In reality what we desire has been started in our direction long ago from the infinitude of God's abundance and plenitude. It is the first approach of the object desired striking us on a higher plane that makes us want to desire it, or even to think of it at all. But we must first relax inwardly, seeking the abiding city interiorly, in the secret place of the Most High, and then God can act for us and on our behalf.

This attitude of mind has been beautifully expressed many years ago in a slight devotional book entitled *Light on the Path* by Mabel Collins. She inculcates this point of view vigorously and beautifully. "Stand aside in the coming battle, and though thou fightest be not thou the warrior. Look for the Warrior, and let him fight in thee. Take his orders for battle, and obey them. Obey him, not as though he were a general, but as though he were thyself, and his spoken words were the utterance of thy secret desires; for his is thyself, yet infinitely wiser and stronger than thyself...If thy cry meet his listening ear, then will he fight in thee, and fill the dull void within. And if this is so, then canst thou go through the fight cool and unwearied, standing aside and letting him battle for thee. Then it will be impossible for thee to strike one blow amiss...He is thyself. Yet though art but finite and liable to error; he is eternal and is sure. He is eternal truth. When once he has entered thee and become thy Warrior he will never utterly desert thee; and at the day of the great peace he will become one with thee."

So far as concerns technical procedure towards realising these desires, a similar procedure is followed here as in all of the metaphysical systems. It is realised that when a person seeks acquaintance with Unity, or to gain a more profound knowledge of spiritual laws, he does so with a definite motive. It is usually because of some personal dissatisfaction with his past, and the general conditions of life with which he finds himself surrounded. Possibly some great sorrow has overtaken him. Or he realises himself to have come to an impasse, and he can go no further. Perhaps, money or position have been lost, health has suffered, and all else beside seems to be in jeopardy. Some solutions to these unsatisfactory conditions must be sought. A way out must be found somewhere. And seeking, he finds. Mind inflamed by a single urge to overcome the difficulties that besets him, he turns around, feeling that somewhere, somehow, something exists which would enable him to realise his deepest and most spiritual desires. And so he comes to metaphysics.

The first step inculcated by these modern spiritual systems is that one must have faith. He is urged to develop faith by belief in God, by believing in spiritual forces which he is told are capable of accomplishing that which seems at first sight impossible. Metaphysics urges that he affirm a propitious outcome for everything he plans, and never to admit of failure in anything.

Here we come to the first difficulty. It is easy enough for the man who has retained something of his early religious training and belief to have faith. But for the individual who has lost his faith, who has become the so-called hard-headed business man—who is really the most gullible of all—or who has had a philosophic, classical or scientific training, to recover that primal child faith is by no means as simple as it sounds.

Here I think is where metaphysics is defective. It is asked of a man who, inherently, is incapable of believing, to believe. It asks a man who has lost everything, including his own faith in himself, in life, in God, to employ just that which he has lost. There is no scientific, systematic approach to this problem. If faith is so all-important, a suitable technique must be devised whereby it may be recovered. Scientifically-minded, modern man has become subject to a valid desire to demonstrate that which he believes. In a chemical laboratory, the presence of sugar in any liquid can be readily demonstrated by the use of Benedict's solution. A diseased gall-bladder can be visualised by means of the appropriate dyes and Roentgen rays. Pathogenic micro-organisms can be demonstrated either by the microscope or by serological tests, by cultural growths or by animal inoculation. We are not asked in any of these scientific spheres to have faith. Patience, yes but not faith. Consequently, faith has taken, rightly, a back seat in the order of our lives. It is not one of the simplicities therefore to ask those of us who have no faith, to have faith.

But what anyway is meant by faith? What is this attitude of mind which appears to be so important. Charles Fillmore attempts in *Teach Us To Pray* to answer this question in these words: "Faith is the most mysterious of the spiritual faculties and has so far eluded the descriptive powers of man. Many attempts have been made to describe faith, but with indifferent success. All spiritual metaphysicians agree that faith is an apprehension by man of a mind power that connects matter and spirit. Faith handles ideas with a facility similar to that with which we handle pumpkin seeds. We plant the little seeds in good soil and watch them grow in a few months into large pumpkins. This is as great a miracle as any that Jesus performed, the difference being that it takes time and an adjustment of material instead of spiritual conditions."

Only in part is this an explanation, and does not inform us too clearly. Let us see what Dr. Cady has to say. She quotes St. Paul who says that faith is a substance of things hoped for, the evidence of things not seen. After this, she adds: "Faith takes right hold of the substance of the things desired, and brings into the world of evidence the things which before were not seen. Further speaking of faith, Paul said, 'Things which are seen were not made of things which do appear'; *i.e.* things which are seen are not made out of visible things, but out of the invisible. In some way, then, we understand that whatever we want is in this surrounding invisible substance, and faith is the power which can bring it out into reality for us." I shall have something to say further on this in the chapter on prayer, relative to images of wish-fulfilment.

The Unity teachings also speak of relaxing and going into the silence. Technical considerations are none too well delineated, and the person who does not find relaxation easy to achieve is bound to strike a snag there. Dr. Cady's instructions on prayer and going into the silence are forceful and clear, but actual descriptions of how to let go, how to achieve quiescence, and how to discover "the secret place of the Most High" must remain vague for the non-mystically inclined person. The individual who has no faith, and no mystical inclination needs such detailed instruction, needs to learn technical methods by which this may be achieved. I have come to believe from a fairly wide experience with patients and students seeking interviews, that relaxation is an almost imperative necessity for most moderns.

In facts, it could easily be said that relaxation is the clue to one phase of metaphysical teaching, and the *sine qua non* of success. From a physical point of view, we know that it is difficult for the psycho-somatic forces to rehabilitate the organism if all the electro-neural energy is being wasted prodigally in metabolism by unnecessary muscular tensions. Although a certain amount of tonicity or tension is necessary for both the voluntary skeletal and the smooth involuntary muscles to function constantly, nonetheless the requisite degree of myo-tonicity is in reality low. With involuntary muscular tensions present in high degree, vast quantities of energy are being wasted. Not only so, but nerve fibres are compressed by muscle contraction, blood vessels are constricted forcing the blood pressure ever higher and higher, tissues are starved of blood and nutritive elements, the viscera are crowded together, and so functional disorders insidiously commence. During sleep, the body's ability to do repair work is ignorantly interfered with, so great is the tension. Sleep is not synonymous with relaxation unfortunately, with the result that during the night these day-time tensions are retained in all their severity.

If therefore an individual should learn the art of relaxation, there is a spontaneous release of all the body forces. Sometimes miracles occur from no more than showing a patient how to "let go." Blood circulation immediately improves, nerve impingements are eradicated, and all the metabolic and nutritional functions are enhanced. Not only do these phenomena occur, but since neuro-muscular tensions are related directly as well as inversely to psychological and emotional tensions, the endeavor to release muscular tension tends to remove psychic tension. Hence, far-reaching alterations occur throughout the whole personality, which experiences a wide sense of relief and expansiveness. This can have vast ramifications not merely on physical health, but on his spiritual attitude towards life—which is the more important factor.

This is why I believe that behind many metaphysical teachings is unconsciously concealed an attempt to provide a kind of system for relaxation. Faith, the belief in the universality and immanence of God, and the transitory nature of the material world which is subject to God's will, all these things have the ultimate effect of relaxing one's tense attitude to problems that have loomed large and fearfully before. By viewing these terrifying factors—material, social, and economic—that have provoked inner storms from the standpoint, not of the personality, but of God, their size and significance decreases. A more relaxed attitude can easily be adopted towards them, which readily permits of conquest. But I shall look at this problem of "letting go" from a wider and more technical point of view elsewhere in this book, and attempt to deal more fully with it there.

Meanwhile, several points of Unity teaching remain to be discussed. One of Mr. Fillmore's statements in *Teach Us To Pray* has it that all fears rest upon thoughts, and if the thought foundation be broken up the fear will vanish. Psychologically speaking, this is undoubtedly true. But one of the major difficulties in dealing with fear, is that the thought-bases are not conscious. Metaphysical systems of today have not been too wise in ignoring the wealth of data revealed to us by the various systems of modern depth psychology. It may be true, as some metaphysicians contend, that prayer reaches far above all the contents of the conscious and unconscious psyche, tending to dissolve all the unwanted thought-formations and complex emotional constellations and syndromes. In some instances, this may be quite true. I strongly doubt it in most cases. They simply push the symptoms further back into the unconscious recesses of the mind. I have seen entirely too many instances of metaphysical students whose dreams, which are the symptomatic revelatory symbols of the unconscious psychic status, are far from healthy. But I cannot believe but that sooner or later these hidden thought-constellations will erupt openly in some terrible manifestation far worse than the original condition treated. The ethical attitude adopted by Unity students may sometimes engender such far-reaching changes in the underlying character that modifications may be engineered and none of this result. For instance, in the book *Teach Us To Pray*, the following praiseworthy advice is found, advice which assuredly is invaluable. "We being our overcoming by thought mastery. We begin to master thoughts of hate and force by first thinking and doing the little component acts that constitute love. Begin today to be a little more patient. Practice kindness. Be generous in thought and act."

This very lofty ethical attitude is probably one of the finest aspects of Unity work. It inculcates an attitude of love and praise even in the face of adversity. I am deeply impressed by its philosophy with regard to uttering words and feelings of benediction when troubled, and blessing that which caused the trouble and concern. Ernest Wilson who wrote a book entitled *Adventures in Prosperity* discusses the biblical story of the conflict between Jacob and the Angel of God. You will recall that Jacob swore that he would not let the angel go until it had blessed him. And this author writes "To the angels of the Lord you and I should say the same thing. There is a blessing to be had from every experience. Finding these blessings overcomes resistance, either by their being removed from your life, or else by their being so transformed that we rejoice to have them stay."

Praise and gratitude and thanksgiving have the dynamic effect of expanding, of releasing and in every way of radiating energy. We all know how much better we feel when we have expressed our gratitude to somebody for a favour bestowed, or a gift received. Our entire personality flows outward, stream like, in love and boundless joy. On the other hand, so Unity teaches, words of failure or impotence contract our minds, acting even as cold does, restricting us, and making us withdraw into our shells. And Dr. Cady admits that while for those who are in serious straits and dire circumstances it may appear travesty at first sight to praise and give thanks to God, nevertheless "thousands of those who have endured poverty and sickness for years find that their prison doors open when they praise and give thanks, like Paul and Silas, as related in the 16th chapter of Acts. They were praying and singing hymns to God when suddenly there was a great earthquake, all the prisoners' chains were loosened, and Paul and Silas stepped forth free men. So you will find that you can be freed from all the prison cells of man's blind thinking and lifting up your voice and heart in song of praise and thanksgiving to the God of freedom, light and life."

This too is not difficult to comprehend psychologically. Conversion phenomena have long been known to psychologists the world over. We know that it is quite possible for men to exceed themselves, performing superhuman tasks under the stimulus of powerful emotion. A man in love will oft-times surprise himself and everyone else by his achievements. Under the stimulus of love, poets and artists and musicians have completed their finest creative work. In any event, creative work needs an emotional exaltation or spiritual frenzy can be aroused or encouraged by prayer, by praise and by thanksgiving, so much the better. He who employs the technique has a first-rate chance of overcoming his limitations and realising the deepest desires of his heart. The use of prayer and song and psalm as a means of exalting the mind and stimulating an emotional mood is a highly valid and successful technique—and no psychological criticism can injure it. It stands by the satisfactory and desirable results that it produces. "You can praise a weak body into strength; a fearful heart into peace and trust; shattered nerves into poise and power; a failing business into prosperity and success; want and insufficiency into supply and support." This is Unity at its best, as expressed by Charles Fillmore. "Do not beg in your prayers, but praise and give thanks for now self-manifesting God of abundance fulfilling every desire of your heart...Make a 'date' daily with God and keep it."

One of the least admirable phases, however, of popular metaphysical teaching is unfounded speculation upon scientific processes not too well understood. Some of the physiological and anatomical notions appearing in *Teach Us To Pray* are curious, to put it mildly. For example, "The solar plexus is the organ of intuition and the brain the organ of telepathy." The solar plexus, as we know, is a large nerve plexus, consisting of crisscross patterns and pathways of sympathetic and parasympathetic nerve fibres, situated behind the stomach, below the diaphragm. The nerve impulses traversing its fibres supply all the abdominal viscera and vessels. For that reason it is often termed the abdominal brain, an excellent name for its function. As such it is concerned with the welfare of the animal life, the function of the glands, the digestive organs, elimination and assimilation, and the genital apparatus. It is far more likely to be considered the organ or centre of instinct, rather than that of intuition—though it may be in the final analysis, these two are identical, and instinct may be the divine power expressing itself through body function, while intuition is the same power expressing itself through mental processes.

The medulla oblongata, or the intra-cranial spinal cord, is also given a function which would find no corroboration in scientifically conducted physiological laboratories. *Teach Us To Pray* informs us that the medulla "is the seat of the animal soul, and its office is to vaporise the fine nerve fluid and distribute it to the senses. The medulla performs in the body the work of a carburetor in a motorcar. An intense desire to carry out some idea forces the nerve fluid into the medulla, where it is atomised with inspiration (air) and then flared through the optic nerve to the eye, where the Spirit ignites it, and it flashes into light... When the Spirit moves a man from within to the accomplishment of some cherished ideal and the intellect steps in and says it can't be done, a conflict ensues and the natural flow of the volatile body is impeded. Congestions and clots form in the circulation, the man gradually slows down, and what are called the marks of old age appear..."

Anatomically, the medulla oblongata, often called the Bulb, is the lowest part of the brain. It is very small in size, and weighs about an ounce. It connects the different structures of the brain with the spinal cord, and here are found the pyramids where occur that phenomenal decussation or crossing of nerve fibres from opposite sides. Physiologically speaking, the medulla is a highly significant neurological structure. Here are located the reflex centres of swallowing, respiration, circulation, and by means of the tenth cranial nerve, the heart and the alimentary tract are affected. Insofar as it is connected with such important vital functions as breathing and swallowing and circulation, the medulla is indeed the seat of the animal soul, if the latter be defined as pertaining to the life of the body. Probably it might be more accurate to call the hypothalamus, the region around the pituitary gland, the seat of the animal soul. For not only is the pituitary gland the controlling agency of most of the endocrine glands besides a number of other functions as well, but in the hypothalamic area various emotional impulses appear to be generated. Sometimes these impulses are at variance with the cerebral cortex, that outer white portion of the brain concerned with reflective rather than reflexive thought. The cortex and the hypothalamus are conflicting and equilibriating structures, even as the parasympathetic and sympathetic nervous systems are conflicting and balancing each other all the time.

Unity offers some highly illuminating interpretations of the Bible which is the source of its inspiration and ministry. It has issued a metaphysical Bible dictionary in the preface of which is found a brief statement which is an excellent summary of Unity teaching. "All is mind, and all material forms are pictures of ideas. By studying a picture we may get a concept of the idea that it represents...Divine Mind has ideas, and they become embodies through natural processes. The Hebrew Scriptures give a series of pictures representing those ideas...The New Testament is a veiled textbook for the initiate who is seeking degrees in the inner life. It gives rules for working out every mental state that may be found in the mind. It is like a textbook on mathematics, a textbook in which are acted out by living figures all the rules for working every problem that may come up in human life." It is for this obvious reason, that Unity students turn to the Bible for inspiration, solace and aid.

Many of its interpretations of Biblical themes show deep insight into and appreciation of human nature, and more than a penchant for understanding the value and meaning of symbols. For example, Mr. Fillmore deals with the story in the second chapter of Kings, of Naaman, a captain of the Syrian armies, who was stricken with leprosy. A Jewish captive girl who was the maid of Naaman's wife, suggested he go to Canaan to find the great prophet Elisha. Elisha gives him the simple prescription of bathing seven times in the river of Jordan. But such a formula is too simple for those of us who expect advice to be complex in order to be effectual. After much conflict and resistance, Naaman does so, however, and emerges from the river, healed and whole, with a skin radiating good health. And Mr. Fillmore, interpreting this mythical story, states that "the little maiden" is representative of a rudimentary intuition that has been captured by the intellectual and is being made to serve its ends. The river Jordan is the life current flowing into man's subconscious nature from the one great life. This 'river of life' is the source of the natural healing impulse that constantly reconstructs and restores the organism."

In another place, while attempting to throw light on the Star of Bethlehem that arose to shine at the birth of Christ he says that for the individual embarking upon the spiritual way of life, this star represents a speck of light shining from the east. Eternally the east has been a symbol of the interior life of the soul, thus revealing to the illumined person what was taking place, the coming to birth of the Christ child within, the symbol of potentiality. It expresses infinite possibility, for the inner self of man which, in its apex, is God, the great I AM, has finally made its appearance and is spiritual power manifest upon the earth.

Describing the verses in Genesis where all creation is given name by Adam, Mr. Fillmore says that all created beings there mentioned represent certain forces in the field of man's activity, over which man will have complete control when he achieves a final realisation of his divine origin and nature. "These forces are symbolically described as 'birds,' 'fish,' 'cattle,' and 'crawling things,' through which man replenishes the earth...The 'birds of the heavens' are their high ideals, the 'cattle' or 'beasts of the field' are of a low order, the 'fish of the sea,' are their generated or accumulated impulses, and the 'creeping things' represent the micro-organisms of modern science that are claimed to be the cause of most diseases."

And of that classical play of wills and purposes between Esau and Jacob, Unity tells us that Esau, a person who was a hunter, subservient to his bodily appetites, was a man of flesh, and so represents symbolically the flesh, the body. But Jacob was a person of a different turn of mind, a man who loved home and the quiet spiritual things of life, the intellectual man. I doubt whether this can wholly be agreed with, upon any basis of symbolism, for the most outstanding feature of this story is that Jacob cheated Esau out of his inheritance by a mean and sordid trick. And of a man who loved the spiritual things of life, we would expect rather different behaviour, a more integrated and socially responsible ethical attitude. The story is hardly an example, symbolism or no symbolism, of how we should behave to others or to ourselves.

A final example of biblical exegesis is the story of the widow's stock of oil which, under the treatment of the prophet Elisha, was found to be plentiful and more than ample for her needs. Mr. Fillmore explains that "the widow typifies a belief in lack, a thought or a line of thought in consciousness that has fallen away from that inner union with the divine source (husband) and as a result is suffering from lack of supply. Elisha (meaning also "God is rich") showed this woman how to shut the door and realise that her supply came from within. Then he revealed to how to pour out the oil (love) of plenty, and how it would prove a permanent supply. Any thought is a prayer in which we realise that our desires, God directed, are answered the very moment they are expressed."

Another very interesting feature, rather unusual, of the metaphysical teachings of Unity is its attention to dreams and their possible significance. While what they have to state does not fully accord with the modern scientific view of the subject, as attested to by the varying pure or mixed schools adhering either to Freud or to Jung, nevertheless an attempt is made to deal with what for most people is a realm either of pure superstition or ignorance. Unity has published a small booklet entitled *Inner Vision* which deals with dreams and a wide range of analysis. It contains a number of ideas and statements which I should like to epitomise as the final aspect of Unity to be described here.

The booklet, at the beginning, states simply that "everyone is more than he consciously knows himself to be." And further, the writer of the booklet also corroborates the modern scientific attitude by stating that our interpretations of dreams would be clearer if there were a knowledge of the background and history of the dreamer. For there is always a connection between the phenomenon of the dream and the entire psychic background and experience of the dreamer. If we had such a case-history of the dreamer, we would be able to divine, not merely the collective or universal significance of the symbols employed, but their particular personal application to the dreamer's problems in life. To attempt dream-interpretation is therefore futile if we are ignorant of dream symbols and the dreamer's life.

The pamphlet proceeds, then, to an account of the famous dreams and visions of the Bible, pointing out that in former times it was believed that God instructed and advised people by means of the agency of dream and vision. The writer also states that "man's body is the sum total of the animal world, because in its evolution it has had experience in nearly every type of elemental form. These memories are part of the soul, and they come to the surface sporadically in the unregenerate. Sometimes whole nations seem to revert from culture to savagery without apparent cause, but there is always a cause. These reversions are the result of some violent wrenching of the soul, or a concentration, to the exclusion of everything else, upon a line of thought out of harmony with divine law." These ideas are remarkably similar to a theme adopted by Jung and expressed in many of his publications.

The effort is made to give meaning to some of the common and more universal symbols found in the dramatic parade of the dream. "In the regeneration man finds that he has, in the part of the soul called the natural man, animal propensities corresponding to the animals in the outer world. In the pictures of the mind, these take form as lions, horses, oxen, dogs, cats, snakes and the birds of the air. The visions of Joseph, Daniel, John, and other Bible seers were of this character. When a person understands that these animals represent thoughts, working in the subconscious realm, he has a key to the many causes of bodily conditions."

In other words, the dream pictures of animals are representations of the instincts. Depending upon the attitude, aggressive or benevolent, of these animals in the dream, we are given a clue to the condition of the repressed libido in man. In large numbers of neurotics and psychotics, the dream animals are almost always discordant and in a dangerously threatening mood, showing the disposition, as it were, of the repressed unconscious with its tendency to produce undesirable symbols endangering psychic and physical health. "Forms are always manifestations of ideas. He who understands this can interpret the symbols shown to him in dreams and visions." If forms are manifestations of ideas, the physical health is an expression of psychic health. And if the integrity of the psyche is in jeopardy because of dangerously aggressive symbols in the Unconscious realm, there can be no true state of health. Hence, the Unconscious and its symbolic manifestations must surely be looked into intelligently and understood—rather than that the physical expression of poor health be merely denied.

A number of dreams sent in by Unity students are then analysed and interpreted. But before I discuss these, I should like to consider the psycho-analytical, that is the Freudian, approach to the same subject. From the Freudian viewpoint, dreams are essentially psychic eruptions from the Unconscious. For the Freudians, the Unconscious is mostly considered to be the repository of repressed material, of likes and dislikes, of loves and hates, of impulses and inhibitions, which the individual has come to regard as repugnant to his evolving moral sense. So feeling, he refuses them permission to gain entry to his consciousness. The faculty of mind mainly responsible for this process of repressing is called the superego, or conscience. In Freudian psychology, the superego has its roots in the child's concept of the attitude of its parents and immediate teachers to the whole host of life problems and situations that arise in infancy. It is this parental attitude which is slowly absorbed or interjected into the psyche, there to act almost as an independent psychic facility. Rather as if the parents were a constant present source of what is wrong and right, it censures and criticises the individual for his lapses from their supposed ethical and social standard. Not exclusively conscious is this superego, for it includes an unconsciously operating factor as well. Being partly concealed, it operates also during dreams, fantasies, and day-dreams, when consciousness temporarily has more or less lapsed into dormancy.

Because of the momentary inhibition of consciousness during sleep, repressed ideas and feelings that have been retained in the unconscious since infancy, attempt to well up from the mental depths into the conscious ego. However, in so doing, they meet with resistance from the moral self. In order to escape this psychic censorship, the impulses and repressions are obliged to alter their tone, as it were, to disguise their true and undesirable nature by obscuring themselves behind a facade of symbolism. Thus the dreams, which is the eruption of infantile repressions from the unconscious psychic side of the mind, consists almost exclusively of symbols, and to obtain the meaning of the dream these symbols required interpretation.

What are the repressions, these inhibited feelings and experiences which attempt to gain entry into consciousness during the dream so as to discharge psychic tension? Freud has a ready, and from one angle a logical answer. Because of our past racial and animal history, an infant recapitulates evolutionary and phylogenetic processes within a short space of time. Since, from a study of history and anthropology, we know that mankind existed on a much lower social standard that we do today, we could well expect the child, during its first few years, to recapitulate a similar primitive behaviour in its own life. And, in fact, this is exactly what we do find. The little child behaves rather as a primitive behaves. It has no ethical or social consciousness. The parents gradually provide that. It will bite, scream, stamp like a young animal, and has primitive impulses and instinctual urges which immediately collide with the parental dictates. In order to retain their love, the whole symbol of its security, the infant is obliged to embark upon a process of repression of it instinctual life. Their continued inhibition develops a psycho-motor strain, a continuous state of psychological tensions. It is this repressed mass of urges, impulses and instincts which, in the main, constantly attempts to well up in the dream as its sole means of release. Inasmuch as the psychic censure of the superego has thrust them wholly outside of the sphere of consciousness, their appearance as wish-fulfillments appears to be an attempt to get rid of some degree of psychic tension.

The Jungian view, while not denying the Freudian concept in any way, attempts to broaden that view. Jung brings into the picture of the psyche, a series of large concepts such as the Collective Unconscious which, embraces all the acquisitions of the personal existence—hence the forgotten, the repressed, the subliminally perceived, thought and felt. But in addition to these personal unconscious contents, there exist other contents which do not originate in personal acquisitions but in the inherited possibility of psychic functioning in general, viz, in the inherited brain-structure. These are the mythological associations—those motives and images which can be spring anew in every age and clime, without historical tradition or migration."

In these layers of what he calls the Collective Unconscious exist primordial images, archetypes of age-old experience, existing under the façade of symbols and quasi-personalities. These may become vivified either by the process of repression, when the libido has been forced into regression, in which case they become vitalised and because not understood erupt dangerously into consciousness. Or else, through the process of analysis, meditation, prayer, or other technical procedures. Then they become transformed into saving and powerfully redeeming symbols. These symbols amongst others, Jung names as the Persona, the Shadow, the Anima, and the Animus, and a whole host of others. These primordial archetypes, Jung seeks to awaken in his patients, by an analytical procedure, that the individual may become whole and individualised, a single discrete entity functioning in an integrated manner. The average person is merely a collection of separate psychic entities, each warring within the interior world with the other. There is not integrity of psychic personality in such a case. By awakening these archaic images, these powerful historical symbols of redemption and salvation, the psyche is enabled to integrate its component elements together, forming a unique dynamic whole, the Self.

Let me now give just a few of the dream interpretations given by the Unity writer in his own small book on inner vision to convey some idea of the exegetical attitude adopted. "The wild, black horse represents the sex vitality, which you have suppressed through will power, instead of disciplining and wisely directing it." This analysis was given to an enquirer who dreamed that a horse was threatening his life, but was prevented from doing so by a large ferocious tiger who wanted the satisfaction himself of killing the dreamer. "The tiger represents the dominant will of the natural man, which would destroy everything that opposes it. The little girl represents the spiritual quality that desires obedience, divine guidance," for this little girl whom the dreamer recognised to be herself was free of all fear of the animals facing her. There are a large number of quite obviously Freudian or sexual themes in this dream, and while the Unity interpretation is in a large measure correct, there are many indications of parental imagos possessing a tremendous emotional surcharge.

There is another dream, obviously of a person with a suicidal tendency, no doubt engendered through guilty experiences with a sister—the self-destructive tendency actually being a desire for punishment to eradicate the guilt. She had many fantasies of leaving her body to spend some time with a dead sister. In the dream, she seemed to be out driving, but because the darkness was not able to see the horses, but only the lines, one of which she pulled wrongly, and all seemed about to be swallowed up in an abyss. The interpretation given her was that "you have been looking to the 'other life' until your mind has inbued it with more reality than your actual life, with the result that our life seems unreal. You are pulling the wrong line when you give your attention to the 'other life.' The horse represents the forces that vitalise your body. These forces need to be guided wisely in order that they may continue to sustain you and to unite you with your body temple...Acknowledge the Christ wisdom that is within you, and give thanks that this wisdom is guiding and directing all your thoughts and your life forces for the purpose of bringing the kingdom of heaven within you into manifestation in our body and affairs..."

Another person dreamed of a snake, which he looked in the eye until it stopped thrusting its tongue in and out, and then it was thrown on a trash heap. The psychological determinants here are wide and varied. But the Unity interpretation of the snake is one which agrees completely with the modern one. "The serpent represents sense consciousness. In the Garden of Eden, it was the serpent that tempted Eve."

In commenting upon another dream, the writer of the booklet gives metaphysical advice, with which I can properly bring to a close this account of the history and teaching of the Unity movement. "A word like this held in the silence daily will help you make your demonstration: *"The forgiving love of Jesus Christ is expressed in me*. The forgiving love of Jesus Christ being expressed in you will enable you to make your future so perfect that you will more than atone for your past mistakes. "Love therefore is the fulfillment of the law..."

New Falcon Publications
**Publisher of Controversial Books and CDs
Invites You to Visit Our Website:
http://www.newfalcon.com**

At the Falcon website you can:

- Browse the online catalog of all our great titles, including books by Robert Anton Wilson, Christopher S. Hyatt, Israel Regardie, Aleister Crowley, Timothy Leary, Osho, Lon Milo DuQuette and many more
- Find out what's available and what's out of stock
- Get special discounts
- Order our titles through our secure online server
- Find products not available anywhere else including:
    - One of a kind and limited availability products
    - Special packages
    - Special pricing
- And much, much more

Get online today at http://www.newfalcon.com